# FIVE PLAYS *by Langston Hughes*

# FIVE PLAYS
## by Langston Hughes

*Edited with an introduction*
*by Webster Smalley*

INDIANA UNIVERSITY PRESS
BLOOMINGTON

# CONTENTS

# INTRODUCTION

LANGSTON HUGHES—poet, playwright, novelist, and short story writer—began writing during the Harlem literary renaissance of the twenties and is today, at the age of sixty, America's outstanding Negro man of letters. His poems and stories are read throughout the world. They have been translated into languages and dialects (Uzbek, for example) that many of us scarcely know exist. All of Hughes' writing has its own intrinsic merit, and his subject matter—the Negro in America—is of vital interest to Americans and, perhaps more than we are aware, to the world. No writer has better interpreted and portrayed Negro life, especially in the urban North, than Langston Hughes.

His primary interest is in the "little people." A critic from the far left might be tempted to say, "the masses," but the critic would be wrong. For Hughes, there are no "masses," there are only people. The problems and aspirations of the rapidly growing, educated Negro middle- and upper-classes concern him only peripherally. He prefers to write about those of his race who live constantly on the edge of financial disaster, who are used to living precariously, occasionally falling over the edge and crawling back up, and who have no time to be pretentious. If there are any cardinal sins in Hughes' canon, they are affectation and intolerance.

The position of the Negro in the United States is one of the facts that any Negro writer must face if he is to write at all. No one has more faith in the strength and dignity of his people than does Hughes, but only a few of his works can be called militant or didactic. Some few readers might wish that he were more belligerent, but he is an artist, not a propagandist. He writes to express those truths he feels need expressing about characters he believes need to be recognized. He has always been tolerant of human weaknesses beneath skins of all colors.

From his plays it is evident that Hughes has more and more identified with and written about the Negro community in Harlem. This crowded section of New York City, its vitality and variety, is his favorite setting, though he was born in Joplin, Missouri, and grew up in Lawrence, Kansas, Cleveland, Ohio, and Toluca, Mexico. Moreover, he has worked as a seaman on voyages to Europe and Africa, lived for some time in Paris and Italy, been a newspaper correspondent in Spain, and traveled extensively in Africa, Europe, Russia, and the Orient. To write of his life and times would be superfluous for he has done so himself in two autobiographical books, *The Big Sea* (1940) and *I Wonder as I Wander* (1956). Cosmopolitan though he is, Hughes prefers to draw most of his fictional characters from the people who live in the vicinity of 125th Street between Amsterdam and Lexington Avenues, the people he calls " just folks."

Not all of his writing is about Harlem and its inhabitants, of course. His first published poem and one of his best, " The Negro Speaks of Rivers," expresses what must be a feeling universal to American Negroes and does so through the evocation of the imagery of a rich historical perspective. His strong feeling for the Negro race and for the past and present problems of the Negro in America made inevitable his concern with the lot of the Negro in the South. This concern is strongly reflected in his first full-length play, *Mulatto*, for which Hughes chose as his subject the still explosive problem of racial intermixture and based the story on the plight of the son of a Negro housekeeper and a white plantation owner. The play ran a year on Broadway in the late thirties and then toured the nation for eight months.

Perhaps because of the commercial nature of our theatre and of dramatic publishing in America, *Mulatto* has never before been printed in English, although it has been translated, performed, and published in Italy, Argentina, and Japan. It should be noted, however, that it is probably quite true that until recently the " amateur market " for Negro plays has been limited. Unfortunately, the Negro theatre in the United States, with the exception of a few vigorous groups such as the Karamu Theatre (formerly called the Gilpin Players) in Cleveland and the Howard University Players in Washington, has been short-lived, inconsequential, or both. What at one time seemed to be the most promising of all, the American Negro Theatre, is dead—perhaps killed by its one big financial success, *Anna Lucasta*.

The role of the playwright is not an easy one, at best, and a Negro playwright has all the woes of a white dramatist, with a number of others thrown in. A playwright must have at least the hope of theatrical production, but the commercial theatre shows only a sporadic interest in Negro drama. Hughes has been writing for a theatre that hardly existed. He solved the problem during the thirties by founding two dramatic groups: the Suitcase Theatre in Harlem and the Negro Art Theatre in Los Angeles. In 1941 he established a third Negro theatre, the Skyloft Players in Chicago. Few playwrights have the heart or the energy for such undertakings, and it is not surprising that the body of Negro drama in America is small. I am quite certain that Hughes' persistent desire to develop a true Negro drama is one reason he has continued to write plays. Negro drama, heralded in the twenties by such men as W. E. B. Du Bois, Alain Locke, Montgomery Gregory, and Ridgely Torrence, has been, until recently, enriched almost single-handedly by Langston Hughes. The younger Negro dramatists, from whom we are just beginning to hear, would do well to emulate his industry and to follow his ideal. If they do so, Negro drama may soon be an important segment of our literary and dramatic heritage.

Hughes has always been drawn toward the drama. Perhaps, like many of us who wish to write for the theatre, he is possessed by a kind of madness that goes beyond reason. It may have begun when, at the age of six or seven, his mother took him to see almost every play that came to Kansas City, Topeka, or Lawrence, Kansas (and this was a considerable number). In any event, his interest came early and has remained. One of his first published efforts was a children's play, written during a visit to his father who had moved to Toluca, Mexico, where he had gained a position of affluence. Hughes was only eighteen at the time, and Toluca was then a very quiet Mexican village—the great highway from the north leading to Mexico City was not yet thought of, and it would be many years before hordes of American tourists would invade the little town on its Friday market day to buy hand-woven cloth and baskets.

The play he wrote, "The Gold Piece," reflects the quiet simplicity of the Mexican village life. It is a straightforward, simply told tale of two children who make a great sacrifice in order that an old woman can help her blind son. It was published (July, 1921) in *The Brownies' Book*, a magazine for children established by W. E. B. Du Bois and the editors of *Crisis*. The editors' interest in this playlet and in two articles Hughes wrote about Mexico led to the publication of his poem, "The Negro Speaks of Rivers," in *Crisis* (June, 1921), and his professional career had begun.

During the next few years, Hughes attended Columbia University, wrote poetry, went to sea, lived in Paris, completed a degree at Lincoln University, wrote a novel, *Not Without Laughter* (1930), and spent some time with Jasper Deeter at the Hedgerow Theatre working on an early draft of *Mulatto*. It was not until 1935, however, that the play was performed on Broadway. Two years later, Hughes founded the Harlem Suitcase Theatre so that his long one-act play, *Don't you Want to be Free?*, might be presented in New York. He directed the play himself, and it ran on weekends during that year and the next for a total of 135 performances, the longest consecutive run any play has had in Harlem. He repeated this procedure in Los Angeles where the play had more than thirty performances. This play is available in the *One Act Play Magazine* (October, 1938).

*Mulatto*, however, was Langston Hughes' first professionally produced play and its text appears for the first time in this volume. This version is somewhat different from the play as presented on Broadway. Readers of *I Wonder as I Wander* will recall that Hughes returned from a tour of Russia and the Orient to find, to his surprise, the play already in production. When he attended rehearsals, he discovered a number of major changes had been made without his knowledge or permission. The producer had presented *White Cargo*, a highly sensational, but very superficial, play of the twenties, with great financial success. This drama had achieved popularity by the exploitation of sex; the producer and director had therefore decided to make *Mulatto* into another *White Cargo*. When Hughes objected to sensationalism in his play, a few minor compromises were arranged, but the major changes remained. For example, since the producer thought that, for box-office reasons, there must always be a beautiful girl in a play, the Broadway production had the young Negro girl, Sallie, a minor character, miss her train to go to boarding school in the first act so that she might be raped in the last.

In the author's version of *Mulatto* printed here, Sallie remains intact, but absent after the first scene, and the focus of the dramatic action is where it should be—on Bert and Cora—if the play is to have meaning. The " germ idea " of this play was first expressed by Hughes in an early poem, " Cross," which clearly suggests the inner conflicts of the play's protagonist:

> My old man's a white old man
> And my old mother's black.
> If I ever cursed my white old man
> I take my curses back.

> If I ever cursed my black old mother
> And wished she were in hell,
> I'm sorry for that evil wish
> And now I wish her well.

My old man died in a fine big house,
My ma died in a shack.
I wonder where I'm gonna die,
Being neither white nor black.

The play, in turn, was the basis for Hughes' libretto of *The Barrier*, an opera with musical score by Jan Meyerowitz that has been often revived since its première at Columbia University's Brander Matthews Theatre.

While reading *Mulatto*, one should remember when it was written. It is very much a play of the thirties, an era when sociopolitical plays dominated American drama. The tendency was to oversimplify moral issues as in melodrama (read *Peace on Earth, Stevedore,* or even *Both Your Houses* for examples). In *Mulatto*, the injustices suffered by Bert, by Cora, and by all the Negroes in the rural South are clearly and forcefully presented. The thesis is there clearly enough. But then the characters of Bert and Cora begin to dominate the action, and the play becomes something more than mere thesis drama. Bert Lewis, the rebellious son of a white plantation owner and his Negro mistress, is placed in an unhappy, untenable situation, but it is his own stubborn, unbending pride—inherited, ironically, from his father— that brings about his downfall and death. The patient love and rich dignity of Cora and Bert's final recognition of the totality of his tragic situation raise *Mulatto* above the level of a mere problem play. One forgives Hughes the sometimes obvious exposition of the opening scenes (as one does the early O'Neill in *Beyond the Horizon*) for the tragedy and power of the play's final scenes. If the reader finds "melo-dramatic" elements in the play, let him look to the racial situation in the deep South as it is even today: it is melodramatic.

*Mulatto* is the only play included here in which a white character is more than peripheral. In the other plays, where white characters do appear, they are little more than symbols—evil, good, or, as in the one-act *Soul Gone Home*, indifferent. The conception of *Soul Gone Home* is that of fantasy, and it contains some ironically comic moments, but its impulse is far removed from comedy. In a vignette-like episode, Hughes creates with great economy the kind of play Zola called for in his preface to *Thérèse Raquin*. Although a fantasy in concept and structure, its atmosphere and effects are those of naturalism. Like one of Hughes' poems, *Soul Gone Home* bristles with implications and reverberates with connotations. That which is unsaid becomes almost more important than what is put into the dialogue. The repressive dominance of the white culture is suggested only by the arrival of ambulance attendants, who are white as the mother knew they would be. The tragedy is that of a people so repressed that they can no longer love, and the ironic implications build to a shocking climax. Its impact is stark and uncomplicated, and it is a difficult play to forget.

Hughes does not always write in a serious vein, as readers of his stories and poems well know. His folk plays of urban Negro life, at once humorous and revealing, are a true contribution to American folk drama. The three included here—*Little Ham, Simply Heavenly,* and *Tambourines to Glory*—are, if one must define them, comedies. But the triple specters of poverty, ignorance, and repression can be seen not far beneath the surface of the comedy. The " numbers racket," " dream books," and the " hot goods man " in *Little Ham,* Simple's wistful sadness that no Negro has seen a flying saucer, and Laura's attitude toward the " religion business " in *Tambourines to Glory,* all indicate the near poverty, the ignorance, and the superstition that prevail in the world of which Hughes writes. Nevertheless, it is a colorful, wonderful world he presents to us, and we cannot but admire the spirit and vigor of his characters. He gives us a dynamic view of a segment of life most of us will never know and can discover nowhere else. At times he may sacrifice dramatic action for the sake of portraying nothing more than the people of Harlem absorbed in living out their lives from day to day, but if the humor of the scene and Hughes' infectious interest in his characters carry us along with him, what more can we ask?

*Little Ham,* " a play of the roaring twenties," is the first of Hughes' urban folk comedies. Its setting is Harlem at the time of the " Negro Renaissance," of *Shuffle Along,* and of the Cotton Club, but it is unlikely that any of its characters knew the meaning of " renaissance," had seen *Shuffle Along,* or had been inside the Cotton Club (which catered to a white clientele). Completed in 1935, *Little Ham* is a period piece, and one should remember the short skirts, tassels, brocades, and bell-shaped trousers of the era as he reads.

The play concerns the affairs (the word is intentionally ambiguous) of Hamlet Jones, a fast-talking, colorful, pint-sized Negro who shines shoes for a living. Little Ham's world is crowded, almost too crowded at times, with Harlemites of every sort except those of conventional respectability and education. It is a lively world, a society of casual morality that the white community either ignores or makes no attempt to understand. Hughes understands it, and this is the Harlem he has made into a literary land exclusively his own. One should not search too hard for profundity in *Little Ham*; it is a high-spirited revel and should be accepted as just that. Little Ham, Madam Bell, Lulu, and generously proportioned Tiny Lee are of the Harlem Hughes remembered as a young man, but are persons clearly recognizable today. If the characters in these folk comedies seem uncomplex, it is simply because these people are, in reality, direct and lacking in subtle complexity. Since they are unaware of the existence of Freud and Jung, Hughes has not hampered them with a burden of subconscious motivation.

Hughes creates his characters from life. He does not create character to fit a preconception, so he is not frightened if some of his creations do things and like things that Negroes are reputed to do and like. There is probably no group of people he dislikes more than the "passers" and pretenders of this world. He accepts, loves, and enjoys every aspect of his heritage and has the wisdom to recognize its richness. He does not write for those Negroes who have turned their backs on the spirituals and blues, nor for the people, Negro and white, who would bowdlerize *Huckleberry Finn*. He writes of what he sees, in his own way.

In *Simply Heavenly*, Hughes answered his pretentious and oversensitive critics in the only way they can be answered. When the "Character," an affected façade of a man, accuses the inhabitants of Paddy's Bar of being stereotypes, Mamie replies:

> Why, it's getting so colored folks can't do nothing no more without some other Negro calling you a stereotype. Stereotype, hah! If you like a little gin, you're a stereotype. You got to drink Scotch. If you wear a red dress, you're a stereotype. You got to wear beige or chartreuse. Lord have mercy, honey, do-don't like no blackeyed peas and rice! Then you're a down-home Negro for true—which I is—and proud of it!. . . I didn't come here to Harlem to get away from my people. I come here because there's more of 'em. I loves my race. I loves my people. Stereotype!

This speech, briefly and directly, expresses Hughes' attitude. To ask for analysis of motivation or for character study in depth in either *Little Ham* or *Simply Heavenly* is to miss the point. They should be read—or seen in the theatre—for the fun they project and for the warm understanding Hughes has of the people of Harlem.

A word should be said here about music. Aristotle long ago noted the importance of music in the drama. Fortunately, Hughes is a poet,

and the rhythm of poetry and music is close to him. He is partial to
the blues, jazz, and the spirituals. When he traveled to the far reaches
of Asia in the thirties, he carried a portable phonograph and a set of
Louis Armstrong records wherever he went. And he has more and more
made music central to his dramatic writing. Hughes is at his best when
he fuses drama and music. This he has done in the last two plays,
*Simply Heavenly*, and *Tambourines to Glory*. Full appreciation of these
two plays is possible only in the theatre, but to approximate their
theatrical impact one must use all his imaginative faculties—the aural
and visual imagination must be constantly and vigorously at play. Aural
imagination is essential when the elements of poetry or music are intro-
duced. To appreciate Hughes' most recent work for the theatre, it is
essential that the reader use his musical imagination.

Langston Hughes is a most eclectic writer. In his " Simple " books
and in his play, *Simply Heavenly*, he has created a hero who is almost
no hero at all. Jesse Semple, or " Simple," yields to temptation so
innocently but means so well, that any audience will forgive him more
quickly than does his fiancée. Simple is Hughes' most memorable
comic creation. He is of the same dramatic stripe as Figaro in Beaumarchais' *Figaro's Marriage*—both constantly skirt calamity and get
into a good deal of trouble before they finally succeed in marrying
the girls they love, and each has a unique dignity in spite of their
comic weaknesses.* Like his comic compeer, Simple has more than his
share of these. His power of reasoning is wonderful to follow, even
when his conclusions are unanswerable. " Joyce," he tells his fiancée,
" I don't want to pay for no woman's divorce I don't love. And I do
not love Isabel. Also, I ain't got the money." Simple, like most of
his friends in Paddy's Bar, seldom has much money. What the inhabitants of this " neighborhood club " lack in affluence, they make up
for in high spirits and good humor. There are no villains in *Simply
Heavenly*; indeed, the only character for whom we feel antipathy is
the pretentious little man mentioned earlier. The values of this play
are not built on dramatic clash and suspense, rather, they are inherent
in Hughes' intimate and warmly affectionate picture of the unique
inhabitants of this city within a city.

The intimacy of the writing and of David Martin's musical setting
call for a special kind of theatre. I suspect that audiences who saw it in
a large theatre on Broadway and who viewed the " Play of the Week "

---

* The Figaro in the Mozart-da Ponte opera is simplified and is more of a
buffoon than in Beaumarchais' great revolutionary play.

televised production missed some of its true quality and value. Though
its plot is of the slenderest comic fabric, its characters and straightforward humor make *Simply Heavenly* the definitive folk comedy of
life in Harlem.

Hughes' point of view and purpose in his Harlem folk plays is
summed up in his description of the final play in this collection:

> *Tambourines to Glory* is a fable, a folk ballad in stage
> form, told in broad and very simple terms—if you will,
> a comic strip, a cartoon—about problems which can only
> convincingly be reduced to a comic strip if presented very
> cleanly, clearly, sharply, precisely, and with humor.

Hughes has done just this in all three plays. Technically, each is a
comedy, but, however tongue-in-cheek his approach in *Tambourines to
Glory*, Hughes has made the problem of good and evil central to the
action. Thus, it is at once the most serious and the most dramatic of
his comedies. Neither Ham nor Simple ever comes to grips with a
moral issue. Part of Ham's charm is that he is unaware that moral
issues exist. Simple knows right from wrong, but there are so very
many pleasant little sins lying in wait for him that we hardly blame
him for straying, especially since he is such a gregarious being and his
intended wife-to-be goes to bed so early.

Essie and Laura, in *Tambourines to Glory*, are presented as simply
and forthrightly as are Ham and Simple, but there is no similarity of
character. Essie and Laura are both strong individuals—Essie, in her
goodness, and Laura, in her prediliction toward chicanery. Symboli-
cally, they represent two very real aspects of all revivalist, perhaps
all religious, movements. The saint and the charlatan often live side
by side, even in established religions, and sometimes exist in a single
personality. Hughes chose to write a rousing musical melodrama about
some aspects of Harlem religion. The result is a skillfully created, well-
integrated musical play, written with humor, insight, and compassion.

It is the latter quality—Hughes' compassionate understanding of all
his characters—that oftentimes minimizes dramatic action and conflict
in his plays. Perhaps he likes his sinners too well, for he is inclined
to justify their evil by mitigating circumstances. But it may be that he
has never forgotten an early experience, gained shortly after his grandmother's death. He lived for a time in Kansas with a couple named
Reed. Hughes has written that " Auntie Reed " was a devout Christian
but " Uncle Reed " was a sinner, and has said, " No doubt from them

I learned to like both Christians and sinners equally well." There can be no doubt that Hughes prefers the healthy sinner to the pretentious fake.

Villains are not plentiful in Hughes' Harlem plays. Big-Eyed Buddy Lomax (who informs us that he is really the Devil) is unique. Even he is a threat only through Laura's weakness for him (and all he represents). Hughes is not as interested in a conventional conflict between protagonist and antagonist as in revealing the cracks in the self-protecting façades humans erect to conceal their weaknesses. His characters are never merely subservient to plot. Thus, even within the confines of melodrama, he is able to write a moving and honest play.

*Tambourines to Glory* is more than musical melodrama; it is a play of redemption. It is a Faust-like tale, told with the simplicity of a medieval morality play. Hughes tells the story with great good humor, but he never asks us to laugh derisively or to smile sardonically. Behind the laughter is a touch of pity and a great quantity of warm understanding. As broadly and simply as the characters are sketched, they are utterly believable. When they show weakness, their frailties stem directly from problems that plague the average Negro in our largest metropolis. Laura's grasping drive for material things, for example, is a natural reaction to the deprivation and poverty she has suffered all her life, and Essie's honest faith is a triumph over tribulation and temptation. Both characterizations are true.

Finally, this play is in effect a " dramatic song," to use one of Hughes' descriptive terms. It has a pervasive rhythm. The integration of action, original lyrics, traditional spirituals, and the gospel music of Jobe Huntley, adds to the richness of the drama and contributes to characterization. Music is central to the lives—one might say, even to the spiritual being—of these characters. Nowhere has Hughes more skillfully interwoven and integrated music into the fabric of drama.

Since Hughes has worked and hoped for a vigorous Negro theatre movement in America, it is my wish that the publication of these five plays may help to stimulate that movement. His plays, and the plays of younger Negro playwrights such as Lorraine Hansberry, William Branch, Loften Mitchell, Alice Childress, and Ossie Davis, need to be seen and heard—projected by actors on stages before living audiences. For in the final analysis plays exist only in the theatre. Langston Hughes has long been one of the most effective literary spokesmen for the American Negro. His poetry and prose have been published both in this country and abroad. Now, thanks to Indiana University Press, these plays, representing his dramatic writing from the twenties to the sixties, are for the first time available to a wide audience. I am honored to write this introductory note. The dramatic world of Langston Hughes is a quite different world from that of any other playwright, and the discovery of that world is, in itself, an entertaining, wonderful, and enlightening experience.

*Urbana, Illinois*                                        WEBSTER SMALLEY

# MULATTO

*A Tragedy of the Deep South*

# CHARACTERS

COLONEL THOMAS NORWOOD  *Plantation owner, a still vigorous man of about sixty, nervous, refined, quick-tempered, and commanding; a widower who is the father of four living mulatto children by his Negro housekeeper*

CORA LEWIS  *A brown woman in her forties who has kept the house and been the mistress of Colonel Norwood for some thirty years*

WILLIAM LEWIS  *The oldest son of Cora Lewis and the Colonel; a fat, easy-going, soft-looking mulatto of twenty-eight; married*

SALLIE LEWIS  *The seventeen-year-old daughter, very light with sandy hair and freckles, who could pass for white*

ROBERT LEWIS  *Eighteen, the youngest boy; strong and well-built; a light mulatto with ivory-yellow skin and proud thin features like his father's; as tall as the Colonel, with the same gray-blue eyes, but with curly black hair instead of brown; of a fiery, impetuous temper— immature and willful—resenting his blood and the circumstances of his birth*

FRED HIGGINS  *A close friend of Colonel Norwood; a county politician; fat and elderly, conventionally Southern*

SAM  *An old Negro retainer, a personal servant of the Colonel*

BILLY  *The small son of William Lewis; a chubby brown kid about five*

TALBOT  *The overseer*

MOSE  *An elderly Negro, chauffeur for Mr. Higgins*

A STOREKEEPER

AN UNDERTAKER

UNDERTAKER'S HELPER  *Voice off-stage only*

THE MOB

# ACT ONE

TIME: *An afternoon in early fall.*

THE SETTING: *The living room of the Big House on a plantation in Georgia. Rear center of the room, a vestibule with double doors leading to the porch; at each side of the doors, a large window with lace curtains and green shades; at left a broad flight of stairs leading to the second floor; near the stairs, downstage, a doorway leading to the dining room and kitchen; opposite, at right of stage, a door to the library. The room is furnished in the long out-dated horsehair and walnut style of the nineties; a crystal chandelier, a large old-fashioned rug, a marble-topped table, upholstered chairs. At the right there is a small cabinet. It is a very clean, but somewhat shabby and rather depressing room, dominated by a large oil painting of* NORWOOD'S *wife of his youth on the center wall. The windows are raised. The afternoon sunlight streams in.*

ACTION: *As the curtain rises, the stage is empty. The door at the right opens and* COLONEL NORWOOD *enters, crossing the stage toward the stairs, his watch in his hand. Looking up, he shouts:*

NORWOOD   Cora! Oh, Cora!

CORA   (*Heard above*)   Yes, sir, Colonel Tom.

NORWOOD   I want to know if that child of yours means to leave here this afternoon?

CORA   (*At head of steps now*)   Yes, sir, she's goin' directly. I's gettin' her ready now, packin' up an' all. 'Course, she wants to tell you goodbye 'fore she leaves.

NORWOOD   Well, send her down here. Who's going to drive her to the railroad? The train leaves at three—and it's after two now. You ought to know you can't drive ten miles in no time.

CORA   (*Above*)   Her brother's gonna drive her. Bert. He ought to be back here most any time now with the Ford.

NORWOOD   (*Stopping on his way back to the library*)   Ought to be *back* here? Where's he gone?

CORA   (*Coming downstairs nervously*)   Why, he driv in town 'fore noon, Colonel Tom. Said he were lookin' for some tubes or some-thin' 'nother by de mornin' mail for de radio he's been riggin' up out in de shed.

NORWOOD  Who gave him permission to be driving off in the middle of the morning? I bought that Ford to be used when I gave orders for it to be used, not . . .

CORA  Yes, sir, Colonel Tom, but . . .

NORWOOD  But what? (*Pausing. Then deliberately*) Cora, if you want that hardheaded yellow son of yours to get along around here, he'd better listen to me. He's no more than any other black buck on this plantation—due to work like the rest of 'em. I don't take such a performance from nobody under me—driving off in the middle of the day to town, after I've told him to bend his back in that cotton. How's Talbot going to keep the rest of those darkies working right if that boy's allowed to set that kind of an example? Just because Bert's your son, and I've been damn fool enough to send him off to school for five or six years, he thinks he has a right to privileges, acting as if he owned this place since he's been back here this summer.

CORA  But, Colonel Tom. . .

NORWOOD  Yes, I know what you're going to say. I don't give a damn about him! There's no nigger-child of mine, yours, ours—no darkie —going to disobey me. I put him in that field to work, and he'll stay on this plantation till I get ready to let him go. I'll tell Talbot to use the whip on him, too, if he needs it. If it hadn't been that he's yours, he'd-a had a taste of it the other day. Talbot's a damn good overseer, and no saucy, lazy Nigras stay on this plantation and get away with it. (*To* CORA) Go on back upstairs and see about getting Sallie out of here. Another word from you and I won't send your (*Sarcastically*) pretty little half-white daughter anywhere, either. Schools for darkies! Huh! If you take that boy of yours for an example, they do 'em more harm than good. He's learned nothing in college but impudence, and he'll stay here on this place and work for me awhile before he gets back to any more schools. (*He starts across the room*)

CORA  Yes, sir, Colonel Tom. (*Hesitating*) But he's just young, sir. And he was mighty broke up when you said last week he couldn't go back to de campus. (COLONEL NORWOOD *turns and looks at* CORA *commandingly. Understanding, she murmurs*) Yes, sir. (*She starts upstairs, but turns back*) Can't I run and fix you a cool drink, Colonel Tom?

NORWOOD   No, damn you! Sam'll do it.

CORA   (*Sweetly*)   Go set down in de cool, then, Colonel. 'Taint good for you to be going' on this way in de heat. I'll talk to Robert maself soon's he comes in. He don't mean nothing—just smart and young and kinder careless, Colonel Tom, like ma mother said you used to be when you was eighteen.

NORWOOD   Get on upstairs, Cora. Do I have to speak again? Get on! (*He pulls the cord of the servants' bell*)

CORA   (*On the steps*)   Does you still be in the mind to tell Sallie good-bye?

NORWOOD   Send her down here as I told you. (*Impatiently*) Where's Sam? Send him here first. (*Fuming*) Looks like he takes his time to answer that bell. You colored folks are running the house to suit yourself nowadays.

CORA   (*Coming downstairs again and going toward door under the steps*)   I'll get Sam for you.

(CORA *exits left.* NORWOOD *paces nervously across the floor. Goes to the window and looks out down the road. Takes a cigar from his pocket, sits in a chair with it unlighted, scowling. Rises, goes toward servants' bell and rings it again violently as* SAM *enters, out of breath*)

NORWOOD   What the hell kind of a tortoise race is this? I suppose you were out in the sun somewhere sleeping?

SAM   No, sah, Colonel Norwood. Just tryin' to get Miss Sallie's valises down to de yard so's we can put 'em in de Ford, sah.

NORWOOD   (*Out of patience*)   Huh! Darkies waiting on darkies! I can't get service in my own house. Very well. (*Loudly*) Bring me some whiskey and soda, and ice in a glass. Is that damn Frigidaire working right? Or is Livonia still too thickheaded to know how to run it? Any ice cubes in the thing?

SAM   Yes, sah, Colonel, yes, sah. (*Backing toward door left*) 'Scuse me, please sah, but (*as* NORWOOD *turns toward library*) Cora say for me to ask you is it all right to bring that big old trunk what you give Sallie down by de front steps. We ain't been able to tote it down them narrer little back steps, sah. Cora, say, can we bring it down de front way through here?

NORWOOD   No other way? (*Sam shakes his head*) Then pack it on through to the back, quick. Don't let me catch you carrying any of Sallie's baggage out of that front door here. You-all'll be wanting to go in and out the front way next. (*Turning away, complaining to himself*)  Darkies have been getting mighty fresh in this part of the country since the war. The damn Germans should've . . . (*To* SAM) Don't take that trunk out that front door.

SAM  (*Evilly, in a cunning voice*)  I's seen Robert usin' de front door—when you ain't here, and he comes up from de cabin to see his mammy.

(SALLIE, *the daughter, appears at the top of the stairs, but hesitates about coming down*)

NORWOOD  Oh, you have, have you? Let me catch him and I'll break his young neck for him. (*Yelling at* SAM)  Didn't I tell you some whiskey and soda an hour ago?

(SAM *exits left.* SALLIE *comes shyly down the stairs and approaches her father. She is dressed in a little country-style coat-suit ready for traveling. Her features are Negroid, although her skin is very fair.* COLONEL NORWOOD *gazes down at her without saying a word as she comes meekly toward him, half-frightened*)

SALLIE  I just wanted to tell you goodbye, Colonel Norwood, and thank you for letting me go back to school another year, and for letting me work here in the house all summer where mama is. (NORWOOD *says nothing. The girl continues in a strained voice as if making a speech*)  You mighty nice to us colored folks certainly, and mama says you the best white man in Georgia. (*Still* NORWOOD *says nothing. The girl continues*)  You been mighty nice to your— I mean to us colored children, letting my sister and me go off to school. The principal says I'm doing pretty well and next year I can go to Normal and learn to be a teacher. (*Raising her eyes*)  You reckon I can, Colonel Tom?

NORWOOD  Stand up straight and let me see how you look. (*Backing away*)  Hum-m-m! Getting kinder grown, ain't you? Do they teach you in that school to have good manners, and not be afraid of work, *and to respect white folks?*

SALLIE  Yes, sir, I been taking up cooking and sewing, too.

NORWOOD  Well, that's good. As I recall it, that school turned your sister out a right smart cook. Cora tells me she's got a good job in some big hotel in Chicago. I'm thinking about you going on up North there with her in a year or two. You're getting too old to be around here, and too womanish. (*He puts his hands on her arms as if feeling her flesh*)

SALLIE  (*Drawing back slightly*)  But I want to live down here with

mama. I want to teach school in that there empty school house by
the Cross Roads what hasn't had a teacher for five years.
(SAM *has been standing with the door cracked, overhearing
the conversation. He enters with the drink and places it on
the table, right.* NORWOOD *sits down, leaving the girl standing, as* SAM *pours out a drink*)
NORWOOD Don't get that into your head, now. There's been no
teacher there for years—and there won't be any teacher there, either.
Cotton teaches these pickaninnies enough around here. Some of
'em's too smart as it is. The only reason I did have a teacher there
once was to get you young ones o' Cora's educated. I gave you all
a chance and I hope you appreciate it. (*He takes a long drink*)
Don't know why I did it. No other white man in these parts ever
did it, as I know of. (*To* SAM) Get out of here! (SAM *exits left*)
Guess I couldn't stand to see Cora's kids working around here dumb
as the rest of these no good darkies—need a dozen of 'em to chop
one row of cotton, or to keep a house clean. Or maybe I didn't want
to see Talbot eyeing you gals. (*Taking another drink*) Anyhow,
I'm glad you and Bertha turned out right well. Yes, hum-m-m!
(*Straightening up*) You know I tried to do something for those
brothers of yours, too, but William's stupid as an ox—good for work,
though—and that Robert's just an impudent, hardheaded, yellow
young fool. I'm gonna break his damn neck for him if he don't
watch out. Or else put Talbot on him.
SALLIE (*Suddenly frightened*) Please, sir, don't put the overseer on
Bert, Colonel Tom. He was the smartest boy at school, Bert was.
On the football team, too. Please, sir, Colonel Tom. Let brother
work here in the house, or somewhere else where Talbot can't mistreat him. He ain't used . . .
NORWOOD (*Rising*) Telling me what to do, heh? (*Staring at her
sternly*) I'll use the back of my hand across your face if you don't
hush. (*He takes another drink. The noise of a Ford is heard outside*) That's Bert now, I reckon. He's to take you to the railroad
line, and while you're riding with him, you better put some sense into
his head. And tell him I want to see him as soon as he gets back
here. (CORA *enters left with a bundle and an umbrella.* SAM *and*
WILLIAM *come downstairs with a big square trunk, and exit hurriedly, left*)
SALLIE Yes, sir, I'll tell him.
CORA Colonel Tom, Sallie ain't got much time now. (*To the girl*)

Come on, chile. Bert's here. Yo' big brother and Sam and Livonia and everybody's all waiting at de back door to say goodbye. And your baggage is being packed in. (*Noise of another car is heard outside*) Who else is that there coming up de drive? (CORA *looks out the window*) Mr. Higgins' car, Colonel Tom. Reckon he's coming to see you . . . Hurry up out o' this front room, Sallie. Here, take these things of your'n (*Hands her the bundle and parasol*) while I opens de door for Mr. Higgins. (*In a whisper*) Hurry up, chile! Get out! (NORWOOD *turns toward the front door as* CORA *goes to open it*)

SALLIE    (*Shyly to her father*)  Goodbye, Colonel Tom.

NORWOOD    (*His eyes on the front door, scarcely noticing the departing* SALLIE, *he motions*)  Yes, yes, goodbye! Get on now! (CORA *opens the front door as her daughter exits left*)  Well, well! Howdy do, Fred. Come in, come in! (CORA *holds the outer door of the vestibule wide as* FRED HIGGINS *enters with rheumatic dignity, supported on the arm of his chauffeur,* MOSE, *a very black Negro in a slouchy uniform.* CORA *closes the door and exits left hurriedly, following* SALLIE)

NORWOOD    (*Smiling*)  How's the rheumatiz today? Women or licker or heat must've made it worse—from the looks of your speed!

HIGGINS    (*Testily, sitting down puffing and blowing in a big chair*)  I'm in no mood for fooling, Tom, not now. (TO MOSE)  All right. (*The* CHAUFFEUR *exits front.* HIGGINS *continues angrily*)  Norwood, that damned yellow nigger buck of yours that drives that new Ford tried his best just now to push my car off the road, then got in front of me and blew dust in my face for the last mile coming down to your gate, trying to beat me in here—which he did. Such a deliberate piece of impudence I don't know if I've ever seen out of a nigger before in all the sixty years I've lived in this county. (*The noise of the Ford is heard going out the drive, and the cries of the* NEGROES *shouting farewells to* SALLIE. HIGGINS *listens indignantly*)  What kind of crazy coons have you got on your place, anyhow? Sounds like a black Baptist picnic to me. ( *Pointing to the window with his cane*).  Tom, listen to that.

NORWOOD    (*Flushing*)  I apologize to you, Fred, for each and every one of my darkies. (SAM *enters with more ice and another glass*)  Permit me to offer you a drink. I realize I've got to tighten down here.

HIGGINS    Mose tells me that was Cora's boy in that Ford—and that young black fool is what I was coming here to talk to you about today. That boy! He's not gonna be around here long—not the way he's acting. The white folks in town'll see to that. Knowing he's one of your yard niggers, Norwood, I thought I ought to come and tell you. The white folks at the Junction aren't intending to put up with him much longer. And I don't know what good the jail would do him once he got in there.

NORWOOD  (*Tensely*)  What do you mean, Fred—jail? Don't I always take care of the folks on my plantation without any help from the Junction's police force? Talbot can do more with an unruly black buck than your marshal.

HIGGINS  Warn't lookin' at it that way, Tom. I was thinking how weak the doors to that jail is. They've broke 'em down and lynched four niggers to my memory since it's been built. After what happened this morning, you better keep that yellow young fool out o' town from now on. It might not be safe for him around there—today, nor no other time.

NORWOOD  What the hell? (*Perturbed*)  He went in just now to take his sister to the depot. Damn it, I hope no ruffians'll break up my new Ford. What was it, Fred, about this morning?

HIGGINS  You haven't heard? Why, it's all over town already. He sassed out Miss Gray in the post office over a box of radio tubes that come by mail.

NORWOOD  He did, heh?

HIGGINS  Seems like the stuff was sent C. O. D. and got here all smashed up, so he wouldn't take it. Paid his money first before he saw the box was broke. Then wanted the money order back. Seems like the post office can't give money orders back—rule against it. Your nigger started to argue, and the girl at the window—Miss Gray—got scared and yelled for some of the mail clerks. They threw Bert out of the office, that's all. But that's enough. Lucky nothing more didn't happen. (*Indignantly*)  That Bert needs a damn good beating—talking back to a white woman—and I'd like to give it to him myself, the way he kicked the dust up in my eyes all the way down the road coming out here. He was mad, I reckon. That's one yellow buck don't know his place, Tom, and it's your fault he don't—sending 'em off to be educated.

NORWOOD  Well, by God, I'll show him. I wish I'd have known it before he left here just now.

HIGGINS  Well, he's sure got mighty aggravating ways for a buck his color to have. Drives down the main street and don't stop for nobody, white or black. Comes in my store and if he ain't waited on as quick as the white folks are, he walks out and tells the clerk his money's as good as a white man's any day. Said last week standing out on my store front that he wasn't *all* nigger no how; said his name was Norwood—not Lewis, like the rest of his family—and part of your plantation here would be his when you passed out—and all that kind of stuff, boasting to the walleyed coons listening to him.

NORWOOD  (*Astounded*)  Well, I'll be damned!

HIGGINS  Now, Tom, you know that don't go 'round these parts 'o Georgia, nor nowhere else in the South. A darkie's got to keep in his place down here. Ruinous to other niggers hearing that talk, too. All this postwar propaganda on the radio about freedom and democracy—why the niggers think it's meant for them! And that Eleanor Roosevelt, she ought to been muzzled. She's driving our niggers crazy—your boy included! Crazy! Talking about civil rights. Ain't been no race trouble in our country for three years—since the Deekin's lynching—but I'm telling you, Norwood, you better see that that buck of yours goes away from here. I'm speaking on the quiet, but I can see ahead. And what happened this morning about them radio tubes wasn't none too good.

NORWOOD  (*Beside himself with rage*)  A black ape! I——I . . .

HIGGINS  You been too decent to your darkies, Norwood. That's what's the matter with you. And then the whole county suffers from a lot of impudent bucks who take lessons from your crowd. Folks been kicking about that, too. Guess you know it. Maybe that's the reason you didn't get that nomination for committeeman a few years back.

NORWOOD  Maybe 'tis, Higgins. (*Rising and pacing the room*)  God damn niggers! (*Furiously*)  Everything turns on niggers, niggers, niggers! No wonder Yankees call this the Black Belt! (*He pours a large drink of whiskey*)

HIGGINS  (*Soothingly*)  Well, let's change the subject. Hand me my glass, there, too.

NORWOOD  Pardon me, Fred. (*He puts ice in his friend's glass and passes him the bottle*)

HIGGINS  Tom, you get excited too easy for warm weather . . . Don't ever show black folks they got you going, though. I think sometimes that's where you make your mistake. Keep calm, keep calm—and then you command. Best plantation manager I ever had never raised his voice to a nigger—and they were scared to death of him.

NORWOOD  Have a smoke. (*Pushes cigars toward* HIGGINS)

HIGGINS   You ought've married again, Tom—brought a white woman
out here on this damn place o' yours. A woman could help you run
things. Women have soft ways, but they can keep things humming.
Nothing but blacks in the house—a man gets soft like niggers are
inside. (*Puffing at cigar*) And living with a colored woman! Of
course, I know we all have 'em—I didn't know you could make use
of a white girl till I was past twenty. Thought too much o' white
women for that—but I've given many a yellow gal a baby in my
time. (*Long puff at cigar*) But for a man's own house you need a
wife, not a black woman.

NORWOOD   Reckon you're right, Fred, but it's too late to marry again
now. ( *Shrugging his shoulders*) Let's get off of darkies and women
for awhile. How's crops? (*Sitting down*) How's politics going?

HIGGINS   Well, I guess you know the Republicans is trying to stir up
trouble for us in Washington. I wish the South had more men like
Bilbo and Rankin there. But, say, by the way, Lawyer Hotchkiss
wants to see us both about that budget money next week. He's got
some real Canadian stuff at his office, in his filing case, too—brought
back from his vacation last summer. Taste better'n this old mountain
juice we get around here. Not meaning to insult your drinks, Tom,
but just remarking. I serve the same as you myself, label and all.

NORWOOD   (*Laughing*) I'll have you know, sir, that this is prewar
licker, sir!

HIGGINS   Hum-m-m! Well, it's got me feelin' better'n I did when I
come in here—whatever it is. (*Puffs at his cigar*) Say, how's your
cotton this year?

NORWOOD   Doin' right well, specially down in the south field. Why
not drive out that road when you leave and take a look at it? I'll
ride down with you. I want to see Talbot, anyhow.

HIGGINS   Well, let's be starting. I got to be back at the Junction by
four o'clock. Promised to let that boy of mine have the car to drive
over to Thomasville for a dance tonight.

NORWOOD   One more shot before we go. (*He pours out drinks*) The
young ones must have their fling, I reckon. When you and I grew up
down here it used to be a carriage and the best pair of black horses
when you took the ladies out—now it's an automobile. That's a good
lookin' new car of yours, too.

HIGGINS   Right nice.

NORWOOD   Been thinking about getting a new one myself, but money's
been kinder tight this year, and conditions are none too good yet,

either. Reckon that's why everybody's so restless. (*He walks toward stairs calling*) Cora! Oh, Cora! . . . If I didn't have a few thousand put away, I'd feel the pinch myself. (*As* CORA *appears on the stairs*) Bring me my glasses up there by the side of my bed . . . Better whistle for Mose, hadn't I, Higgins? He's probably 'round back with some of his women. (*Winking*) You know I got some nice black women in this yard.

HIGGINS  Oh, no, not Mose. I got my servants trained to stay in their places—right where I want 'em—while they're working for me. Just open the door and tell him to come in here and help me out. (NOR-WOOD *goes to the door and calls the* CHAUFFEUR. MOSE *enters and assists his master out to the car.* CORA *appears with the glasses, goes to the vestibule and gets the* COLONEL'S *hat and cane which she hands him*)

NORWOOD  (*To* CORA) I want to see that boy o' yours soon as I get back. That won't be long, either. And tell him to put up that Ford of mine and don't touch it again.

CORA  Yes, sir, I'll have him waiting here. (*In a whisper*) It's hot weather, Colonel Tom. Too much of this licker makes your heart upset. It ain't good for you, you know. (NORWOOD *pays her no attention as he exits toward the car. The noise of the departing motor is heard.* CORA *begins to tidy up the room. She takes a glass from a side table. She picks up a doily that was beneath the glass and looks at it long and lovingly. Suddenly she goes to the door left and calls toward the kitchen*) William, you William! Com'ere, I want to show you something. Make haste, son. (*As* CORA *goes back toward the table, her eldest son,* WILLIAM *enters carrying a five-year-old boy*) Look here at this purty doily yo' sister made this summer while she been here. She done learned all about sewing and making purty things at school. Ain't it nice, son?

WILLIAM  Sho' is. Sallie takes after you, I reckon. She's a smart little crittur, ma. (*Sighs*) De Lawd knows, I was dumb at school. (*To his child*) Get down, Billy, you's too heavy. (*He puts the boy on the floor*) This here sewin's really fine.

BILLY  (*Running toward the big upholstered chair and jumping up and down on the spring seat*) Gityap! I's a mule driver. Haw! Gee!

CORA  You Billy, get out of that chair 'fore I skins you alive. Get on into de kitchen, sah.

BILLY  I'm playin' horsie, grandma. (*Jumps up in the chair*) Horsie! Horsie!

CORA  Get! That's de Colonel's favorite chair. If he knows any little darkie's been jumpin' on it, he raise sand. Get on, now.

BILLY  Ole Colonel's ma grandpa, ain't he? Ain' he ma white grandpa?

WILLIAM  (*Snatching the child out of the chair*)  Boy, I'm gonna fan your hide if you don't hush!

CORA  Shs-ss-s! You Billy, hush yo' mouth! Chile, where you hear that? (*To her son*) Some o' you all been talking too much in front o' this chile. (*To the boy*) Honey, go on in de kitchen till yo' daddy come. Get a cookie from 'Vonia and set down on de back porch. (*Little* BILLY *exits left*)

WILLIAM  Ma, you know it 'twarn't me told him. Bert's the one been goin' all over de plantation since he come back from Atlanta remindin' folks right out we's Colonel Norwood's chilluns.

CORA  (*Catching her breath*)  Huh!

WILLIAM  He comes down to my shack tellin' Billy and Marybell they got a white man for grandpa. He's gonna get my chilluns in trouble sho'—like he got himself in trouble when Colonel Tom whipped him.

CORA  Ten or 'leven years ago, warn't it?

WILLIAM  And Bert's sho' in trouble now. Can't go back to that college like he could-a if he'd-a had any sense. You can't fool with white folks—and de Colonel ain't never really liked Bert since that there first time he beat him, either.

CORA  No, he ain't. Leastwise, he ain't understood him. (*Musing sadly in a low voice*)  Time Bert was 'bout seven, warn't it? Just a little bigger'n yo' Billy.

WILLIAM  Yes.

CORA  Went runnin' up to Colonel Tom out in de horse stables when de Colonel was showin' off his horses—I 'members so well—to fine white company from town. Lawd, that boy's always been foolish! He went runnin' up and grabbed a-holt de Colonel and yelled right in front o' de white folks' faces, " O, papa, Cora say de dinner's ready, papa!" Ain't never called him papa before, and I don't know where he got it from. And Colonel Tom knocked him right backwards under de horse's feet.

WILLIAM  And when de company were gone, he beat that boy unmerciful.

CORA  I thought sho' he were gonna kill ma chile that day. And he were mad at me, too, for months. Said I was teaching you chilluns who they pappy were. Up till then Bert had been his favorite little colored child round here.

WILLIAM  Sho' had.

CORA  But he never liked him no more. That's why he sent him off to school so soon to stay, winter and summer, all these years. I had to beg and plead to have him home this summer—but I's sorry now I ever got that boy back here again.

WILLIAM  He's sho' growed more like de Colonel all de time, ain't he? Bert thinks he's a real white man hisself now. Look at de first thing he did when he come home, he ain't seen de Colonel in six years— and Bert sticks out his hand fo' to shake hands with him!

CORA  Lawd! That chile!

WILLIAM  Just like white folks! And de Colonel turns his back and walks off. Can't blame him. He ain't used to such doings from colored folks. God knows what's got into Bert since he come back. He's acting like a fool—just like he was a boss man round here. Won't even say "Yes, sir" and "No, sir" no more to de white folks. Talbot asked him warn't he gonna work in de field this mornin'. Bert say "No!" and turn and walk away. White man so mad, I could see him nearly foam at de mouth. If he warn't yo' chile, ma, he'd been knocked in de head fo' now.

CORA  You's right.

WILLIAM  And you can't talk to him. I tried to tell him something the other day, but he just laughed at me, and said we's all just scared niggers on this plantation. Says he ain't no nigger, no how. He's a Norwood. He's half-white, and he's gonna act like it. (*In amazement at his brother's daring*)  And this is Georgia, too!

CORA  I's scared to death for de boy, William. I don't know what to do. De Colonel says he won't send him off to school no mo'. Says he's mo' sassy and impudent now than any nigger he ever seed. Bert never has been like you was, and de girls, quiet and sensible like you knowed you had to be. (*She sits down*)  De Colonel say he's gonna make Bert stay here now and work on this plantation like de rest of his niggers. He's gonna show him what color he is. Like that time when he beat him for callin' him "papa." He say he's gwine to teach him his place and make de boy know where he belongs. Seems like me or you can't show him. Colonel Tom has to take him in hand, or these white folks'll kill him around here and then—oh, My God!

WILLIAM  A nigger's just got to know his place in de South, that's all, ain't he, ma?

CORA  Yes, son. That's all, I reckon.

WILLIAM   And ma brother's one damn fool nigger. Don't seems like he knows nothin'. He's gonna ruin us all round here. Makin' it bad for everybody.

CORA   Oh, Lawd, have mercy! (*Beginning to cry*) I don't know what to do. De way he's acting up can't go on. Way he's acting to de Colonel can't last. Somethin's gonna happen to ma chile. I had a bad dream last night, too, and I looked out and seed de moon all red with blood. I seed a path o' living blood across this house, I tell you, in my sleep. Oh, Lawd, have mercy! (*Sobbing*) Oh, Lawd, help me in ma troubles. (*The noise of the returning Ford is heard outside.* CORA *looks up, rises, and goes to the window*) There's de chile now, William. Run out to de back door and tell him I wants to see him. Bring him in here where Sam and Livonia and de rest of 'em won't hear ever'thing we's sayin'. I got to talk to ma boy. He's ma baby boy, and he don't know de way.

> (*Exit* WILLIAM *through the door left.* CORA *is wiping her eyes and pulling herself together when the front door is flung open with a bang and* ROBERT *enters*)

ROBERT   (*Running to his mother and hugging her teasingly*) Hello, ma! Your daughter got off, and I've come back to keep you company in the parlor! Bring out the cookies and lemonade. *Mister* Norwood's here!

CORA   (*Beginning to sob anew*) Take yo' hands off me, boy! Why don't you mind? Why don't you mind me?

ROBERT   (*Suddenly serious, backing away*) Why, mamma, what's the matter? Did I scare you? Your eyes are all wet! Has somebody been telling you 'bout this morning?

CORA   (*Not heeding his words*) Why don't you mind me, son? Ain't I told you and told you not to come in that front door, never? (*Suddenly angry*) Will somebody have to beat it into you? What's got wrong with you when you was away at that school? What am I gonna do?

ROBERT   (*Carelessly*) Oh, I knew that the Colonel wasn't here. I passed him and old man Higgins on the road down by the south patch. He wouldn't even look at me when I waved at him. (*Half playfully*) Anyhow, isn't this my old man's house? Ain't I his son and heir? (*Grandly, strutting around*) Am I not Mr. Norwood, Junior?

CORA   (*Utterly serious*) I believes you goin' crazy, Bert. I believes you wants to get us all killed or run away or something awful like that. I believes . . . (WILLIAM *enters left*)

WILLIAM  Where's Bert? He ain't come round back——(*Seeing his brother in the room*) How'd you get in here?

ROBERT  (*Grinning*)  Houses have front doors.

WILLIAM  Oh, usin' de front door like de white folks, heh? You gwine do that once too much.

ROBERT  Yes, like de white folks. What's a front door for, you rabbit-hearted coon?

WILLIAM  Rabbit-hearted coon's better'n a dead coon any day.

ROBERT  I wouldn't say so. Besides you and me's only half-coons, anyhow, big boy. And I'm gonna act like my white half, not my black half. Get me, kid?

WILLIAM  Well, you ain't gonna act like it long here in de middle o' Georgy. And you ain't gonna act like it when de Colonel's around, either.

ROBERT  Oh, no? My stay down here'll be short and sweet, boy, short and sweet. The old man won't send me away to college no more—so you think I'm gonna stick around and work in the fields? Like fun? I might stay here awhile and teach some o' you darkies to think like men, maybe—till it gets too much for the old Colonel— but no more bowing down to white folks for me—not Robert Norwood.

CORA  Hush, son!

ROBERT  Certainly not right on my own old man's plantation— Georgia or no Georgia.

WILLIAM  (*Scornfully*)  I hears you.

ROBERT  *You* can do it if you want to, but I'm ashamed of you. I've been away from here six years. (*Boasting*) I've learned something, seen people in Atlanta, and Richmond, and Washington where the football team went—real colored people who don't have to take off their hats to white folks or let 'em go to bed with their sisters— like that young Higgins boy, asking me what night Sallie was comin' to town. A damn cracker! (*To* CORA) 'Scuse me, ma. (*Continuing*) Back here in these woods maybe Sam and Livonia and you and mama and everybody's got their places fixed for 'em, but not me. (*Seriously*) Nobody's gonna fix a place for me. I'm old man Norwood's son. Nobody fixed a place for him. (*Playfully again*) Look at me. I'm a 'fay boy. (*Pretends to shake his hair back*) See these gray eyes? I got the right to everything everybody else has. (*Punching his brother in the belly*), Don't talk to me, old slavery-time Uncle Tom.

WILLIAM  (*Resentfully*)  I ain't playin', boy.  (*Pushes younger brother back with some force*)  I ain't playin' a-tall.

CORA  All right, chilluns, stop.  Stop!  And William, you take Billy and go on home.  'Vonia's got to get supper and she don't like no young-uns under her feet in de kitchen.  I wants to talk to Bert in here now 'fore Colonel Tom gets back.  (*Exit* WILLIAM *left*. CORA *continues to* BERT)  Sit down, child, right here a minute, and listen.

ROBERT  (*Sitting down*)  All right, ma.

CORA  Hard as I's worked and begged and humbled maself to get de Colonel to keep you chilluns in school, you comes home wid yo' head full o' stubbornness and yo' mouth full o' sass for me, an' de white folks an' everybody.  You know can't no colored boy here talk like you's been doin' to no white folks, let alone to de Colonel and that old devil of a Talbot.  They ain't gonna stand fo' yo' sass.  Not only you, but I 'spects we's all gwine to pay fo' it, every colored soul on this place.  I was scared to death today fo' yo' sister, Sallie, scared de Colonel warn't gwine to let her go back to school, neither, 'count o' yo' doins, but he did, thank Gawd—and then you come near makin' her miss de train.  Did she have time to get her ticket and all?

ROBERT  Sure!  Had to drive like sin to get there with her, though.  I didn't mean to be late getting back here for her, ma, but I had a little run-in about them radio tubes in town.

CORA  (*Worried*)  What's that?

ROBERT  The tubes was smashed when I got 'em, and I had already made out my money order, so the woman in the post office wouldn't give the three dollars back to me.  All I did was explain to her that we could send the tubes back—but she got hot because there were two or three white folks waiting behind me to get stamps, I guess.  So she yells at me to move on and not give her any of my " educated nigger talk."  So I said, " I'm going to finish showing you these tubes before I move on "—and then she screamed and called the mail clerk working in the back, and told him to throw me out.  (*Boasting*)  He didn't do it by himself, though.  Had to call all the white loafers out in the square to get me through that door.

CORA  (*Fearfully*)  Lawd have mercy!

ROBERT  Guess if I hadn't-a had the Ford then, they'd've beat me half-to-death, but when I saw how many crackers there was, I jumped in the car and beat it on away.

CORA  Thank God for that!

ROBERT  Not even a football man (*Half-boasting*) like me could
tackle the whole junction. 'Bout a dozen colored guys standing
around, too, and not one of 'em would help me—the dumb jigga-
boos! They been telling me ever since I been here, (*Imitating darky
talk*) " You can't argue wid whut folks, man. You better stay out
o' this Junction. You must ain't got no sense, nigger! You's a
fool " . . . Maybe I am a fool, ma—but I didn't want to come back
here nohow.

CORA  I's sorry I sent for you.

ROBERT  Besides you, there ain't nobody in this country but a lot of
evil white folks and cowardly niggers. (*Earnestly*) I'm no nigger,
anyhow, am I, ma? I'm half-white. The Colonel's my father—the
richest man in the county—and I'm not going to take a lot of stuff
from nobody if I do have to stay here, not from the old man either.
He thinks I ought to be out there in the sun working, with Talbot
standing over me like I belonged in the chain gang. Well, he's got
another thought coming! (*Stubbornly*) I'm a Norwood—not a
field-hand nigger.

CORA  You means you ain't workin' no mo'?

ROBERT  (*Flaring*) No, I'm not going to work in the fields. What
did he send me away to school for—just to come back here and be
his servant, or pick his hills of cotton?

CORA  He sent you away to de school because *I* asked him and begged
him, and got down on my knees to him, that's why. (*Quietly*) And
now I just wants to make you see some sense, if you can. I knows,
honey, you reads in de books and de papers, and you knows a lot
more'n I do. But, chile, you's in Georgy—and I don't see how it is
you don't know where you's at. This ain't up North—and even up
yonder where we hears it's so fine, yo' sister has to pass for white
to get along good.

ROBERT  (*Bitterly*) I know it.

CORA  She ain't workin' in no hotel kitchen like de Colonel thinks.
She's in a office typewriting. And Sallie's studyin' de typewriter, too,
at de school, but yo' pappy don't know it. I knows we ain't s'posed
to study nothin' but cookin' and hard workin' here in Georgy. That's
all I ever done, or knowed about. I been workin' on this very place
all ma life—even 'fore I come to live in this Big House. When de
Colonel's wife died, I come here, and borned you chilluns. And de
Colonel's been real good to me in his way. Let you all sleep in this
house with me when you was little, and sent you all off to school

when you growed up. Ain't no white man in this county done that
with his cullud chilluns before, far as I can know. But you—Robert,
be awful, awful careful! When de Colonel comes back, in a few
minutes, he wants to talk to you. Talk right to him, boy. Talk
like you was colored, 'cause you ain't white.

ROBERT (*Angrily*) And I'm not black, either. Look at me, mama.
(*Rising and throwing up his arms*) Don't I look like my father?
Ain't I as light as he is? Ain't my eyes gray like his eyes are? (*The
noise of a car is heard outside*) Ain't this our house?

CORA That's him now. (*Agitated*) Hurry, chile, and let's we get out
of this room. Come on through yonder to the kitchen. (*She starts
toward the door left*) And I'll tell him you're here.

ROBERT I don't want to run into the kitchen. Isn't this our house?
(*As* CORA *crosses hurriedly left,* ROBERT *goes toward the front door*)
The Ford is parked out in front, anyway.

CORA (*At the door left to the rear of the house*) Robert! Robert!
(*As* ROBERT *nears the front door,* COLONEL NORWOOD *enters, almost
runs into the boy, stops at the threshold and stares unbelievingly at
his son.* CORA *backs up against the door left*)

NORWOOD Get out of here! (*He points toward the door to rear of
the house where* CORA *is standing*)

ROBERT (*Half-smiling*) Didn't you want to talk to me?

NORWOOD Get out of here!

ROBERT Not that way. (*The* COLONEL *raises his cane to strike the
boy.* CORA *screams.* BERT *draws himself up to his full height, taller
than the old man and looking very much like him, pale and proud.
The man and the boy face each other.* NORWOOD *does not strike*)

NORWOOD (*In a hoarse whisper*) Get out of here. (*His hand is
trembling as he points*)

CORA Robert! Come on, son, come on! Oh, my God, come on.
(*Opening the door left*)

ROBERT Not that way, ma. (ROBERT *walks proudly out the front
door.* NORWOOD, *in an impotent rage, crosses the room to a small
cabinet right, opens it nervously with a key from his pocket, takes out
a pistol, and starts toward the front door.* CORA *overtakes him, seizes
his arm, stops him*)

CORA He's our son, Tom. (*She sinks slowly to her knees, holding his
body*) Remember, he's our son.

CURTAIN

# ACT TWO

## SCENE ONE

TIME: *After supper. Sunset.*

SETTING: *The same.*

ACTION: *As the curtain rises, the stage is empty. Through the windows the late afternoon sun makes two bright paths toward the footlights.* SAM, *carrying a tray bearing a whiskey bottle and a bowl of ice, enters left and crosses toward the library. He stoops at the door right, listens a moment, knocks, then opens the door and goes in. In a moment* SAM *returns. As he leaves the library, he is heard replying to a request of* NORWOOD'S.

SAM    Yes, sah, Colonel! Sho' will, sah! Right away, sah! Yes, sah, I'll tell him. (*He closes the door and crosses the stage muttering to himself*) Six o'clock. Most nigh that now. Better tell Cora to get that boy right in here. Can't nobody else do nothin' with that fool Bert but Cora. (*He exits left. Can be heard calling*) Cora! You, Cora . . .

(*Again the stage is empty. Off stage, outside, the bark of a dog is heard, the sound of Negroes singing down the road, the cry of a child. The breeze moves the shadows of leaves and tree limbs across the sunlit paths from the windows. The door left opens and* CORA *enters, followed by* ROBERT)

CORA    (*Softly to* ROBERT *behind her in the dining room*) It's all right, son. He ain't come out yet, but it's nearly six, and that's when he said he wanted you, but I was afraid maybe you was gonna be late. I sent for you to come up here to de house and eat supper with me in de kitchen. Where'd you eat yo' vittuals at, chile?

ROBERT    Down at Willie's house, ma. After the old man tried to hit me you still want me to hang around and eat up here?

CORA    I wanted you to be here on time, honey, that's all. (*She is very nervous*) I kinder likes to have you eat with me sometimes, too, but you ain't et up here more'n once this summer. But this evenin' I just wanted you to be here when de Colonel sent word for you, 'cause we's done had enough trouble today.

ROBERT    He's not here on time, himself, is he?

CORA   He's in de library. Sam couldn't get him to eat no supper tonight, and I ain't seen him a-tall.

ROBERT   Maybe he wants to see me in the library, then.

CORA   You know he don't 'low no colored folks in there 'mongst his books and things 'cept Sam. Some o' his white friends goes in there, but none o' us.

ROBERT   Maybe he wants to see *me* in there, though.

CORA   Can't you never talk sense, Robert? This ain't no time for foolin' and jokin.' Nearly thirty years in this house and I ain't never been in there myself, not once, 'mongst de Colonel's papers. (*The clock strikes six*) Stand over yonder and wait till he comes out. I's gwine on upstairs now, so's he can talk to you. And don't aggravate him no mo' fo' God's sake. Agree to whatever he say. I's scared fo' you, chile, de way you been actin,' and de fool tricks you done today, and de trouble about de post office besides. Don't aggravate him. Fo' yo' sake, honey, 'cause I loves you—and fo' all de po' colored folks on this place what has such a hard time when his humors get on him—agree to whatever he say, will you, Bert?

ROBERT   All right, ma. (*Voice rising*) But he better not start to hit me again.

CORA   Shs-ss-s! He'll hear you. He's right in there.

ROBERT   (*Sullenly*) This was the day I ought to have started back to school—like my sister. I stayed my summer out here, didn't I? Why didn't he keep his promise to me? You said if I came home I could go back to college again.

CORA   Shs-ss-s! He'll be here now. Don't say nothin', chile. I's done all I could.

ROBERT   All right, ma.

CORA   (*Approaching the stairs*) I'll be in ma room, honey, where I can hear you when you goes out. I'll come down to de back door and see you 'fore you goes back to de shack. Don't aggravate him, chile.

(*She ascends the stairs. The boy sits down sullenly, left, and stares at the door opposite from which his father must enter. The clock strikes the quarter after six. The shadows of the window curtains have lengthened on the carpet. The sunshine has deepened to a pale orange, and the light paths grow less distinct across the floor. The boy sits up straight in his chair. He looks at the library door. It opens.* NORWOOD *enters. He is bent and pale. He looks across the room and sees the boy. Suddenly he straightens up. The*

*old commanding look comes into his face. He strides
directly across the room toward his son. The boy, half
afraid, half defiant, yet sure of himself, rises.* Now that
ROBERT *is standing, the white man turns, goes back to a
chair near the table, right, and seats himself. He takes out
a cigar, cuts off the end and lights it, and in a voice of
mixed condescension and contempt, he speaks to his son.*
ROBERT *remains standing near the chair*)

NORWOOD   I don't want to have to beat you another time as I did
when you were a child. The next time I might not be able to control
myself. I might kill you if I touched you again. I been runnin'
this plantation for thirty-five years, and I never had to beat a Nigra
as old as you are. I never had to beat one of Cora's children either—
but you. The rest of 'em had sense 'nough to keep out of my sight,
and to speak to me like they should . . . I don't have any trouble
with my colored folks. Never have trouble. They do what I say,
or what Mr. Talbot says, and that's all there is to it. I give 'em a
chance. If they turn in crops they get paid. If they're workin' for
wages, they get paid. If they want to spend their money on licker,
or buy an old car, or fix up their cabins, they can. Do what they
choose long as they know their places and it don't hinder their work.
And to Cora's young ones I give all the chances any colored folks
ever had in these parts. More'n many a white child's had. I sent
you all off to school. Let Bertha go on up North when she got grown
and educated. Intend to let Sallie do the same. Gave your brother
William that house he's living in when he got married, pay him for
his work, help him out if he needs it. None of my darkies suffer.
Sent you to college. Would have kept on, would have sent you back
today, but I don't intend to pay for no darky, or white boy either
if I had one, that acts the way you've been acting. And certainly for
no black fool. Now I want to know what's wrong with you? I don't
usually talk about what I'm going to do with anybody on this place.
It's my habit to tell people *what to do*, not discuss it with 'em. But I
want to know what's the matter with you—whether you're crazy or
not. In that case, you'll have to be locked up. And if you aren't,
you'll have to change your ways a damn sight or it won't be safe
for you here, and you know it—venting your impudence on white
women, parking the car in front of my door, driving like mad
through the Junction, and going, everywhere, just as you please.
Now, I'm going to let you talk to me, but I want you to talk right.

ROBERT  (*Still standing*)  What do you mean, "talk right?"

NORWOOD  I mean talk like a nigger should to a white man.

ROBERT  Oh! But I'm not a nigger, Colonel Tom. I'm your son.

NORWOOD  (*Testily*)  You're Cora's boy.

ROBERT  Women don't have children by themselves.

NORWOOD  Nigger women don't know the fathers. You're a bastard.

(ROBERT *clenches his fist.* NORWOOD *turns toward the drawer where the pistol is, takes it out, and lays it on the table. The wind blows the lace curtains at the windows, and sweeps the shadows of falling leaves across the paths of sunlight on the floor*)

ROBERT  I've heard that before. I've heard it from Negroes, and I've heard it from white folks. Now I hear it from you. (*Slowly*) You're talking about my mother.

NORWOOD  I'm talking about Cora, yes. Her children are bastards.

ROBERT  (*Quickly*)  And you're their father. (*Angrily*) How come I look like you, if you're not my father?

NORWOOD  Don't shout at me, boy. I can hear you. (*Half-smiling*) How come your skin is yellow and your elbows rusty? How come they threw you out of the post office today for talking to a white woman? How come you're the crazy young buck you are?

ROBERT  They had no right to throw me out. I asked for my money back when I saw the broken tubes. Just as you had no right to raise that cane today when I was standing at the door of this house where *you* live, while *I* have to sleep in a shack down the road with the field hands. (*Slowly*) But my mother sleeps with you.

NORWOOD  You don't like it?

ROBERT  No, I don't like it.

NORWOOD  What can you do about it?

ROBERT  (*After a pause*)  I'd like to kill all the white men in the world.

NORWOOD  (*Starting*)  Niggers like you are hung to trees.

ROBERT  I'm not a nigger.

NORWOOD  You don't like your own race? (ROBERT *is silent*) Yet you don't like white folks either?

ROBERT  (*Defiantly*)  You think I ought to?

NORWOOD  You evidently don't like me.

ROBERT  (*Boyishly*)  I used to like you, when I first knew you were my father, when I was a little kid, before that time you beat me under the feet of your horses. (*Slowly*) I liked you until then.

NORWOOD (*A little pleased*) So you did, heh? (*Fingering his pistol*) A pickaninny calling me "papa." I should've broken your young neck for that first time. I should've broken your head for you today, too—since I didn't then.

ROBERT (*Laughing scornfully*) You should've broken my head?

NORWOOD Should've gotten rid of you before this. But you was Cora's child. I tried to help you. (*Aggrieved*) I treated you decent, schooled you. Paid for it. But tonight you'll get the hell off this place and stay off. Get the hell out of this county. (*Suddenly furious*) Get out of this state. Don't let me lay eyes on you again. Get out of here now. Talbot and the storekeeper are coming up here this evening to talk cotton with me. I'll tell Talbot to *see* that you go. That's all. (NORWOOD *motions toward the door, left*) Tell Sam to come in here when you go out. Tell him to make a light here.

ROBERT (*Impudently*) Ring for Sam—I'm not going through the kitchen. (*He starts toward the front door*) I'm not your servant. You're not going to tell me what to do. You're not going to have Talbot run me off the place like a field hand you don't want to use any more.

NORWOOD (*Springing between his son and the front door, pistol in hand*) You black bastard! (ROBERT *goes toward him calmly, grasps his father's arm and twists it until the gun falls to the floor. The older man bends backward in startled fury and pain*) Don't you dare put your . . .

ROBERT (*Laughing*) Why don't you shoot, papa? (*Louder*) Why don't you shoot?

NORWOOD (*Gasping as he struggles, fighting back*) . . . black . . . hands . . . on . . . you . . .

ROBERT (*Hysterically, as he takes his father by the throat*) Why don't you shoot, papa? (NORWOOD'S *hands claw the air helplessly.* ROBERT *chokes the struggling white man until his body grows limp*) Why don't you shoot! (*Laughing*) Why don't you shoot? Huh? Why?

> (CORA *appears at the top of the stairs, hearing the commotion. She screams*)

CORA Oh, my God! (*She rushes down.* ROBERT *drops the body of his father at her feet in a path of flame from the setting sun.* CORA *starts and stares in horror*)

ROBERT (*Wildly*) Why didn't he shoot, mama? He didn't want *me* to live. Why didn't he shoot? (*Laughing*) He was the boss. Telling me what to do. Why didn't he shoot, then? He was the white man.

CORA *(Falling on the body)* Colonel Tom! Colonel Tom! Tom! Tom! *(Gazes across the corpse at her son)* He's yo' father, Bert.

ROBERT He's dead. The white man's dead. My father's dead. *(Laughing)* I'm living.

CORA Tom! Tom! Tom!

ROBERT Niggers are living. He's dead. *(Picks up the pistol)* This is what he wanted to kill me with, but he's dead. I can use it now. Use it on all the white men in the world, because they'll be coming looking for me now. *(Stuffs the pistol into his shirt)* They'll want me now.

CORA *(Rising and running toward her boy)* Quick, chile, out that way, *(Pointing toward the front door)* so they won't see you in de kitchen. Make for de swamp, honey. Cross de fields fo' de swamp. Go de crick way. In runnin' water, dogs can't smell no tracks. Hurry, chile!

ROBERT Yes, mama. I can go out the front way now, easy. But if I see they gonna get me before I can reach the swamp, I'm coming back here, mama, and *(Proudly)* let them take me out of my father's house—if they can. *(Pats the gun under his shirt)* They're not going to string me up to some roadside tree for the crackers to laugh at.

CORA *(Moaning aloud)* Oh, O-o-o! Hurry! Hurry, chile!

ROBERT I'm going, ma. *(He opens the door. The sunset streams in like a river of blood)*

CORA Run, chile!

ROBERT Not out of my father's house. *(He exits slowly, tall and straight against the sun)*

CORA Fo' God's sake, hurry, chile! *(Glancing down the road)* Lawd have mercy! There's Talbot and de storekeeper in de drive. They sees my boy! *(Moaning)* They sees ma boy. *(Relieved)* But thank God, they's passin' him! *(CORA backs up against the wall in the vestibule. She stands as if petrified as TALBOT and the STOREKEEPER enter)*

TALBOT Hello, Cora. What's the matter with you? Where's that damn fool boy o' your'n goin', coming out the front door like he owned the house? What's the matter with you, woman? Can't you talk? Can't you talk? Where's Norwood? Let's have some light in this dark place. *(He reaches behind the door and turns on the lights.* CORA *remains backed up against the wall, looking out into the twilight, watching* ROBERT *as he goes across the field*) Good God, Jim! Look at this! (*The* TWO WHITE MEN *stop in horror before the sight of* NORWOOD's *body on the floor*)

STOREKEEPER He's blue in the face. (*Bends over the body*) That nigger we saw walking out the door! (*Rising excitedly*) That nigger bastard of Cora's . . . (*Stooping over the body again*) Why the Colonel's dead!

TALBOT That nigger! (*Rushes toward the door*) He's running toward the swamp now . . . We'll get him . . . Telephone town— there, in the library. Telephone the sheriff. Get men, white men, after that nigger.

> (STOREKEEPER *rushes into the library. He can be heard talking excitedly on the phone*)

STOREKEEPER Sheriff! Sheriff! Is this the sheriff? I'm calling from Norwood's plantation. That nigger, Bert, has just killed Norwood— and run, headed for the swamp. Notify the gas station at the cross-roads! Tell the boys at the sawmill to head him off at the creek. Warn everybody to be on the lookout. Call your deputies! Yes! Yes! Spread a dragnet. Get out the dogs. Meanwhile we'll start after him. (*He slams the phone down and comes back into the room*) Cora, where's Norwood's car? In the barn? (CORA *does not answer*)

TALBOT Talk, you black bitch!

> (*She remains silent.* TALBOT *runs, yelling and talking, out into the yard, followed by the* STOREKEEPER. *Sounds of excited shouting outside, and the roar of a motor rushing down the drive. In the sky the twilight deepens into early night.* CORA *stands looking into the darkness*)

CORA My boy can't get to de swamp now. They's telephoned the white folks down that way. So he'll come back home now. Maybe he'll turn into de crick and follow de branch home directly. (*Protectively*) But they shan't get him. I'll make a place for to hide him. I'll make a place upstairs down under de floor, under ma bed. In a minute ma boy'll be runnin' from de white folks with their hounds and their ropes and their guns and everything they uses to kill po' colored folks with. (*Distressed*) Ma boy'll be out there runnin'. (*Turning to the body on the floor*) Colonel Tom, you hear me? Our boy, out there runnin'. (*Fiercely*) *You* said he was ma boy— *ma* bastard boy. I heard you . . . but he's yours too . . . but yonder in

de dark runnin'—runnin' from yo' people, from white people.
(*Pleadingly*) Why don't you get up and stop 'em? He's *your* boy.
His eyes is gray—like your eyes. He's tall like you's tall. He's
proud like you's proud. And he's runnin'—runnin' from po' white
trash what ain't worth de little finger o' nobody what's got your
blood in 'em, Tom. (*Demandingly*) Why don't you get up from
there and stop 'em, Colonel Tom? What's that you say? He ain't
your chile? He's ma bastard chile? My yellow bastard chile?
(*Proudly*) Yes, he's mine. But don't call him that. Don't you
touch him. Don't you put your white hands on him. You's beat him
enough, and cussed him enough. Don't you touch him now. He
*is* ma boy, and no white folks gonna touch him now. That's finished.
I'm gonna make a place for him upstairs under ma bed. (*Backs
away from the body toward the stairs*) He's ma chile. Don't you
come in ma bedroom while he's up there. Don't you come to my
bed no mo'. I calls you to help me now, and you just lays there.
I calls you for to wake up, and you just lays there. Whenever you
called me, in de night, I woke up. When you called for me to love,
I always reached out ma arms fo' you. I borned you five chilluns and
now one of 'em is out yonder in de dark runnin' from yo' people.
Our youngest boy out yonder in de dark runnin'. (*Accusingly*) He's
runnin' from you, too. You said he warn't your'n—he's just Cora's
po' little yellow bastard. But he *is* your'n, Colonel Tom. (*Sadly*)
And he's runnin' from you. You are out yonder in de dark, (*Points
toward the door*) runnin' our chile, with de hounds and de gun in
yo' hand, and Talbot's followin' 'hind you with a rope to hang
Robert with. (*Confidently*) I been sleepin' with you too long,
Colonel Tom, not to know that this ain't you layin' down there with
yo' eyes shut on de floor. You can't fool me—you ain't never been
so still like this before—you's out yonder runnin' ma boy. (*Scornfully*) Colonel Thomas Norwood, runnin' ma boy through de fields
in de dark, runnin' ma poor little helpless Bert through de fields in
de dark to lynch him . . . Damn you, Colonel Norwood! (*Backing
slowly up the stairs, staring at the rigid body below her*) Damn you,
Thomas Norwood! God damn you!

CURTAIN

## SCENE TWO

TIME: *One hour later. Night.*
SETTING: *The same.*
ACTION: *As the curtain rises, the* UNDERTAKER *is talking to* SAM *at the outer door. All through this act the approaching cries of the man hunt are heard.*

UNDERTAKER    Reckon there won't be no orders to bring his corpse back out here, Sam. None of us ain't seen Talbot or Mr. Higgins, but I'm sure they'll be having the funeral in town. The coroner told us to bring the body into the Junction. Ain't nothin' but niggers left out here now.

SAM    (*Very frightened*)  Yes, sah! Yes, sah! You's right, sah! Nothin' but us niggers, sah!

UNDERTAKER    The Colonel didn't have no relatives far as you know, did he, Sam?

SAM    No, sah. Ain't had none. No, sah! You's right, sah!

UNDERTAKER    Well, you got everything o' his locked up around here, ain't you? Too bad there ain't no white folks about to look after the Colonel's stuff, but every white man that's able to walk's out with the posse. They'll have that young nigger swingin' before ten.

SAM    (*Trembling*)  Yes, sah, yes, sah! I 'spects so. Yes, sah!

UNDERTAKER    Say, where's that woman the Colonel's been living with —where's that black housekeeper, Cora, that murderin' bastard's mother?

SAM    She here, sah! She's up in her room.

UNDERTAKER    (*Curiously*)  I'd like to see how she looks. Get her down here. Say, how about a little drink before we start that ride back to town, for me and my partner out there with the body?

SAM    Cora got de keys to all de licker, sah!

UNDERTAKER    Well, get her down here then, double quick! (SAM *goes up the stairs. The* UNDERTAKER *leans in the front doorway talking to his partner outside in the wagon*) Bad business, a white man having saucy nigger children on his hands, and his black woman living in his own house.

VOICE OUTSIDE    Damn right, Charlie.

UNDERTAKER    Norwood didn't have a gang o' yellow gals, though, like Higgins and some o' these other big bugs. Just this one bitch

far's I know, livin' with him damn near like a wife. Didn't even
have much company out here. And they tell me ain't been a white
woman stayed here overnight since his wife died when I was a baby.
(SAM'S *shuffle is heard on the stairs*) Here comes a drink, I reckon,
boy. You needn't get down off the ambulance. I'll have Sam bring
it out there to you. (SAM *descends followed by* CORA *who comes
down the stairs. She says nothing. The* UNDERTAKER *looks up
grinning at* CORA) Well, so you're the Cora that's got these educated
nigger children? Hum-m! Well, I guess you'll see one of 'em
swinging full of bullet holes when you wake up in the morning.
They'll probably hang him to that tree down here by the Colonel's
gate—'cause they tell me he strutted right out the front gate past
that tree after the murder. Or maybe they'll burn him. How'd you
like to see him swinging there roasted in the morning when you
wake up, girlie?

CORA    (*Calmly*)   Is that all you wanted to say to me?

UNDERTAKER    Don't get smart! Maybe you think there's nobody to
boss you now. We gonna have a little drink before we go. Get out
a bottle of rye.

CORA    I takes ma orders from Colonel Norwood, sir.

UNDERTAKER    Well, you'll take no more orders from him. He's dead
out there in my wagon—so get along and get the bottle.

CORA    He's out yonder with de mob, not in your wagon.

UNDERTAKER    I tell you he's in my wagon!

CORA    He's out there with de mob.

UNDERTAKER    God damn! (*To his partner outside*) I believe this
black woman's gone crazy in here. (*To* CORA) Get the keys out for
that licker, and be quick about it! (CORA *does not move.* SAM *looks
from one to the other, frightened*)

VOICE OUTSIDE    Aw, to hell with the licker, Charlie. Come on, let's
start back to town. We want to get in on some of that excitement,
too. They should've found that nigger by now—and I want to see
'em drag him out here.

UNDERTAKER    All right, Jim. (*To* CORA *and* SAM) Don't you all go
to bed until you see that bonfire. You niggers are getting besides
yourselves around Polk County. We'll burn a few more of you if
you don't be careful. (*He exits, and the noise of the dead-wagon
going down the road is heard*)

SAM    Oh, Lawd, hab mercy on me! I prays, Lawd hab mercy! O, ma
Lawd, ma Lawd, ma Lawd! Cora, is you a fool? *Is* you a fool? Why

didn't you give de mens de licker, riled as these white folks is? In ma old age is I gonna be burnt by de crackers? Lawd, is I sinned? Lawd, what has I done? (*Suddenly stops moaning and becomes schemingly calm*) I don't have to stay here tonight, does I? I done locked up de Colonel's library, and he can't be wantin' nothin'. No, ma Lawd, he won't want nothin' now. He's with Jesus—or with de devil, one. (*To* CORA) I's gwine on away from here. Sam's gwine in town to his chilluns' house, and I ain't gwine by no road either. I gwine through de holler where I don't have to pass no white folks.

CORA   Yes, Samuel, you go on. De Colonel can get his own drinks when he comes back tonight.

SAM   (*Bucking his eyes in astonishment at* CORA) Lawd God Jesus! (*He bolts out of the room as fast as his old legs will carry him.* CORA *comes down stairs, looks for a long moment out into the darkness, then closes the front door and draws the blinds. She looks down at the spot where the* COLONEL'S *body lay*)

CORA   All de colored folks are runnin' from you tonight. Po' Colonel Tom, you too old now to be out with de mob. You got no business goin', but you had to go, I reckon. I 'members that time they hung Luke Jordon, you sent yo' dogs out to hunt him. The next day you killed all de dogs. You were kinder softhearted. Said you didn't like that kind of sport. Told me in bed one night you could hear them dogs howlin' in yo' sleep. But de time they burnt de courthouse when that po' little cullud boy was locked up in it cause they said he hugged a white girl, you was with 'em again. Said you had to go help 'em. Now you's out chasin' ma boy. (*As she stands at the window, she sees a passing figure*) There goes yo' other woman, Colonel Tom, Livonia is runnin' from you too, now. She would've wanted you last night. Been wantin' you again ever since she got old and fat and you stopped layin' with her and put her in the kitchen to cook. Don't think I don't know, Colonel Tom. Don't think I don't remember them nights when you used to sleep in that cabin down by de spring. I knew 'Vonia was there with you. I ain't no fool, Colonel Tom. But she ain't bore you no chilluns. I'm de one that bore 'em. (*Musing*) White mens, and colored womens, and little bastard chilluns—that's de old way of de South—but it's ending now. Three of your yellow brothers yo' father had by Aunt Sallie Deal—what had to come and do your laundry to make her livin'— you got colored relatives scattered all over this county. Them de ways o' de South—mixtries, mixtries. (WILLIAM *enters left, silently, as his mother talks. She is sitting in a chair now. Without looking up*) Is that you, William?

WILLIAM Yes, ma, it's me.

CORA Is you runnin' from him, too?

WILLIAM (*Hesitatingly*) Well, ma, you see. . . don't you think kinder . . . well, I reckon I ought to take Libby and ma babies on down to de church house with Reverend Martin and them, or else get 'long to town if I can hitch up them mules. They's scared to be out here, my wife and her ma. All de folks done gone from de houses down yonder by de branch, and you can hear de hounds a bayin' off yonder by de swamp, and cars is tearin' up that road, and de white folks is yellin' and hollerin' and carryin' on somethin' terrible over toward de brook. I done told Robert 'bout his foolishness. They's gonna hang him sure. Don't you think you better be comin' with us, ma. That is, do you want to? 'Course we can go by ourselves, and maybe you wants to stay here and take care o' de big house. I don't want to leave you, ma, but I . . . I . . .

CORA Yo' brother'll be back, son, then I won't be by myself.

WILLIAM (*Bewildered by his mother's sureness*) I though Bert went . . . I thought he run . . . I thought . . .

CORA No, honey. He went, but they ain't gonna get him out there. I sees him comin' back here now, to be with me. I's gwine to guard him 'till he can get away.

WILLIAM Then de white folks'll come here, too.

CORA Yes, de Colonel'll come back here sure. (*The deep baying of the hounds is heard at a distance through the night*) Colonel Tom will come after his son.

WILLIAM My God, ma! Come with us to town.

CORA Go on, William, go on! Don't wait for them to get back. You never was much like neither one o' them—neither de Colonel or Bert—you's mo' like de field hands. Too much o' ma blood in you, I guess. You never liked Bert much, neither, and you always was afraid of de Colonel. Go on, son, and hide yo' wife and her ma and your chilluns. Ain't nothin' gonna hurt you. You never did go against nobody. Neither did I, till tonight. Tried to live right and not hurt a soul, white or colored. (*Addressing space*) I tried to live right, Lord. (*Angrily*) Tried to live right, Lord. (*Throws out her arms resentfully as if to say, "and this is what you give me."*) What's de matter, Lawd, you ain't with me?

(*The hounds are heard howling again*)

WILLIAM I'm gone, ma. (*He exits fearfully as his mother talks*)
CORA (*Bending over the spot on the floor where the* COLONEL *has lain. She calls*) Colonel Tom! Colonel Tom! Colonel Tom! Look! Bertha and Sallie and William and Bert, all your chilluns, runnin' from you, and you layin' on de floor there, dead! (*Pointing*) Out yonder with the mob, dead. And when you come home, upstairs in my bed on top of my body, dead. (*Goes to the window, returns, sits down, and begins to speak as if remembering a far-off dream*) Colonel Thomas Norwood! I'm just poor Cora Lewis, Colonel Norwood. Little black Cora Lewis, Colonel Norwood. I'm just fifteen years old. Thirty years ago, you put your hands on me to feel my breasts, and you say, " You a pretty little piece of flesh, ain't you? Black and sweet, ain't you? " And I lift up ma face, and you pull me to you, and we laid down under the trees that night, and I wonder if your wife'll know when you go back up the road into the big house. And I wonder if my mama'll know it, when I go back to our cabin. Mama said she nursed you when you was a baby, just like she nursed me. And I loved you in the dark, down there under that tree by de gate, afraid of you and proud of you, feelin' your gray eyes lookin' at me in de dark. Then I cried and cried and told ma mother about it, but she didn't take it hard like I thought she'd take it. She said fine white mens like de young Colonel always took good care o' their colored womens. She said it was better than marryin' some black field hand and workin' all your life in de cotton and cane. Better even than havin' a job like ma had, takin' care o' de white chilluns. Takin' care o' you, Colonel Tom. (*As* CORA *speaks the sound of the approaching mob gradually grow louder and louder. Auto horns, the howling of dogs, the far-off shouts of men, full of malignant force and power, increase in volume*) And I was happy because I liked you, 'cause you was tall and proud, 'cause you said I was sweet to you and called me purty. And when yo' wife died—de Mrs. Norwood (*Scornfully*) that never bore you any chilluns, the pale beautiful Mrs. Norwood that was like a slender pine tree in de winter frost . . . I knowed you wanted me. I was full with child by you then—William, it was—our first boy. And ma mammy said, go up there and keep de house for Colonel Tom, sweep de floors and make de beds, and by and by, you won't have to sweep de floors and make no beds. And what ma mammy said was right. It all come true. Sam and Rusus and 'Vonia and Lucy did de waitin' on you and me, and de washin' and de cleanin' and de cookin'. And all I

did was a little sewin' now and then, and a little preservin' in de summer and a little makin' of pies and sweet cakes and things you like to eat on Christmas. And de years went by. And I was always ready for you when you come to me in de night. And we had them chilluns, your chilluns and mine, Tom Norwood, all of 'em! William, born dark like me, dumb like me, and then Baby John what died; then Bertha, white and smart like you; and then Bert with your eyes and your ways and your temper, and mighty nigh your color; then Sallie, nearly white, too, and smart, and purty. But Bert was yo' chile! He was always yo' child . . . Good-looking, and kind, and headstrong, and strange, and stubborn, and proud like you, and de one I could love most 'cause he needed de most lovin'. And he wanted to call you " papa," and I tried to teach him no, but he did it anyhow and (*Sternly*) you beat him, Colonel Thomas Norwood. And he growed up with de beatin' in his heart, and your eyes in his head, and your ways, and your pride. And this summer he looked like you that time I first knowed you down by de road under them trees, young and fiery and proud. There was no touchin' Bert, just like there was no touchin' you. I could only love him, like I loved you. I could only love him. But I couldn't talk to him, because he hated you. He had your ways—and you beat him! After you beat that chile, then you died, Colonel Norwood. You died here in this house, and you been living dead a long time. You lived dead. (*Her voice rises above the nearing sounds of the mob*) And when I said this evenin', " Get up! Why don't you help me? " You'd done been dead a long time—a long time before you laid down on this floor, here, with the breath choked out o' you—and Bert standin' over you living, living, living. That's why you hated him. And you want to kill him. Always, you wanted to kill him. Out there with de hounds and de torches and de cars and de guns, you want to kill ma boy. But you won't kill him! He's comin' home first. He's comin' home to me. He's comin' home! (*Outside the noise is tremendous now, the lights of autos flash on the window curtains, there are shouts and cries.* CORA *sits, tense, in the middle of the room*) He's comin' home!

A MAN'S VOICE  (*Outside*)  He's somewhere on this lot.

ANOTHER VOICE  Don't shoot, men. We want to get him alive.

VOICE  Close in on him. He must be in them bushes by the house.

FIRST VOICE  Porch! Porch! Porch! There he is yonder—running to the door!

(*Suddenly shots are heard. The door bursts open and* ROBERT *enters, firing back into the darkness. The shots are returned by the mob, breaking the windows. Flares, lights, voices, curses, screams*)

VOICES   Nigger! Nigger! Nigger! Get the nigger!

(CORA *rushes toward the door and bolts it after her son's entrance*)

CORA   (*Leaning against the door*)   I was waiting for you, honey. Yo' hiding place is all ready, upstairs, under ma bed, under de floor. I sawed a place there fo' you. They can't find you there. Hurry— before yo' father comes.

ROBERT   (*Panting*)   No time to hide, ma. They're at the door now. They'll be coming up the back way, too. (*Sounds of knocking and the breaking of glass*) They'll be coming in the windows. They'll be coming in everywhere. And only one bullet left, ma. It's for me.

CORA   Yes, it's fo' you, chile. Save it. Go upstairs in mama's room. Lay on ma bed and rest.

ROBERT   (*Going slowly toward the stairs with the pistol in his hand*) Goodnight, ma. I'm awful tired of running, ma. They been chasing me for hours.

CORA   Goodnight, son.

(CORA *follows him to the foot of the steps. The door begins to give at the forcing of the mob. As* ROBERT *disappears above, it bursts open. A great crowd of white men pour into the room with guns, ropes, clubs, flashlights, and knives.* CORA *turns on the stairs, facing them quietly.* TALBOT, *the leader of the mob, stops*)

TALBOT   Be careful, men. He's armed. (*To* CORA)   Where is that yellow bastard of yours—upstairs?

CORA   Yes, he's going to sleep. Be quiet, you all. Wait. (*She bars the way with outspread arms*)

TALBOT   (*Harshly*)   Wait, hell! Come on, boys, let's go! (*A single shot is heard upstairs*)   What's that?

CORA   (*Calmly*)   My boy . . . is gone . . . to sleep!

(TALBOT *and some of the men rush up the stairway,* CORA *makes a final gesture of love toward the room above. Yelling and shouting, through all the doors and windows, a great crowd pours into the room. The roar of the mob fills the house, the whole night, the whole world. Suddenly*

           TALBOT *returns at the top of the steps and a hush falls*
           *over the crowd*)

TALBOT   Too late, men. We're just a little too late.

           (*A sigh of disappointment rises from the mob.* TALBOT
           *comes down the stairs, walks up to* CORA *and slaps her once*
           *across the face. She does not move. It is as though no*
           *human hand can touch her again*)

           CURTAIN

# SOUL GONE HOME

*A One-Act Play*

## CHARACTERS

THE MOTHER
THE SON
TWO MEN

# SOUL GONE HOME

*Night.*

*A tenement room, bare, ugly, dirty. An unshaded electric-light bulb. In the middle of the room a cot on which the body of a* NEGRO YOUTH *is lying. His hands are folded across his chest. There are pennies on his eyes. He is a soul gone home.*

*As the curtain rises, his* MOTHER, *a large, middle-aged woman in a red sweater, kneels weeping beside the cot, loudly simulating grief.*

MOTHER  Oh, Gawd! Oh, Lawd! Why did you take my son from me? Oh, Gawd, why did you do it? He was all I had! Oh, Lawd, what am I gonna do? (*Looking at the dead boy and stroking his head*) Oh, son! Oh, Ronnie! Oh, my boy, speak to me! Ronnie, say something to me! Son, why don't you talk to your mother? Can't you see she's bowed down in sorrow? Son, speak to me, just a word! Come back from the spirit-world and speak to me! Ronnie, come back from the dead and speak to your mother!

SON  (*Lying there dead as a doornail. Speaking loudly*)  I wish I wasn't dead, so I *could* speak to you. You been a hell of a mama!

MOTHER  (*Falling back from the cot in astonishment, but still on her knees*)  Ronnie! Ronnie! What's that you say? What you sayin' to your mother? (*Wild-eyed*)  Is you done opened your mouth and spoke to me?

SON  I said you a hell of a mama!

MOTHER  (*Rising suddenly and backing away, screaming loudly*)  Awo-ooo-o! Ronnie, that ain't you talkin'!

SON  Yes, it is me talkin', too! I say you been a no-good mama.

MOTHER  What for you talkin' to me like that, Ronnie? You ain't never said nothin' like that to me before.

SON  I know it, but I'm dead now—and I can say what I want to say. (*Stirring*)  You done called on me to talk, ain't you? Lemme take these pennies off my eyes so I can see. (*He takes the coins off his eyes, throws them across the room, and sits up in bed. He is a very dark boy in a torn white shirt. He looks hard at his mother*)  Mama, you know you ain't done me right.

MOTHER   What you mean, I ain't done you right? (*She is rooted in horror*) What you mean, huh?

SON   You know what I mean.

MOTHER   No, I don't neither. (*Trembling violently*) What you mean comin' back to haunt your poor old mother? Ronnie, what does you mean?

SON   (*Leaning forward*) I'll tell you just what I mean! You been a bad mother to me.

MOTHER   Shame! Shame! Shame, talkin' to your mama that away. Damn it! Shame! I'll slap your face. (*She starts toward him, but he rolls his big white eyes at her, and she backs away*) Me, what borned you! Me, what suffered the pains o' death to bring you into this world! Me, what raised you up, what washed your dirty didies. (*Sorrowfully*) And now I'm left here mighty nigh prostrate 'cause you gone from me! Ronnie, what you mean talkin' to *me* like that—what brought you into this world?

SON   You never did feed me good, that's what I mean! Who wants to come into the world hongry, and go out the same way?

MOTHER   What you mean hongry? When I had money, ain't I fed you?

SON   (*Sullenly*) Most of the time you ain't had no money.

MOTHER   'Twarn't my fault then.

SON   'Twarn't *my* fault neither.

MOTHER   (*Defensively*) You always was so weak and sickly, you couldn't earn nothin' sellin' papers.

SON   I know it.

MOTHER   You never was no use to me.

SON   So you just lemme grow up in the street, and I ain't had no manners nor morals, neither.

MOTHER   Manners and morals? Ronnie, where'd you learn all them big words?

SON   I learnt 'em just now in the spirit-world.

MOTHER   (*Coming nearer*) But you ain't been dead no more'n an hour.

SON   That's long enough to learn a lot.

MOTHER   Well, what else did you find out?

SON   I found out you was a hell of a mama puttin' me out in the cold to sell papers soon as I could even walk.

MOTHER   What? You little liar!

SON   If I'm lyin', I'm dyin'! And lettin' me grow up all bowlegged and stunted from undernourishment.

MOTHER  Under-nurse-mint?

SON  Undernourishment. You heard what the doctor said last week?

MOTHER  Naw, what'd he say?

SON  He said I was dyin' o' undernourishment, that's what he said. He said I had TB 'cause I didn't have enough to eat never when I were a child. And he said I couldn't get well, nohow eating nothin' but beans ever since I been sick. Said I needed milk and eggs. And you said you ain't got no money for milk and eggs, which I know you ain't. (*Gently*) We never had no money, mama, not even since you took up hustlin' on the streets.

MOTHER  Son, money ain't everything.

SON  Naw, but when you got TB you have to have milk and eggs.

MOTHER  (*Advancing sentimentally*)  Anyhow, I love you, Ronnie!

SON  (*Rudely*)  Sure you love me—but here I am dead.

MOTHER  (*Angrily*)  Well, damn your hide, you ain't even decent dead. If you was, you wouldn't be sittin' there jawin' at your mother when she's sheddin' every tear she's got for you tonight.

SON  First time you ever did cry for me, far as I know.

MOTHER  Tain't! You's a liar! I cried when I borned you—you was such a big child—ten pounds.

SON  Then *I* did the cryin' after that, I reckon.

MOTHER  (*Proudly*)  Sure, I could of let you die, but I didn't. Naw, I kept you with me—off and on. And I lost the chance to marry many a good man, too—if it weren't for you. No man wants to take care o' nobody else's child. (*Self-pityingly*) You been a burden to me, Randolph.

SON  (*Angrily*)  What did you have me for then, in the first place?

MOTHER  How could I help havin' you, you little bastard? Your father ruint me—and you's the result. And I been worried with you for sixteen years. (*Disgustedly*) Now, just when you get big enough to work and do me some good, you have to go and die.

SON  I sure am dead!

MOTHER  But you ain't decent dead! Here you come back to haunt your poor old mama, and spoil her cryin' spell, and spoil the mournin'. (*There is the noise of an ambulance gong outside. The* MOTHER *goes to the window and looks down into the street. Turns to* SON) Ronnie, lay down quick! Here comes the city's ambulance to take you to the undertaker's. Don't let them white men see you dead, sitting up here quarrelin' with your mother. Lay down and fold your hands back like I had 'em.

SON (*Passing his hand across his head*) All right, but gimme that
comb yonder and my stocking cap. I don't want to go out of here
with my hair standin' straight up in front, even if I is dead.
(*The* MOTHER *hands him a comb and his stocking cap. The* SON *combs
his hair and puts the cap on. Noise of men coming up the stairs*)

MOTHER Hurry up, Ronnie, they'll be here in no time.

SON Aw, they got another flight to come yet. Don't rush me, ma!

MOTHER Yes, but I got to put these pennies back on your eyes, boy!
(*She searches in a corner for the coins as her* SON *lies down and
folds his hands, stiff in death. She finds the coins and puts them
nervously on his eyes, watching the door meanwhile. A knock*)
Come in.

(*Enter two* MEN *in the white coats of city health employees*)

MAN Somebody sent for us to get the body of Ronnie Bailey? Third
floor, apartment five.

MOTHER Yes, sir, here he is! (*Weeping loudly*) He's my boy! Oh,
Lawd, he's done left me! Oh, Lawdy, he's done gone home! His
soul's gone home! Oh, what am I gonna do? Mister! Mister!
Mister, the Lawd's done took him home! (*As the* MEN *unfold the
stretchers, she continues to weep hysterically. They place the boy's
thin body on the stretchers and cover it with a rubber cloth. Each
man takes his end of the stretchers. Silently, they walk out the door
as the* MOTHER *wails*) Oh, my son! Oh, my boy! Come back, come
back, come back! Ronnie, come back! (*One loud scream as the door
closes*) Awo-ooo-o!
(*As the footsteps of the men die down on the stairs, the
MOTHER becomes suddenly quiet. She goes to a broken
mirror and begins to rouge and powder her face. In the
street the ambulance gong sounds fainter and fainter in
the distance. The* MOTHER *takes down an old fur coat from
a nail and puts it on. Before she leaves, she smooths back
the quilts on the cot from which the dead boy has been
removed. She looks into the mirror again, and once more
whitens her face with powder. She dons a red hat. From
a handbag she takes a cigarette, lights it, and walks slowly
out the door. At the door she switches off the light. The
hallway is dimly illuminated. She turns before closing the
door, looks back into the room, and speaks*)

MOTHER Tomorrow, Ronnie, I'll buy you some flowers—if I can pick
up a dollar tonight. You was a hell of a no-good son, I swear!

CURTAIN

# LITTLE HAM

*A Comedy in Three Acts*

# CHARACTERS

MADAM LUCILLE BELL  *Proprietress of Paradise Shining Parlors*
SHINGLE  *A lazy shine boy*
CUSTOMER  *On the shine stand*
JANITOR  *A numbers addict*
SUGAR LOU BIRD  *A Harlem chorus girl*
LITTLE HAM  *A sporty young shoe shiner*
MATTIE BEA  *A married woman*

OLD LADY
SHABBY MAN
BOSS LEROY  *A Harlem racketeer*
MAN IN BOOTS
TINY LEE  *A hairdresser*
LITTLE BOY
1ST DETECTIVE
2ND DETECTIVE
YOUTH
JASPER  *Night shine boy*
WEST INDIAN
DEACONESS
TALL GUY
HOT STUFF MAN
PRETTY WOMAN
MASCULINE LADY
NEWSBOY
BUTCH  *Gangster*
JIGGERS  *Gang leader*
DUTCH  *Gangster*

OPAL  *Manicurist*
LULU  *A hairdresser, Tiny's sister*
MAMA  *A customer*
SNOOKS  *Her child*
STAID LADY  *A customer*
MISSOURI  *Her little girl*
LODGE LADY
DIVINITE
DELIVERY BOY
A COP
NELSON  *A dog*
JACK  *Lulu's boy friend*
GILBERT  *Tiny's used-to-be*
MASTER OF CEREMONIES  *At the Hello Club Ball*
BERIBBONED COMMITTEE MEMBERS
DANCERS
ORCHESTRA

# ACT ONE

TIME: Late 1920's
PLACE: Harlem

*SCENES*

ACT ONE    The Paradise Shining Parlors
ACT TWO    Interior of Tiny's Beauty Shop
ACT THREE
   *Scene One*: Tiny's Boudoir
   *Scene Two*: The Savoy Ballroom

*Late morning.*

*The interior of the Paradise Shining Parlors, three chairs mounted on a dais, a rack of weekly Negro newspapers and Dream Books. At opposite side of stage from door a cigar counter and cash register behind which a stately middle-aged woman called* MADAM BELL *presides, a telephone booth, a closet, a gas stove, a few stools, a radio, a poster announcing the Hello Club's Social Contest and Ball.*

*When the curtain rises, the radio is blaring a blues.* MADAM BELL *sits behind the register taking down a number from a client, the* JANITOR *of the building, who wishes to play.*

MADAM BELL  (*To one of the shine boys*)  Turn that radio down, Shingle, so I can take this number. That noise gets on my nerves.
SHINGLE  (*Leaving customer whose shoes he is shining*)  Yes, ma'am.
JANITOR  (*At cigar stand*)  702 in a box. I drempt it as sure as I'm standing here, last night.
MADAM  How much, a dime?
JANITOR  No'm, a nickel a piece.
MADAM  Thirty cents. (*Opening drawer in stand*)  Haven't you got any change?
JANITOR  Only this here half dollar.
MADAM  I wish you-all'd bring change for these numbers. Shingle,

can you change this? I don't want to ring this register and get my store accounts all mixed up with the number money.

SHINGLE   (*Leaving customer again*)   All I got is 15 cents. (*Drawling*) Tips ain't amounted to nothing today.

MADAM   All right, all right. (*Ringing register and taking change out*) I'll have to give you some pennies.

JANITOR   Well, I tell you—put ten cents on a run down, 702 to 712, 'cause I know 7 something is coming today.

MADAM   Now you're talkin'. That's the way to win. Why don't you put that other dime on bolito, nickel on the first and last?

JANITOR   I believe I will, 7-0 and 0-2.

MADAM   (*Putting the numbers down and making out a slip*)   Them's good numbers, Janitor, I might play 'em myself.

JANITOR   I believes they lucky.

MADAM   Yes, indeed! Well, now, you don't get no change.

JANITOR   That's the last cent I got till payday, so you know I believes in them numbers. I dreampt 702 just as plain last night.

SHINGLE   I hope you warn't in your lickers.

JANITOR   I never drinks 'cept on payday. Don't have nothing to drink on.

CUSTOMER   (*On stand*)   Well, I drink—and don't play. I never play numbers. I'd rather have mine in my belly than in somebody else's pocket.

JANITOR   That's you. But if I ever hit, I'm gonna live on the fat o' the land. (*Exits*)

SHINGLE   (*Pointedly, as* CUSTOMER *descends from stand*)   Well, I never plays neither. I takes *my tips* home to my wife and children.

CUSTOMER   (*Handing him two dimes*)   You're a good man. Here's a dime for yourself.

SHINGLE   (*As* CUSTOMER *exits*)   Thank you, sir! Thank you. (*As soon as* CUSTOMER *is gone*, SHINGLE *goes to the* MADAM, *who rings up a dime for the shine*)   Here, Madam Bell, here's yo' dime, and put my ten cents on 942, will you, straight? That's the number of my new girl friend's house, where she moved in, and I knows it's lucky, 'cause I went by there last night and helped her put up the bed, and she say, "Baby, I feels like something good's gonna happen in this house!"

MADAM   (*Putting down numbers*)   Wife and babies! Shingle, you's an awful liar!

MATTIE BEA  (*Sticking head in door*)  S'cuse me, you all. Ain't Little Ham got here yet?

SHINGLE  No'm, he ain't showed up as yet, lady.

MATTIE BEA  Well, tell him I were here and'll be back directly.

SHINGLE  Yes'm.

(*Exit* MATTIE BEA)

MADAM  (*Handing him paper*)  Here's your slip. That makes about five numbers you played already today.

SHINGLE  Yes'm. I sho' better hold on to my next tip 'cause its almost lunch time, and I's hungry.

MADAM  It's about time for Ham to show up, too. He relieves you, don't he?

SHINGLE  Yes'm. I wish I was as lucky as little old Ham. He sure do have plenty good womens, and he's always hittin' the numbers. For such a little man, he musta done got a charm or something 'nother.

MADAM  Well, if you just work hard, Shingle, you'll have something some day, too, son.

SHINGLE  What kind o' son you mean, Madam Bell?

MADAM  Son of Ethiopia, my boy, waiting to stretch forth your hand. (*Putting scarf about her shoulders*) Shingle, turn up that gas a little. It's getting cold. Looks like snow. And see if you can't get something good on the radio like " Trees," I hate blues.

SHINGLE  Sure is cold. What month is we at now?

MADAM  October.

SHINGLE  (*Going to the radio and monkeying with dials*)  Next month's Christmas, ain't it?

MADAM  No, Thanksgiving.

SHINGLE  Um-uh! I hope I hits 942, by then, so's I can buy my girl friend a turkey.

MADAM  Just keep on playing it. 942's bound to come out some time.

SHINGLE  If I don't run out first.

(*Enter good-looking chorus girl,* SUGAR LOU BIRD)

SUGAR LOU  Quick shine, please. I got a rehearsal today.

SHINGLE  Yes, ma'am. Just mount the chair, Miss Bird, I'll be through with this radio in a minute.

(*All sorts of fantastic and discordant sounds come out of the radio as the two women try to top it with their conversation*)

SUGAR LOU  (*Shouting*)  How you been, Madam Bell?

MADAM   Not bad, not bad, Sugar Lou.

SUGAR LOU   What's been running lately?

MADAM   The fours and sevens. 467 and 347've both come out this week.

SUGAR LOU   Well, put me a quarter straight on 744. That ought to hit it in the bread basket.

MADAM   What'd you say? (*To Shingle*) You Shingle, tone it down.

SUGAR LOU   7 - 4 - 4.

MADAM   That's a good number, girlie.

SHINGLE   (*Drawling as he dials back to the records*)   If I just had a dime, I'd play that number, too.

SUGAR LOU   Put a dime on it for Shingle, then——(*To him*)   And that'll be your tip.

SHINGLE   Thank you! *Thank you!* I'm gonna shine 'em till you can see your pretty face in the toes.

SUGAR LOU   These are handmade shoes from abroad. They take a good shine.

SHINGLE   You been all over Europe, ain't you, Miss Bird? That's what you get for dancin' with a show.

SUGAR LOU   Yep, I been most everywhere. How about you?

SHINGLE   I been to Paris.

SUGAR LOU   Paris, Kentucky?

SHINGLE   No'm. Paris, London. And I took a train and went from there to Chicago. Then I come by zepp'lin here. (*The phone rings loudly.* SHINGLE *goes to answer*)

MADAM   (*Making out slips and calling* SHINGLE *to get them*)   Here, hand that to Miss Bird. (*To the girl*)   How's your show doing, Sugar Lou?

SUGAR LOU   Shaping up right well. Opens next week. Looks like we might go to London after a run here. You know I was over there all last year with the Dixie Vamps, toured the Continent everywhere.

MADAM   How'd you like it?

SUGAR LOU   How'd they like me, you mean? Honey, they musta thought I was chocolate. They nearly ate me up. Looked like I'd never get out of France. (*To* SHINGLE *as he turns from phone*)   Hurry up, boy. I got to get down to the theatre.

MADAM   Who was that for?

SHINGLE   Little Ham.

MADAM   Some woman, I suppose.

SHINGLE   Naturally.

SUGAR LOU  Shingle, please hurry. I've got a rehearsal.

SHINGLE  Yes'm.

MADAM  It must be nearly noon, ain't it?

SUGAR LOU  (*Raising her sleeve and displaying eight or ten wrist watches*)  You mean here in New York, I presume?

MADAM  Yes, darling.

SUGAR LOU  Well, it is 11:30 here.

SHINGLE  (*Noticing her many watches*)  Um-uh!

MADAM  Why so many watches, darling? I ain't never seen the like.

SUGAR LOU  I got one for each European capital, honey. I collected 'em while I was over there, and I wear 'em all just to tell the time o' day in each place. They came from Paris, Berlin, Monaco. Now, for instance, an Indian Prince, Naboo, gave me this little platinum thing in Paris, and I told him I'd never let it run down, nor change the hour until we met in Paris again. (*Sighing*)  It's 6:30 in the evening in Paris right now.

SHINGLE  Well, I be a Abyssinian! Miss Bird, what time is it in Ethiopia?

SUGAR LOU  I'm sorry, but I never met Haile Selassie.

SHINGLE  (*As he finishes with her shoes*)  I knows it's lunch time in Harlem, and I ain't got nary dime to get myself a pig's foot.

SUGAR LOU  You broke?

SHINGLE  Always broke. Look like I just can't hit them numbers.

MADAM  Shingle. (*To girl*)  Don't pay him no mind, Sugar Plum. That boy's always got his hand out. I'm gonna fire him if he don't watch out—asking for tips.

SUGAR LOU  That's all right! Here, Shingle, pay for my numbers and yours, and keep the change. (*Hands him fifty cents*)

SHINGLE  Yes, ma'am. Thank you. Thank you.

SUGAR LOU  Be seeing you, Madam Bell.

> (*As she exits, she bumps into* LITTLE HAM, *who enters in a hurry—late, as usual. He steps back with a flourish, tips his hat, and bows*)

HAM  Howdy do, Miss Sugar Lou.

SUGAR LOU  Hello, Little Ham! How're you?

HAM  I'm your man! If you ain't busy after the show, lemme know.

SUGAR LOU  I might at that, Little Ham. You got any new trucking steps you can teach me?

HAM  Sure have. Look here! (*He trucks across the room toward the*

*Madam to the music of the radio. Laughs aloud and turns and waves at Sugar Lou)*

SUGAR LOU (*Smiling*) Goodbye, boy! That sends me!

HAM (*Still trucking*) I sure likes to dance, Lucille. When I'm dancing, feels like I'm loving a million women all at once!

MADAM (*Peeved*) You better get here, Ham. You devil! You know you s'pose to come at eleven. Shingle, turn down that radio!

SHINGLE (*As he turns dial*) That joker can't keep time. Ham can't do nothin' but truck and love.

HAM (*In surprise*) What time is it?

SHINGLE Six o'clock in Paris.

HAM How do you know?

SHINGLE Sugar Lou just told me.

HAM You keep your mind off Sugar Lou, boy. She's got her eye on me.

SHINGLE She don't know you livin', less'n she see you.

HAM Didn't you glimpse her just givin' me that " truck on up and see me some time " look as she went out the door?

MADAM You come on in here and truck them shoebrushes. Shingle's got to go get his lunch, and some of you boys clean up that shine stand too, before Boss LeRoy comes. It's filthy.

SHINGLE Yes'm. I sure will, but just lemme play a dime on 645 first.

MADAM (*Making out a slip*) 645 straight?

SHINGLE Um-um. And put this other dime on bolito, back and front.

MADAM Bolito, each way.

SHINGLE Ham, you lend me a dime to get a hot dog, please, being I ain't kicked about you being late, and tips is poor.

HAM (*Tossing him a dime*) Money's nothing to me. Here, boy. Lemme see you go! Has Mattie Bea been here asking for me?

SHINGLE Some woman or 'nother stuck her head in here about half hour ago, say she'd be back.

HAM What she look like? (*Beginning to unbutton his street clothes*)

SHINGLE Like a chocolate blonde with purple powder.

HAM That's Mattie Bea. She promised to bring me a muffler today. My neck is cold.

SHINGLE Why don't you buy one yourself?

HAM I likes to give the women pleasure. They loves to present me with things.

SHINGLE How come they never presents *me* with nothing, I wonder?

HAM You just not the type, Shingle, you not the type.

SHINGLE  Some woman named Laura called up here, too.

HAM  I ain't interested in Laura.

SHINGLE  How come?

HAM  She's just a used blade, and I got a new razor.

MADAM  Shingle, go get your lunch.

> (*Meanwhile,* HAM *has been taking off his sporty overcoat with the extra broad shoulders and removing his coat and vest, while* SHINGLE *takes his old coat out of the closet and puts it on.* HAM *dons a snappy white jacket and begins to straighten up the shoeshine stand*)

SHINGLE  (*Moving toward the door*)  Don't you go grabbing off all the women customers this afternoon after I gets back. I wants to look at some legs, too.

HAM  Aw, go on eat your pigs feet. Lemme miss you! You know you ain't no Clark Gable like I am. (SHINGLE *exits*)

MADAM  Ham, you're a mess!

HAM  (*Coming toward her*)  That's why the women like me, Lucille. You still likes me a little bit your ownself, don't you?

MADAM  I let you stay around here even if you is late all the time.

HAM  (*Sadly*)  But you done got yourself all tied up with that numbers baron now and can't go for nobody else.

MADAM  We makin' money though, Ham. You know yourself, I didn't hardly make my rent out of this place before I met LeRoy, and he set me up as one of his agents for takin' bets. You must admit, LeRoy's way up yonder with the big shots when it comes to writing numbers. Why the biggest gangster in New York's behind LeRoy's outfit. Manny made LeRoy chief of this section of Harlem himself. 'Fore long you'll see me wearing more diamond wrist watches than Sugar Lou brought back from the Old Country.

HAM  Well I hope you'll gimme just one to put on my big old arm so I can tell time.

MADAM  I sure will, Ham, for old time's sake. (*They hold hands. She sighs*)

HAM  Lucille, is there anything I can do for you?

MADAM  (*Coming to herself*)  You might give me a shine. (*Leaves cash register and mounts shine stand*)

HAM  (*Suddenly busy*)  You know I'll do that.

MADAM  (*Looking down at* HAM)  Ham, honey, sometimes I worries about you. Honest I do, even if we did bust up. You fool around with too many women. And you don't take none of them serious.

Someday, some one of 'em's gonna get mad and cut you from here to yonder.

HAM   Not me, baby! Oh, no! When it comes to cuttin' and shootin', that's when I'm gone. Me and weapons don't mix.

MADAM   That's why I couldn't let myself like you any more than I did. I'd a-been in the electric chair by now and you'd a-been in your grave.

HAM   Aw, baby, don't talk so mean.

MADAM   But I'm glad I didn't hurt you.

HAM   Why?

MADAM   You too cute, Ham, to get all cut up.

HAM   You tellin' me?

                    (*Enter* MATTIE BEA)

MATTIE BEA   Oh, here you is, Hamlet. I been up here three or four times tryin' to catch you. (*Noticing* MADAM BELL *glaring at her*) Ham, I wants to talk to you—when you gets through.

HAM   Just sit down. I'll be with you in a minute, baby.

                    (MATTIE BEA *sits down as an* OLD LADY *enters, poorly dressed*)

OLD LADY   Is I too late to play my numbers back today?

MADAM   Plenty of time, plenty of time. They ain't collected yet.

OLD LADY   (*As* MADAM *gets down*) I just got a few pennies my daughter give me. I wants to play 403, 862, and 919, and put . . .

                    (*She and* MADAM *talk at the cigar counter as* HAM *and* MATTIE BEA *get together*)

HAM   Girl, you oughtn't to bother me during my working hours. Don't you know I don't 'low no women to mix in with my profession?

MATTIE BEA   Well, honey, I just had to see you. (*Pulling out a package from beneath her coat*) Didn't you tell me your neck was cold? I done brought you this nice warm muffler. (*Unwraps and offers him a bright red muffler.* HAM *tries it on*)

HAM   (*Looking in glass*) I reckon it'll do. It's mighty red, though. Liable to burn me up!

MATTIE BEA   Don't you like red, honey?

HAM   I reckon so, since you brought it to me.

MATTIE BEA   Are you coming by the Silver Dollar tonight?

HAM   Well, er . . . er, now my business . . .

MATTIE BEA   (*Impatiently*) Now, you know you ain't got no business . . .

HAM   Shss—ss-s. How you know what I got?

MATTIE BEA   (*Loudly*)   I know—you just getting tired of me, that's all, or else you actin' like it. You must think I enjoy staying home with my husband.

HAM   No, baby. I don't. But can't you see this ain't no place to talk like that. (*Enter a shabby but neatly dressed* MAN *who mounts the shine stand*)   I got a customer.

MATTIE BEA   Well, I'll be back by and by. I want you to go with me to the Hello Social Club tomorrow night, anyhow. They havin' a Charleston contest.

HAM   Baby, you know you can't Charleston. (*Beginning to shine the shabby* MAN'S *shoes*)

MATTIE BEA   I know I can't, but we can sit there and look.

HAM   Well, I wants to dance, not look, when I go to a party.

MATTIE BEA   I can two-step.

HAM   You can't do that good, much less Lindy hop.

MATTIE BEA   Well, you goin' with me, whether you want to or not.

HAM   Shss-ss! Here comes the boss, anyhow.

MATTIE BEA   I'll be coming back. (*Starts toward door*)

HAM   O.K.

MATTIE BEA   You go hang your muffler up, Ham, so you won't get it dirty.

>  (*She exits, as* BOSS LEROY *enters and looks around importantly*)

OLD LADY   (*At cigar counter*)   And if I don't catch today, don't know how I'm gonna play tomorrow, but the Lawd will provide, I reckon. Fact is, I know he will.

MADAM   He always does, don't he?

OLD LADY   Yes, he do!

LEROY   (*To* HAM)   Get them papers and cigar butts off that shine stand. It looks like a pigpen in here.

HAM   (*Insolently*)   O.K., big boy.

LEROY   What'd you mean—big boy?

HAM   Big boss, ain't you?

LEROY   (*Satisfied*)   Well, all right then. (*Approaches register and greets* MADAM BELL)   Hello, dear. Got the slips ready for me to check up on? We ain't got much time.

>  (*Puts his arm around her as they check over the numbers. The* OLD LADY *exits*)

MADAM   Hello babe! I ain't seen you all day, LeRoy, honey.

LEROY   Been busy as hell, darling. Didn't get a chance to run by.

One of our best writers is in jail, too. The damn fool sold a slip to a plain-clothes man. I've got to try to replace him, if I can. (*Looking over the slips*) Now, let's see . . . (*They check up and converse as* HAM *shines the* SHABBY MAN'S *shoes*)

HAM   Gettin' kinder cold, ain't it?

SHABBY MAN   Yes, it is, for certain. But I had some good luck today. First time in two years.

HAM   What'd you do, hit the numbers?

SHABBY MAN   No, I got a job! At least, I think I did. That's why I'm getting a shine. They told me to come back at three this afternoon, dressed up. It's waiting table.

HAM   Kinder hard to shine shoes as old as these is.

SHABBY MAN   I know it, but they all I got. I ain't hardly got a nickel to get downtown after I pay for this shine, either.

HAM   Then, that's all right, buddy. You don't have to pay, I been broke too. You just keep it.

              (*Enter* SHINGLE)

SHABBY MAN   (*Getting down*)   Thank you! Thank you! (*Bowing as he exits*) Thank you!

SHINGLE   Ham, you must-a done give the *man* a tip.

HAM   I ain't give him nothin', but a shine. (*Loudly*) But as long as you stayed out, you must-a done et up a whole hog, not just the feet.

              (BOSS *and* MADAM *both look at* SHINGLE)

LEROY   I think I'll have to get a time clock in here. (*Lowering his voice*) And I want you to get rid of that fresh Little Ham.

SHINGLE   (*Turning up the radio*)   I had to drop by on Pauline a minute.

HAM   I lets the women drop by on me.

SHINGLE   They gonna gang up on you some day, and then you'll be sorry they knows where you at.

HAM   Don't worry 'bout me, big boy.

SHINGLE   (*Pointing at* HAM'S *neck and the red muffler*)   What's the matter, forest fire burnin' you up?

HAM   (*Taking off muffler*)   This here's my present from Mattie Bea, so don't touch it.

SHINGLE   Don't worry. I wouldn't put my neck in nothin' that red. They liable to take me for a Roosian Red.

MADAM   (*Loudly*)   Turn down that radio so I can hear my ears.

SHINGLE   (*As he takes off his overcoat*)   Yes'm. (*Looking at Contest poster*) Ham, what do that mean—*Social* Charleston Contest?

HAM   Social—meanin' don't nobody get mad. Don't draw no guns nor knives.

SHINGLE   Oh! Then I might go.

HAM   Ugly as you are, though, you liable to make 'em get mad anyhow. (*Phone rings*)

SHINGLE   (*To* HAM)   Go on! I know it's for you. (HAM *enters phone booth*)

LEROY   (*Putting money into a chamois bag which he secretes in an inner pocket*)   Not bad, darling. But we gonna run our intake up to a hundred bucks a day, you wait and see! Now, I'll just take these duplicate tickets and run on. Also the cash. I've got to report to Manny's secretary. (*Whispering*)   There's a little shake-up going on in the racket today, but I reckon it'll come out all right. I'm just sitting tight. (*Looking at watch*)   You can let 'em play until two, then close up till the papers come out.

(A MAN *in muddy riding boots enters and mounts the shine stand, but* SHINGLE *avoids him, lazily continuing to clean the shine stand*)

SHINGLE   (*Singing to himself*)   In my solitude . . .

LEROY   (*To* MADAM)   See you later, babe. I'll drop back by and pick up the other entries in half an hour or so. (*Suddenly*)   Did you play today, Lucille?

MADAM   My usual 6-7-8, in a box.

LEROY   For how much?

MADAM   Quarter apiece.

HAM   (*In the phone booth, speaking loudly in a feminine voice*)   I tell you Ham don't work here no more . . . No, indeed! There ain't nobody here by the name o' Ham. (*Hangs up the receiver with a bang and emerges from the booth. To* SHINGLE)   That warn't nobody but Laura, tryin' to find out is Ham here. (*Mimicking her voice*)   And come talkin' 'bout a winter coat somebody by the name o' Little Ham done promised to buy her a month ago, and ain't sent it to her yet.

SHINGLE   (*Dryly*)   Here's a customer for you. (*Indicating the* MAN IN BOOTS)

HAM   (*Noting size and dirtiness of the boots*)   Go on boy, it's your turn.

SHINGLE   I ain't got my cleanin' done yet.

HAM   Well, I got to go to de washroom myself.

LEROY   (*Barking*)   Give that customer service!

HAM and SHINGLE   Yes, suh! (*Soon as* BOSS LEROY's *back is turned,*
HAM *eases toward the door, so* SHINGLE *is forced to take the hard
job. Begins to wipe off the boots*)

SHINGLE   (*Mumbling to* HAM)   All you wants to do is wait on the
women.

HAM   You sure is right.

SHINGLE   Well, I gets tired . . .
(*Just then a large fat brownskin* WOMAN *enters*)

HAM   Step right up, lady. (*Helps her on stand, holding her hand
until she is well seated*)   You desires a shine?

TINY   I don't want no *shampoo*!

HAM   Well, I am at your service. (*As he shines*) I ain't seen you in
these parts before.

TINY   I just moved up this way. My business is down on 128 Street.

HAM   You's a business woman?

TINY   (*Placidly chewing gum*)   I'm a hairdresser. And I own my
own beauty parlor.

HAM   Now that is what I like in a woman. That she be her own boss.

TINY   That I am.

HAM   You don't need nobody private-like to boss you, does you?

TINY   You mean a man?

HAM   That's just what I mean.

TINY   I don't see nary one I could use.

HAM   You must not be lookin' down then, is you?

TINY   Oh, you mean yourself? I ain't acquainted with you.

HAM   That's no difficulty. I'm Ham, just Little Hamlet Hitchcock
Jones.

TINY   And I'm Tiny Lee, that's all.

HAM   Baby, you could be a Christmas doll to me.

TINY   I hope you don't mean a rag doll.

HAM   Woman, I mean a sugar doll. (*Confidentially*) I could set
you up, plump as you is.
(*Noise of people running down the street and shouting*)

SHINGLE   What's goin' on out there?
(A LITTLE BOY *cracks the door and sticks his head in*)

LITTLE BOY   Joe Louis is goin' by down at the corner.

SHINGLE   (*Dropping his brushes*)   Well, black my soul: Joe Louis!
(*Exits*)

MAN IN BOOTS   I got to see him! (*Exits also*)

LEROY   I'm ready to go anyhow. See you later, Lucille. (*Exits*)

MADAM  I'd like to see that boy, too, world's greatest prize fighter. Ham, you watch the cash register. (*Takes coat from closet and exits also*)

HAM  Ain't nothin' in the cash register—now that LeRoy's been here.

TINY  I done seen Joe Louis. I was at his last fight.

HAM  You was? Who took you, high as them seats were?

TINY  I took myself. I make money.

HAM  Don't you need somebody to escort you places?

TINY  Where'd you get that idea?

HAM  A sweet little woman like you's got no business at a fight all alone by her little she-self.

TINY  Now you know I ain't little. (*Coyly*) Don't nobody like me 'cause I'm fat.

HAM  Well, don't nobody like me 'cause I'm so young and small.

TINY  You a cute little man. You mean don't *nobody* like you?

HAM  (*Woefully*) Nobody that amounts to nothin.'

TINY  (*Impulsively*) Well, from now on Tiny likes you.

HAM  (*Holding his shine rag*) You really gonna like me, baby?

TINY  Sure I'm gonna like you, and they better not nobody else dare look at you neither.

HAM  Who would want to look at me? I know I won't look at nobody myself. But, I'm gonna be the boss, ain't I, Tiny?

TINY  Certainly—long as I boss you! But first, I got to know something about you. Ham, is this your place?

HAM  Yes'm. (*Shining shoes*)

TINY  You tellin' the truth?

HAM  No'm.

TINY  Then this ain't your place?

HAM  I mean it ain't my place.

TINY  That's what I thought! Where you from?

HAM  Alabam.

TINY  Alabam?

HAM  Yes, but I don't give a damn about it.

TINY  You got any relatives?

HAM  None a-tall.

TINY  Neither've I. I'm all alone.

HAM  You all alone?

TINY  All alone.

HAM  Well, from now on you ain't! Not with Ham around.

TINY  Neither're you, long as Tiny's here.

HAM    (*Looking up soulfully*)  Darling!

TINY   Honey! Come on up here and kiss me, 'cause I'm too stout to get down to you.

(HAM *climbs up on the stand and* TINY *takes him in her arms. Just then the door opens and* SHINGLE *and* MADAM *return*)

SHINGLE   Dog take my soul!

MADAM   (*Acidly*)  After all, Ham, you ain't John Barrymore.

TINY   No, but I'm Jean Harlow, folks, and nobody yet has took a man from me.

SHINGLE   Ham has met his match.

HAM   (*Getting down*)  What you mean, match?

SHINGLE   I mean a woman that can hold you down now.

HAM   (*Embarrassed*)  I ain't had no womens before, long as you knowed me.

SHINGLE   Then I was born tomorrow.

TINY   Well, what he *has* had, and what he *will* have, is two different things! He belongs to Tiny now, don't you, Hamlet, honey?

HAM   I sure do. (*Mannishly*)  That is, you belong to me. You my little Tiny.

TINY   And you're Tiny's little Ham.

(*Enter* JANITOR *to play numbers again*)

JANITOR   Did you all see Joe Louis passing?

SHINGLE   Sure!

MADAM   I not only saw him, I touched him! What a man!

JANITOR   Madam, I got a penny here. Believe I'll put it on 8-8-8. Tribles. There's just 8 letters in Joe Louis' name.

MADAM   (*Beginning to write out slip*)  Tribles is always good. I used to play 3-3-3 and 7-7-7 all the time.

HAM   Babe, I sure feels lucky, findin' you. I feels so lucky I believes I sees a number in the toe of your shoe.

EVERYBODY   What number?

HAM   (*Staring*)  1 - 1 - 6, yes sir! 116!

SHINGLE   Damn if I ain't gonna play it. Is I got time, Madam?

MADAM   Two minutes. I believe I'll play it myself. Ham might really be lucky.

TINY   (*Opening her pocketbook*)  Course he's lucky. Put a dollar on it for me, straight.

JANITOR   (*Woefully*)  I wish somebody'd lend me a dime. I come in here to get a pack o' cigarettes on credit until Sat'day, but I just got to play this one mo' number if Ham say it's good.

HAM (*Tossing him a dime*) Here, buddy, try yo' luck. (*To* MADAM) And Madam, put this quarter on it for me.

TINY (*Looking down*) Ain't you got no mo'n a quarter, Ham?

HAM I really ain't.

TINY (*Hands him a dollar*) Here, take this buck.

HAM And right on 116 it goes. We gonna be rich tomorrow.

MADAM We gonna bust the bank.

SHINGLE I'm gonna buy my gal a hot stuff dress right straight from Fifth Avenue—by way o' some fire escape.

TINY Help me down, 'cause I got to go now. My customers is waiting to get they hair ironed out. Don't you forget, Little Ham, you mine! Here, honey, is my card, shop number, house number, telephone, and everything, written down, printed, so you can't go wrong.

HAM I couldn't never go wrong on you, sweet chile.

TINY (*Pinching his cheek*) You a cute little man! You keep my slip, and if the number comes out, we share and share alike.

HAM Okeydoke! Sweetheart, I'll see you tonight.

TINY I'll see you tonight. I mean *tonight*. (*Exit*)

SHINGLE (*To* MADAM) You see that Ham! He's just got a way with women, that's all!

MADAM A taking way, I'd say. If this number does hit, she'll never see Ham nor the money either. (*Hands out the slips.* JANITOR *Exits*)

HAM Now you all hush. (*Musingly*) You know, I believes I really does like that big old fat girl.

SHINGLE For what?

HAM To boss around. The bigger the woman, the bigger boss I be's.

SHINGLE You mean the more bossed you *will* be, 'cause you really got a something on your hands now.

MADAM (*Acidly*) He's got an elephant.

HAM (*Hurt*) Now, Lucille, don't say that.

MADAM Well, I will say it! You got an elephant. But even at that, she looks like a better woman than that corn-colored hussy that brought you that muffler.

SHINGLE That one's married, ain't she?

HAM You all mean Mattie Bea? Yes, she's married—but she's broad-minded.

MADAM (*Acidly*) Her mind's so broad you could lay on it!

SHINGLE Ham ain't studyin' 'bout her mind.

HAM    Now, I'm studyin' 'bout Tiny now. You know, I believe I loves her.

SHINGLE    You always loves the last female you just meets.

HAM    Well, she's the last.

SHINGLE    You don't know what love is no how.

HAM    Sure I know what love is.

SHINGLE    What is love?

HAM    Love is taking till you can't give no mo'.

SHINGLE    And what does you ever give?

HAM    Myself.

SHINGLE    What does you take?

MADAM    He takes the soul-case out of you, that's what he takes. He drives me mad.

HAM    Now, Lucille, you . . .

(*Enter* TWO WHITE MEN)

SHINGLE    (*Under his breath*)    Uh-oh! I know these two don't want no shines.

(MADAM *begins to secrete the file of number slips hurriedly in her bosom.* HAM *is very busy with the blacking cans, hiding his slips therein.* SHINGLE *looks as if he is paralyzed. They all know the men are detectives*)

1ST DETECTIVE    I judge you give shines here?

HAM    Yes, sir! Oh, yes, sir! Black or tan shoes, gray, yellow, or white.

2ND DETECTIVE    You say you shine white shoes, too?

HAM    If you wants 'em shined. I'm a shiner, that's what I am.

1ST DETECTIVE    Is that all you are?

HAM    Most nigh all.

2ND DETECTIVE    (*Savagely*)    What do you mean, most nigh?

HAM    (*Nonchalantly*)    Don't you understand the English language? Who are you?

SHINGLE    (*Frightened—to* HAM)    Here, here, now! Ham, hush!

2ND DETECTIVE    I guess you don't know who I am?

HAM    I don't.

2ND DETECTIVE    Well, looky here! (*Pulls back coat and reveals badge*)

SHINGLE    I knowed it all the time.

2ND DETECTIVE    Well, come here then you, if you know so much.

(SHINGLE *approaches like molasses in the wintertime, slower than slow. Meanwhile, the other* DETECTIVE *examines the cigar stand, the cash register, etc., looking for number slips, but* MADAM *has hidden them all in her bosom*)

MADAM  A poor woman can't run a decent business without being suspicioned. I never wrote a number in my life, nor played one either.

HAM  Numbers? What is that? I can't even count.

2ND DETECTIVE  Never went to school, did you?

HAM  I skipped that and went to barber college.

MADAM  You just must look in my cash register?

1ST DETECTIVE  We just must, lady. (*Opens register, finds nothing*)

2ND DETECTIVE  (*Suddenly shaking* SHINGLE *while two or three dozen number slips fall out of his pockets*)  Aw, here's the evidence!

SHINGLE  And all of 'em due to win today!

2ND DETECTIVE  Where'd you get 'em?

SHINGLE  (*Stuttering*)  God knows.

1ST DETECTIVE  The judge'll find out then—and not from God!

SHINGLE  I-I-I was movin' and I just packed up some old papers . . .

2ND DETECTIVE  Did you play 'em here in this shine parlor?

HAM  He sure didn't.

MADAM  I should say not!

SHINGLE  Naw, sir.

1ST DETECTIVE  Where'd you get 'em from?

SHINGLE  Well, I can't tell you the name o' the place, but I can take you to the street, and see maybe can I find it.

1ST DETECTIVE  You can?

SHINGLE  I reckon I can.

MADAM  (*Clamping her hand over her mouth as she stares at window*) LeRoy! (*Nearly faints, then looks relieved as he evidently goes on*)

2ND DETECTIVE  Well, Biggs, we didn't find nothing here, so let's take this fellow and let him lead us on. And he better lead us right, or else he'll get a year in jail for every slip he's got on his person.

SHINGLE  I ain't got no slips now, you all got 'em all.

HAM  (*To* SHINGLE)  Then they'll give the years to you—and the money to them, if any one of 'em hit.

2ND DETECTIVE  You shut up.

SHINGLE  This ain't no laughin' matter. Send somebody to come and bail me out.

MADAM  I will, Shingle. Don't worry.

1ST DETECTIVE  (*To the* MADAM)  Don't hire boys that play the numbers, sister. It ain't wise. It's a bad habit. They're liable to steal your money to play with.

MADAM   Thank you for the good advice. You all certainly gave me a shock coming in here like this. My nerves are all jittering.

2ND DETECTIVE   Next time we'll give you a warning.

MADAM   (*Taking them seriously*)   Please do. Won't you have a cigar before you go? (*Offers box*)

1ST DETECTIVE   Don't mind if I do. (*Takes one. To his pal*)   Go ahead, Bill.

2ND DETECTIVE   Thank you, lady.

HAM   (*As they start out*)   Have a shine, too?

DETECTIVES   No, thanks. (*Nodding at* SHINGLE)   We got one, that's enough. (*They exit with* SHINGLE)

MADAM   (*Nearly hysterical*)   Lord! Oh, my Father, oh! oh! oh! I near had heart failure! Did you see LeRoy come right there to the door and notice 'em just in time not to come in? If he'd-a come in here then, the game would've been up. They'd-a found all them slips and money and everything on him.

HAM   But, Lucille, now it'll be too late to put in my 116. All them last slips we made out, Boss LeRoy done passed on by and didn't collect 'em. Now it's past the time, ain't it? Suppose my number do come out?

MADAM   (*Distressed*)   They had to come around just before the number comes out!

HAM   Just before our number got in, you mean. (*Then remembering*) But this here's a depot. They oughta pay off here, anyhow. You done wrote it down.

MADAM   Ham, that's got me scared. They must-a suspicioned this place, or they never would-a come here. And you know I don't want to go to jail! Oh, I don't care if we are makin' a lot o' money. I wish I'd never met LeRoy. My nerves can't stand it. He's the first racketeer I ever loved.

HAM   If this had just stayed a nice little shine shop like it was when I first met you and you took me for your little Ham.

MADAM   Yes, till you got wild and went runnin' off with other women! Oh, Lord, life's nothing but troubles, nothing but troubles! And oh! poor Shingle! They'll get him down to that police station maybe and beat him, and just make him tell where he played those numbers.

HAM   They ain't gonna make Shingle tell nothing. He's more afraid of Boss LeRoy and the white gangsters what runs the numbers, than he is of any cops.

MADAM   I'm just so distressful!

HAM   I feels right blue myself.
> (*Enter an* EFFEMINATE YOUTH)

YOUTH   Can I get a polish?

HAM   You mean your nails?

YOUTH   I mean my slippers. (*Mounting the stand*)

HAM   Well, . . . er, are you . . . er, what nationality?

YOUTH   Creole by birth, but I never draw the color line.

HAM   I know you don't. Is you married?

YOUTH   Oh no, I'm in vaudeville.

HAM   I knowed you was in something. What do you do?

YOUTH   I began in a horse-act, a comic horse-act.

HAM   A who?

YOUTH   A horse-act. I played the hind legs. But I got out of that. I've advanced.

HAM   To what?

YOUTH   I give impersonations.

HAM   Is that what they call it now?

YOUTH   I impersonate Mae West.

HAM   Lemme see.

YOUTH   Of course. (*Begins to talk like Mae West, giving an amusing impersonation of that famous screen star*)

HAM   You a regular moving picture!

YOUTH   Indeed I am.
> (*Enter* JASPER, *the third shine boy*)

JASPER   Hello!

YOUTH   Who is that?

HAM   That's the night shine boy.

JASPER   None o' your cracks now, Hamlet, first thing soons I get here. I know I'm dark.

HAM   Who's crackin'? I'm tellin' de truth, ain't I, Jasper? You do work at night.

JASPER   Yes, and I work in the daytime too, from two o'clock on. Is the number out yet?

MADAM   (*Jumping*) Shss—ss! Don't mention numbers here.

JASPER   How come, don't mention numbers here?

HAM   Ssh-ssh! The man has been here, him and his brother.

JASPER   Who?

YOUTH   What man?

HAM   Two bulls lookin' for numbers.

YOUTH   Oh, those kind o' men!

JASPER    (*Frightened*)   They have? If they come here again, you gonna miss me!

MADAM    They arrested poor Shingle.

JASPER    For what? He don't write no numbers.

HAM    No, but he plays 'em.

YOUTH    Can you play here?

HAM    Not after two o'clock.

MADAM    Not a-tall! Not a-tall! Not now!

(*Enter a* WEST INDIAN)

JASPER    (*Motioning to chair*)   Right up here, sir.

WEST INDIAN    I wahnt a parfick shine!

JASPER    You got perfect shoes?

WEST INDIAN    Naw sawh, but whan I pay me maney, I wahnt a parfick shine.

JASPER    You ain't pay your money yet.

MADAM    Shine the gentleman's shoes, Jasper, and don't talk so much, please. And turn down the radio, it's ruining my nerves.

WEST INDIAN    Yes, 'cause I dadn't come in here to hear no tunes nor to play no number.

YOUTH    (*Ecstatically*)   I just love that dialect.

WEST INDIAN    (*Glares at him*)   Air you tawlkin' 'bout me?

YOUTH    Oh, no. I realize you're giving an impersonation. I give impersonations too, that's why I'm interested in your art!

(*Enter a* DEACONESS *in her church bonnet and carrying a hymnbook*)

DEACONESS    Gawd bless you all!

HAM    Gawd bless you too, sister.

DEACONESS    I would like to have a shine for the glory of Gawd.

HAM    Well, get right up here and your toes'll twinkle like de mornin' star when I get through wid you.

DEACONESS    (*Taking chair between* YOUTH *and* WEST INDIAN)   That's a precious lamb. (*As* HAM *helps her up*) We got to help one another now—because in 397 years this world will end.

(HAM, JASPER, *and the* YOUTH *all draw out pencils and take that number down*)

YOUTH    3 - 9 - 7.

HAM    I'm gonna play that number tomorrow, 397.

MADAM    (*With a start, clasping her breast where the slips are hidden*) Don't mention numbers!

WEST INDIAN    They are an abawmination, the numbers!

DEACONESS  That's right! Are you a Christian?

WEST INDIAN  I'm a Church of Englander, lady. Firm and true.

DEACONESS  Well, I'm a Wash Foot Baptist. Touch my foot and you'll find it clean. My soul's the same way! How about you, son?

YOUTH  Oh, you're speaking to me? I'm New Thought—and we don't bother with such common things as washing feet.

DEACONESS  Well, you better, 'cause God ain't gonna let nobody in heaven 'thout their feet is clean. How about you, son?

HAM  I was baptized and reverted when I were 10 years old, and I ain't had a dirty foot since. Amen!

JASPER  Amen, hell!

DEACONESS  Hallelujah! How about that other young man, so industrious here?

HAM  Who? Old Jasper? He smokes reefers!

JASPER  That's a damn lie.

YOUTH  (*Gasps*) Oh!

HAM  Don't tell me you don't. 'Cause I seen you smokin'.

JASPER  But I don't run with married womens.

YOUTH  Neither do I.

WEST INDIAN  Sister, I think you have come to a nest o' devils.

HAM  That Jasper just ain't got no business o' his own to mind, that's all.

DEACONESS  You all is sweet boys, and I'm gonna save your souls. Now you all listen fluently.

HAM and JASPER  Yes'm. (*They listen and shine, tapping their cloths on the toes of the shoes in rhythm*)

DEACONESS  I'am gonna recite you all a little verse, that I made up myself.

> Don't you drink no licker.
> Don't you shoot no dice.
> Don't you do nothing
> You think ain't nice.
> Don't you dance on Sunday.
> Don't forget to pray.
> And you'll get to heaven
> On Judgment Day!

WEST INDIAN  Amen!

HAM  Hallelujah! I'm heaven bound.

JASPER  The green pastures is sure gonna see a black sheep!

YOUTH  Well, we believe in mind over matter, spirit over flesh.

WEST INDIAN   And I believe in the Bri-tish faith.

DEACONESS   And I believe in washin' feet.

JASPER   And I believe in shining shoes, 'cause I got the shoeshine blues.

HAM   Let's go, boy. (HAM *and* JASPER *begin to pop their rags as they shine in syncopated time, each shining three shoes at once, so that they finish with the three people on the stand the same time. Meanwhile another customer, a* TALL GUY, *comes in, and shortly after him, the* HOT STUFF MAN, *who goes across to* MADAM *and begins to show her some silk stockings he pulls from a traveling bag. As they finish shining*) Yes, sir! Yes, ma'am!

> (*They help the* DEACONESS *and the* YOUTH *down, and collect for their work. The* WEST INDIAN *sits there critically inspecting his shine a moment. The* TALL GUY *approaches the stand just as the* WEST INDIAN *steps down. He steps on the* TALL GUY'S *toe*)

WEST INDIAN   I beg your pardon.

TALL GUY   I'm just tryin' to be a gentleman. But if you want to get tough about it, then step on my corns again and see what I'll do.

DEACONESS   My! My! My! He's gonna start some stuff!

WEST INDIAN   What'll you do?

TALL GUY   Knock you half way into next week, that's what I'll do.

WEST INDIAN   (*Raising his cane like a sword*)   Yes, and you'll have a duel on your hands.

TALL GUY   (*Raising his fists*)   I don't duel, I duke, and I'll choose you out.

WEST INDIAN   (*Contemptuously*)   Aw, mawn, hush! I'll take you outside and wrop you round the downside o' that manhole where the sewer run.

DEACONESS   Do, Jesus!

YOUTH   My dear!

TALL GUY   Who you gonna wrap around the downside of a manhole?

WEST INDIAN   You!

DEACONESS   God don't love ugly! You boys behave!

TALL GUY   Well, all right, then, start wrapping.

> (*They go into a clinch. The women and the* YOUTH *scream and wring their hands. The* HOT STUFF MAN *puts his suitcase down, still open.* HAM *lifts a velvet evening coat out of it*)

MADAM (*Coming between them*) Stop that! Just stop! I don't allow no fighting here.

WEST INDIAN I kill you so quick you won't know the death you died, 'cause mawn, I'm a fightin' cock and my spurs is out.

TALL GUY (*His hand going toward his back pocket*) Yes, and if I draw my gun and start burnin' powder, you'll be so full o' holes your wife can use you for a tea strainer.

(*At the mention of a gun the* YOUTH *and* DEACONESS *huddle near the door*)

WEST INDIAN (*Hand going to back pocket also*) And if I pull mine, I'll blow you from here back before prohibition, and then some.

MADAM Jasper, call the cops! (*Clutching her breast and remembering the numbers*) No, don't . . . Oh, my nerves!

HAM (*With the evening coat on his arm*) You all stop that foolishness now. Here's the Hot Stuff Man and I want to pick out a present for my woman, if he got anything big enough. (*Raising up the belligerents' coattails*) Ain't neither one of you all got a gun, no how.

WEST INDIAN I know it.

TALL GUY You know what?

WEST INDIAN You ain't got no gun.

TALL GUY You'd be surprised. (*Pulls out a pistol*) Now get out!

WEST INDIAN (*Still belligerent, but moving*) Don't tell me what to do! I don't have to do but four things—eat, sleep, stay black, and die.

TALL GUY Well, you sure will die if you fool with me.

(*He raises gun and snaps it once.* MADAM *dives behind the cash register,* JASPER *behind the cigar stand, the* YOUTH *and the* DEACONESS *out the door, and the* WEST INDIAN *starts to bolt, but* HAM *grabs him by his coattail*)

HAM Pay me for that shine first.

WEST INDIAN (*Running his hand in his pockets and producing a coin*) Here, mawn, here! Lemme go! (*Bolts out the door, as the* TALL GUY *again clicks his gun which fails to go off*)

HAM (*Looking at coin*) He gimme a Canadian dime!

JASPER (*Peeping over cigar stand*) It's better'n a Canadian nickel.

TALL GUY What's the matter with this gun? It's loaded.

HAM Whatever's the matter with it, put it down, or up, one, or leave here!

MADAM (*Coming out angrily*) Put that thing away! You're ruining my nerves!

JASPER (*Scornfully*) Huh! I thought it would shoot!

TALL GUY (*Puzzled*) I just bought it. It ought to. (*Inspecting it*) Aw, no wonder! (*Begins to fire, with the result that everybody goes back into hiding, and* HAM *out the door*) I had the safety on. *Ceases firing and sits calmly down on the stand to await a shine.* HAM *pokes his head back in the door*)

HAM Is you through yet?

TALL GUY Of course, of course! I knew that gun would shoot.

(*The others come out of hiding,* MADAM, *the* HOT STUFF MAN, *and* JASPER. *The* YOUTH, *returning, has fainted on the footboard on the shine stand*)

HAM Get some water and throw on Mae West there.

MADAM Somebody attend to me! I can't stand it! Jasper, go get me a bucket of beer! I'm about gone.

JASPER Yes'm. (*Exit* JASPER)

HAM (*To* HOT STUFF MAN) How much is this here coat? With another piece o' goods in it, 'bout two feet wide, it'd fit Tiny.

HOT STUFF MAN That's one of the finest things I've got a-hold of this season. A man that worked right in a Fifth Avenue store got me this. An inside job, wholesale. Brand new, right off the counter. I'll let you have it cheap. For a little o' nothing 'cause it's too hot for me to hold. How about ten dollars spot cash.

HAM I'll give you nine.

(*The* YOUTH *begins to come to, smoothing his hair and preparing to rise*)

TALL GUY I want a shine.

HAM Jasper'll be back in a minute. I only shines white shoes. (*Going on with his deal*) Is that there coat velvet?

RADIO (*Suddenly loud*) Ladies, use the Venus lipstick to achieve that ravishing virginal look. (*Continuing until* MADAM *turns it down*) No other lipstick on the market gives the same demure yet fascinating tint to the lips. And it cost less than any other . . .

HOT STUFF MAN Pure gelatine velvet with a Frigidaire collar, this coat is!

YOUTH (*Listening to radio*) Shss-ss! You all be quiet so I can hear the beauty news.

HAM (*Feeling coat again*) I might take it. That is, I think I will. Nine?

HOT STUFF MAN No. Ten.

(*Enter* MATTIE BEA)

MATTIE BEA  Hello, there, Little Ham. I tole you I'd be back. (*Sniffing*) Smells like smoke in here. Are you buyin' me a present, baby? I could go for that coat.

HAM  I wouldn't want you to wear no hot stuff honey. You might get arrested. These is stolen goods.

MATTIE BEA  Everything I got on is hot. Lemme try on that coat. (HOT STUFF MAN *gives her the coat. She admires herself*)

YOUTH  (*Hovering around*)  Oh, ain't that a sweet garment!

MATTIE BEA  Ham, I just got to have this.

TALL GUY  (*Yelling*)  I want a shine!

HAM  Jasper be right back. (*Offers him a Dream Book*) Here, take this here Dream Book and pick out your numbers for tomorrow while you're waiting.

TALL GUY  I don't believe in dreams. Gimme a *Baltimore Afro-American.* (HAM *hands him the Negro paper, for which he pays ten cents*)

MATTIE BEA  Buy this coat for me, honey.

HOT STUFF MAN  (*To* HAM)  You said you liked it.

HAM  I like it, and I'm gonna take it. But by and by, by and by. Just hold it for me.

MATTIE BEA  (*Returning coat*)  Oh Ham, you're just too sweet. I'll wear it to the Hello Club Social tomorrow.

HAM  Um-hum.

MATTIE BEA  That's why I stopped by, to leave you a couple o' tickets for the Ball. One for you and one for me. I thought I'd better buy 'em in advance. Here, you keep 'em, daddy. (*Reading tickets*) Hello Club Social Charleston Contest. Saturday. Tomorrow night.

HAM  All right! Now you run on home, Mattie Bea, and I'll see you by and by. In the chop suey joint.

MATTIE BEA  You gonna bring the coat?

HAM  I'll have the coat when I come.

MATTIE BEA  (*As she exits*)  Goodbye, sweetheart.

HAM  So long. (*After door closes*) If I ever come! That woman's got a husband anyhow.

TALL GUY  (*Shouting angrily*)  I'll shoot you all if I don't get a shine.

YOUTH  (*Nearly fainting again*)  Aw-ooooo!

HAM  (*To* HOT STUFF MAN)  Leave me that coat. But it's not for her. (*Indicating the departed* MATTIE BEA) Here's ten bucks! (*Gives him the money*) And help this Creole (*Pointing to the* YOUTH) out of here when you go—before he faints again.

YOUTH   (*Leaving on the arm of the* HOT STUFF MAN)   Goodbye, Little Ham.

HAM   (*To* TALL GUY)   Stick 'em up—I mean your feet. (*Begins to shine his shoes as* JASPER *returns with the beer*)

JASPER   Refreshments is served.

MADAM   Jasper, if LeRoy don't come in a few minutes, you better call him up. I want to get rid of these slips. I can't keep 'em in my bosom all day. I wonder why don't he phone, or come. He seen I was in trouble, them dicks in here. (*Drinks her beer*) And he's got to go down to the station and bail out Shingle besides.

JASPER   Poor Shingle! He in jail, ain't he? I tell him 'bout playing them numbers so much.

MADAM   If somebody didn't play, how would we live?

         (JANITOR *enters*)

JASPER   Go on relief, I reckon.

JANITOR   Ain't the number out yet? I ain't got a cent to buy a paper to see.

HAM   T'ain't out yet. 'Bout time though.

JANITOR   I think I'm due to catch today on some one o' them numbers.

HAM   I know we gonna catch! Ain't I done seen the number in the toe o' my baby's shoe—1-1-6, and ain't I done bought her a coat on the strength o' what I know is coming?

JANITOR   What's coming?

JASPER   Christmas.

         (*Phone rings,* HAM *starts, but* MADAM *answers it*)

MADAM   No, the numbers not out yet. Paper's due here any minute.

         (A PRETTY WOMAN *enters limping slightly*)

PRETTY WOMAN   I've got a tack in my shoe.

HAM   (*Forgetting the* TALL GUY *whose shoes he is shining*)   Lemme see!

PRETTY WOMAN   (*Mounting the shine stand*)   Please do. It hurts.

HAM   I certainly am sorry. (*Leaving* TALL GUY *entirely*) Jasper, you finish this man's shoes, here. A lady is in trouble. (*Begins to remove her shoe, fondling her foot tenderly*) You married?

PRETTY WOMAN   Yes, but my husband is taking a rest cure.

HAM   A who?

PRETTY WOMAN   A rest cure.

HAM   Rest from what?

PRETTY WOMAN   He overexerted himself.

HAM   Over which?

PRETTY WOMAN  Exerted, overworked, tired himself out.

HAM  One blip I bet he never gets rested long as he's got you. (*Begins to hammer loudly on the tack in her toe*)

JASPER  I bet two blips, if you was him, you'd be dead!

JANITOR  (*To* MADAM)  You know, lady, if I ever hit that number, I'm gonna take me a vacation. I been janitor o' this building for four years, ain't had me a week off yet.

MADAM  'Bout the only vacation you get is coming in here to play, ain't it?

JANITOR  Sure is.

(*Enter* SUGAR LOU BIRD)

SUGAR LOU  Rehearsal's off until eight o'clock. Thought I'd drop by and wait for the number.

MADAM  Just sit down, honey. We'll know in no time. I'm bettin' on 1-1-6 today, myself, so I'm anxious, too.

(*Enter* OLD LADY)

OLD LADY  Hit ain't out yet, is it?

JASPER  Not yet, but soon.

OLD LADY  (*Tottering up to cigar stand*)  You can't sell a body a little snuff on credit, can you?

MADAM  Sorry, but we don't have snuff, Mis' Dobson.

JANITOR  Why, that's out o' style now, ma.

OLD LADY  Style or no style, snuff is snuff, and I likes it.

(TALL GUY *leaves stand and pays* JASPER *for his shine*)

JASPER  Thank you, sir.

TALL GUY  I might as well wait around and see what the number is, too, so I'll know how to play tomorrow.

JASPER  Sure, make yourself at home.

(TALL GUY *goes to cigar stand and buys a pack of cigarettes. Lights one and sits down on a stool with his paper. A big masculine* WOMAN *walks in and straight across to the cigar stand*)

MASCULINE LADY  (*In bass voice*)  Gimme a five-cent cigar. (MADAM *offers her the box and accepts payment as everybody in the shop stares*)  Is the number out yet?

MADAM  Not yet.

MASCULINE LADY  Then I'll pick it up later. (*Turns and strides out*)

HAM  Whew! What's the world coming to?

JANITOR  I don't care what it comes to, just so I hits the numbers.

MADAM  Numbers! Numbers! Numbers!

SUGAR LOU   That's one thing I sure miss in Europe, the numbers. They don't seem to know how to play 'em over there.

HAM   They know in Harlem.

MADAM   And they'll be the end of Harlem, too. They've just about whipped my nerves to a frazzle.

PRETTY WOMAN   (*Her shoe fixed, leaves stand, opens her purse*) Thank you! How much?

HAM   Nothing a-tall! No charge—to you.

PRETTY WOMAN   That's awfully nice of you.

HAM   I hopes to see you again.

PRETTY WOMAN   That's very possible.

HAM   Then come again.

PRETTY WOMAN   Maybe I will. Goodbye. (*She exits*)

HAM   Goodbye.

SUGAR LOU   Untrue to me already, huh, Little Ham?

HAM   Untrue as I can be—at a shine stand.

JANITOR   (*Hearing newsboy's cry*) Listen! There they come! (*Sound of* NEWSBOY *crying off stage. Enters*)

NEWSBOY   Racing edition of the evening paper. Get the number.

EVERYBODY   Gimme one . . . What's the number, boy? . . . Here, you got change? . . . Let's have a copy.

HAM   (*Opening paper to sporting page. Shouting*) Dog-gone my soul! I won!

JANITOR   Thank God-a-mighty, I won too, then.

MADAM   Ham, your number hit!

SUGAR LOU   What was it?

HAM   1-1-6, folks, 116! I mean good ole 1-1-6 has done come out— that I seen in the toe o' my baby's shoe. Damn! Lemme call her up and tell her. Where is that card she gimme? (*Searches in his pocket for card, finds it, and goes to phone*) Done hit the number!

JASPER   You lucky rascal! You must carry a black cat's bone.

SUGAR LOU   Well, it's luck for you all. Ham wins, but I lose!

OLD LADY   I lose too! Lawd, I lose!

SUGAR LOU   But' maybe I'll hit tomorrow. If I don't, I'll pawn a wrist watch till that show opens.

MADAM   Which watch, darling?

SUGAR LOU   Oh, I think the one a duke gave me in Budapest. Nobody cares what time it is in Budapest.

JASPER   Where's that, Miss Bird?

SUGAR LOU   Somewhere, in . . . er . . . Norway, I believe.

OLD LADY (*Weeping*) I can't never hit. My last penny, and I can't never hit. My daughter give me that money to get some matches with to light the gas.

MADAM Here, grandma, I'll give you a box of matches. (*Hands her matches*)

OLD LADY But ain't you got no snuff?

MADAM No snuff! No snuff!

(*Exit* OLD LADY)

HAM (*At telephone*) Hello! Hello! Tiny's Hairdressin' Parlor? Well, is Tiny there? . . . Yes. Is this Tiny? Well, this is Little Ham! Baby, we done hit the numbers! Yeah! That number I saw in the toe o' your shoe . . . You's a lucky old big old sweet something, you is! Come on up here and get your money! I want to see you anyhow. I got a present for you. . . . Yes, I is . . . And two tickets to the Hello Club Ball, too. O-key-do-ky!

JASPER Some woman, as usual, on the phone.

MADAM Ham, call LeRoy, see is he coming back here. We want to collect what we won.

HAM What's his number—Edgecombe 4-1909?

MADAM That's it.

(HAM *dials and listens*)

HAM Hello—er . . . er . . . (*Hangs up suddenly, looks scared*)

MADAM What's the matter?

HAM I don't get nothing but a funny noise. Then somebody answers sounds like cops or gangsters, one! The toughest voice I ever heard.

MADAM (*Clutching her breast*) Oh, my God!

(*Suddenly the door opens, and in comes* LEROY, *wild and disheveled. The afternoon begins to darken*)

LEROY (*Hurrying across to cash register*) Lucille, baby, I got to talk to you.

HAM Man, I done hit the numbers. Stop right here!

JANITOR Me, too.

LEROY Just a minute! Just a minute! I ain't payin' off no numbers today. Harlem's all torn up now. The Danny Jiggers gang's trying to muscle in against Manny Hudgins, and there's hell to pay. I just saw two big New Jersey cars outside my apartment, so I didn't go in.

MADAM (*As* SUGAR LOU, TALL GUY, *leave*) Oh, my nerves! My nerves!

JANITOR Well, what about my number that come out, 1-1-6?

LEROY It never went in. Didn't no numbers from my route go in

**today.** I tell you, Harlem's on the spot. Who's gonna report numbers with the Jiggers gang in town?

HAM   I just knowed something'd go wrong.

JANITOR   De Lawd never intended a poor man to win money! My last fifty cents gone, and payday two weeks off yet! I tell you I want to be paid off on that number. (*Hysterical*) I hit it: 1-1-6!

LEROY   (*Hand to pocket*)   Hush, and get out of here! Or I'll blow you to bits. The gang's on my trail now, more'n likely, and you talkin' 'bout payin' off on a lousy ten-cent number.

JANITOR   It's a racket! That's what it is! A racket!

LEROY   Sure, we know it.

JANITOR   Everyday, all my money gone on the numbers.

LEROY   You have something to look forward to, don't you? Some day you might win.

JANITOR   Not from lousy cheaters like you!

LEROY   Get out of here! (JANITOR *exits*)

MADAM   Put that gun away! If another shot's fired this afternoon, I'll die! I'll die! Here—(*Reaching into her bosom*)—take these slips. I just want to get 'em out of my hands. Why did I ever go into this game? Why? Oh, why!

LEROY   Quiet, Lucille, quiet! Everything'll be all right. I got three thousand dollars here, which ever way the gang war goes. That's yours and mine, darling. Understand?

   (*Just as he is about to hand it to her, three strange* WHITE MEN *enter. They are obviously gangsters. Each has one hand in his pocket*)

BUTCH   So here's where little Boss LeRoy holds forth after the number comes out?

DUTCH   No wonder his apartment's empty.

JIGGERS   Hand us over today's collection, you. We told that punk of a Hudgins we were taking over this field way last week. But he just kept right on, and you helpin' him. Well, now he's where the daisies'll tickle his nose when they come up in the spring. (*Savagely*) And that's where you'll be if you don't act right.

MADAM   (*Loudly*)   My heart! My nerves! My heart! (*She glares at the gangsters*)

JIGGERS   Just hold tight, sister. It'll be over in a minute. (*Referring to* JASPER *and* HAM)  Who're these two there?

MADAM   They're my shine boys.

DUTCH   They look like men to me. (*To* JASPER)  Who're you?

JASPER   John Jasper Armstrong Smith.

DUTCH   What do you do?

JASPER   Shine shoes, that's all.

BUTCH   (*To* HAM)   How about you?

HAM   Oh, I'm just here. Part of the decorations. Take the place, you take me. I just hit this afternoon for a dollar with 1-1-6.

JIGGERS   One of these lucky birds, heh? Well, you're the kind of a guy we need to write for us, don't we, Butch? Fly and lucky. Folks like to play with personality lads like you. Come over here. (HAM *approaches*) What's your name?

HAM   Little Ham Jones—Hamlet Hitchcock Jones.

JIGGERS   Your age?

HAM   Indiscriminate.

JIGGERS   Well, if you're old enough to play numbers, you're old enough to write 'em. Ever do it?

HAM   No, indeed!

LEROY   (*Interrupting*)   I always choose my own writers in this district.

JIGGERS   You'll be lucky to choose yourself from here on in. We're running this racket in Harlem now.

DUTCH   You're going for a ride, more'n likely.

JIGGERS   (*To* HAM)   Report tomorrow to our headquarters over on Lenox. (*To* MADAM BELL) Are you with us, lady? I guess you are if you want to stay in business. Keep this here Shine Parlor as your base and *keep on* writing numbers. Only we'll send *our* man to collect.

MADAM   I'm with you—if my nerves'll stand it.

DUTCH   You'll pull through.

JIGGERS   Listen, both of you. (*To* HAM *and* MADAM) If you ever get in any trouble, just give my fixer's name to the cop, the judge, the jailer, anybody, and they'll turn you loose. We're payin' heavy protection. Just say—Schnabel.

HAM   Schnabel, Schnabel, Schnabel. I sure will try to remember that.

JIGGERS   That's it, Schnabel. He's the pay-off from now on.

DUTCH   (*To the* MADAM)   How about you?

MADAM   I'll recall it.

JIGGERS   (*To* LEROY)   As for you, didn't you get word yesterday to lay off writing for Manny?

LEROY   I didn't get nothing.

JIGGERS   Well, come with us now, and we'll talk it over. There might be some hope for you then. But we can't use you no more, no how. You was too thick with the old crowd.

(*Enter* TINY *puffing and blowing*)

TINY   Bless God, we won! Little Ham, I come for you and our money.

HAM   You sure come at a busy time, baby.

TINY   Didn't you phone for me?

HAM   Yes, but that was before the crisis.

TINY   What do you mean? They ain't payin' off?

JIGGERS   Of course, we're paying off. Our outfit always pays off. Did you hit today, lady? Where's your slips?

TINY   (*To* HAM)   Ain't you give 'em the slips, baby?

HAM   I ain't had time. (*Fumbling in his pockets*) Here they is, one for me and one for you, 1-1-6. (*Hands them to* JIGGERS.)

JIGGERS   Perfectly good. (*To* LEROY) Pay 'em off, you. They hit for a dollar a-piece. We're not going to start our business with no dissatisfied clients. (*As* LEROY *hesitates*) Pay 'em off!

LEROY   We're short on cash. I done turned mine in.

JIGGERS   (*To* DUTCH *and* BUTCH)   Search him, boys! If I find a dollar on him, I'll blow his brains out.

MADAM   (*Screams*)   Don't shoot no gun in here.

LEROY   Wait, wait, wait! Here, lemme see. I might have a few bills. (*He produces a wad of several thousand dollars*)

JIGGERS   Two or three grand, that's all. Pay 'em off, and give me the rest.

LEROY   (*Hesitantly to* HAM)   You hit for a dollar, heh?

HAM   Dollar and a quarter.

LEROY   Then you gets 675 dollars.

HAM   I sure do. (LEROY *begins to count out the money*)

TINY   You both lucky *and* cute, Ham!

HAM   You tellin' me?

JIGGERS   That's real money. That's just how my bank'll pay off from now on.

LEROY   (*To* TINY)   And you hit for a dollar?

TINY   That's right.

LEROY   540 then.

TINY   540 gets it.

DUTCH   If I wasn't toting a gun, I'd play these fool numbers myself.

MADAM   (*To* LEROY)   I had a quarter on that too, LeRoy. Here's my slip.

LEROY   135 to you then, baby.

MADAM   That small change is just right.

LEROY   (*Sadly*)  I won't have a thing left.

JIGGERS   Only about two thousand bucks. Give it here! We'll use it to buy cigarettes. (LEROY *hands over the money angrily*) And come on! (*They start toward the door*)

LEROY   (*Looking back*)  Lucille! Lucille!

MADAM   My nerves won't stand it! Go on! I can't help you! (*Savagely as he hesitates*) Go on! (*They exit*)

JASPER   I wish I'd-a played that number—1-1-6.

TINY   Baby, who's them strange men?

HAM   They the new bosses o' this shop.

TINY   I thought it belonged to colored folks.

HAM   It do, but whites run it. How about it, Madam?

MADAM   Little bit more, and they can have it! My nerves won't stand this number racket. They just won't. (*As* HAM *begins to take off his coat*) Ham, are you going off and leave me, too?

HAM   I'm off at four, ain't I? Jasper's the night man. (*Begins to don his street clothes*)

MADAM   Come back and talk to me later. I need comfort.

TINY   Not this evening, no sir. *Comfort* is with me! Come on here, boy! From now on you Tiny's Little Ham. (*As he hands her the velvet coat*) Um-huh! Is that my present? Ain't you sweet! It looks kinder small, but I'll have me a nice gold-brocaded back put in it in the morning, and wear it to the Hello Club's Ball tomorrow night. You got tickets, ain't you, sugar?

HAM   Sure, I got tickets. They havin' a Charleston contest. And just like we hit that number today, we gonna win that contest tomorrow. Girl, can you Charleston?

TINY   Sure, I can Charletson. Where you s'pose I been at all my life?

HAM   Well, come on then. Let's dance on away from here! (JASPER *turns up the radio and* TINY *and* HAM *dance toward the door*) Hey, now!

CURTAIN

# ACT TWO

*Saturday afternoon.*

*Interior of* TINY'S *Beauty Shop on Lenox Avenue. Street door center. At immediate left of door, manicurist's table. At right an overstuffed chair and a floor lamp. Two operator's booths, one on either side of door.* TINY *presides over the booth at the left.* LULU *over the booth at right. At extreme right, just outside* LULU'S *booth, a radio beside a door marked "Ladies Room." At extreme left, next to* TINY'S *booth, a kind of little open storeroom, sink, and closet where coats, street clothes, etc., are hung.*

*As the curtain rises, both* TINY *and* LULU *are busily engaged straightening heads of hair.* SUGAR LOU *is in* TINY'S *chair. The manicurist,* OPAL, *is occupied applying red polish to the nails of a customer.* A LITTLE GIRL, *waiting for her* MAMA, *is in the big chair. All the women are chattering full blast, the radio going, smoke rising from oily heads, noise of traffic outside.*

TINY  (*Yelling to manicurist*)  Opal, have you seen Bradford today?

OPAL  No, Tiny, there's been not a single number writer in here today. They must be all scared out by the gang war I read about in the *News*.

CUSTOMER  (*At table*)  I hear they just a-switchin' and a-changin' all them writers up here in Harlem. Looks like a new lot of downtown chiselers done took over things. I hear they chased out LeRoy.

TINY  Well, my new fella's writin' for the new outfit. They the ones what paid off my hit yesterday, and they give him a job right then and there. We sure knocked 1-1-6 for a row.

OPAL  Did you box it?

TINY  Naw, I didn't box it. Didn't need to this time.

OPAL  Always box your numbers, girl. If they don't come straight they might come some other way. You're lucky you caught it right straight out like you did.

TINY  You right, I'm lucky. I'm gonna play that same number back today. This time I'll box it and bolito it, too. 116's a good number! And sometimes them pari-mutuels repeats figures, you know!

LULU  No, they don't either, sister. I ain't never seen a number repeat hand-running no two times yet.

SUGAR LOU  Me neither.

OPAL  Well, I have, girl! 417 come out twice hand-running not more'n two or three months ago.

LULU  Well, I must-a been in Jalopy, cause I ain't seen it, and I play every day in the year, and ain't left New York in ten years.

OPAL  I don't believe you ever leave Harlem even much, do you, Lulu?

LULU  Not hardly. What business I got downtown? I can get everything I wants right here in Harlem, even to Fifth Avenue dresses so hot they just stole 'em fresh the night before.

OPAL  Girl, don't believe all this stuff they call hot up here in Harlem is really stolen. They buy it at wholesale, then tell you it's stole—to make you think you're getting something worth more than it is.

LULU  Cheaper than in stores though.

OPAL  But if you don't know what you're buying, you can get cheated, too.

TINY  Girl, my new man bought me the prettiest velveteen evening coat you ever seen yesterday from a hot selling huck.

SUGAR LOU  (In TINY's chair)  He did?

TINY  Naturally the coat wasn't made to fit my size, exactly, but I took it early this morning to a seamster and am having a gold brocaded back put in it so I can shine like the sun at that there Hello Club Ball tonight.

OPAL  Say, what time does that Charleton Contest come off?

TINY  I don't know, but whatever time it comes off, me and my little short papa's gonna be there rarin' to go.

SUGAR LOU  Comes off at midnight, they tell me. I'm gonna try and make it, if rehearsal's over.

LULU  We gonna close up early, sis?

TINY  You all can stay here if you want, but I'm gonna be gone. Stay if you need to make up that extra commission. If you don't leave early—just like me. I don't care. After I been fryin' heads all day and all week, I need myself a little recreation on Saturday nights.

OPAL  Me, too.

SUGAR LOU  I sure am glad I got my appointment this afternoon. You all get so busy late on Saturdays.

TINY  Busy all day Saturdays, no matter what time you come. That's the day we really take in the money. But I just hit for 540 bucks yesterday, so you know I'm gonna have myself one *really* good time tonight.

MAMA    (*In* LULU's *chair*)    So am I, kid! I'm goin' to that Ball.

SNOOKS    (*The child in the big armchair*)    Mama, hurry up!

MAMA    How can I hurry up, and one half o' my head's still looking like a gooseberry bush in August?

SNOOKS    Well, I'm tired.

MAMA    Well, get yourself a funny paper and see can't you find me a good number. Look in Popeye, or else in Skippy.

LULU    Child, I gets the best numbers out of Little Orphan Annie.

MAMA    I never win nothing on the Annie numbers.

LULU    Maybe you don't play them the right way.

MAMA    Something's wrong, something's wrong. To tell the truth, the only thing I ever catches on is funeral wreaths. Everytime I see a crape on the door, anywhere, I take down the house number. Them kind o' sad numbers is always my best bet.

OPAL    (*Calling*)    How about the numbers of hymns in church?

TINY    Them ain't no good. They give out too many of 'em. Seven or eight hymns every service.

MAMA    Yes, and some o' them ministers is such devils. They ain't got Christ in 'em. Naturally their numbers ain't no good.

OPAL    'Bout the best way is to pick some number that's hit good once, like Tiny's 1-1-6, and play it every day for two or three months.

LULU    No, 'taint, neither. I don't believe in them repeats, I tell you. You gotta wait too long.

TINY    Sometimes you wait that long anyhow. Turn down that radio, Lulu, so I can hear my ears.

LULU    All right, sis! (LULU *turns down radio*)

CUSTOMER    (*At* OPAL's *table*)    Well, I'm telling you, if 'twarn't for the numbers, I don't know how I'd get along. I plays six or eight dollars a week, and I always wins three or four dollars, every week.

OPAL    Do you?

CUSTOMER    Why, everything I own 'cept my husband I bought with my winnings. But I drempt a dream last night that I sure don't know how to play. I got to look it up. You all got a Dream Book around here?

TINY    I might have one back yonder by the sink. I'll look in a minute.

LULU    What were the dream?

CUSTOMER    I drempt about a yellow woman washing a green dress in a white lady's back yard. Now what do that mean?

MAMA    Lemme think.

CUSTOMER    What number should I play? Any o' you all know?

MAMA   Well, er . . . green is 448, if I remembers rightly.

TINY   Yes, 'tis, that's right. In Rajah Simm's Book it's 448.

LULU   Yes, but she say a *yellow* woman washing a *green* dress in a *white* lady's back yard. That's more colors than one.

SUGAR LOU   Certainly is!

CUSTOMER   Yes, and the dress faded, too.

MAMA   Do, Jesus!

CUSTOMER   When she got through washing it it weren't no color a-tall.

LULU   There now! Then you wouldn't look up green.

MAMA   No, you wouldn't.

TINY   I think you'd look up *dress.*

SUGAR LOU   I think you add all them colors together, subtract the difference, and play that.

LULU   What kind o' dress were it?

CUSTOMER   Seems like to me it were a calico dress.

OPAL   Then look up *calico.* Who knows what that would be?

TINY   I'll go see can I find that book right now.

> (*She leaves her booth and goes back where the shelves are. Searches until she finds the book. Meanwhile, a* STAID LADY *enters with a* LITTLE GIRL *of ten or twelve*)

STAID LADY   I want a hot-oil treatment, and I want you all to see if you can do anything with my child's hair, too, to try and bring out the Indian blood that's in her. Her head sure went back on her.

OPAL   Just have a seat. One of the operators'll take you in a minute now.

STAID LADY   (*To* SNOOKS)   Get up, child, and let me sit down. You children can sit on the arms of the chair.

SNOOKS   Why don't *you* sit on the arm of the chair yourself and let us sit here?

STAID LADY   Because I'm grown, that's why, and you and Missouri are nothing but tots.

SNOOKS   Her name's Missouri?

STAID LADY   That's it.

SNOOKS   That's a state, ain't it?

MISSOURI   Yes, but it's a name, too. What's your name?

SNOOKS   Samantha. But they call me Snooks for short.

MISSOURI   That sounds like a funny-paper name to me.

SNOOKS   Well, your name sounds like mud to me.

MAMA   (*Yelling from* LULU'S *booth*)   You Snooks! Just hush. I'm ashamed o' you.

STAID LADY  (*To her offspring*)  Sit over here and keep still. I told
you not to speak to every stranger you meet.

TINY  (*Returning to front with the Dream Book*)  Here's the Dream
Book. Now, I'd advise you to look up wash, cause that's what you
was doin' in the dream, washing a dress. Lemme see what it is.
(*Searches in book*)

OPAL  Yes, but she was washing a *green* dress, girl.

TINY  Well, if it was me, I'd play the number for wash and let the
colors and dress and white lady and all go. Here it is—wash—964.
That's it. (*Hands book to* OPAL'S *customer*) Howdy-do! (*To the
new arrival in chair*)

STAID LADY  Howdy do! I'm in need of a hot-oil treatment. And a
pull for this child.

TINY  Yes'm. Just a few minutes now, and I'll be with you.

>          (TINY *returns to* SUGAR LOU *and takes the apparatus out of
>          her hair.* SUGAR LOU *has a beautiful croquinolle. Looks at
>          herself in the glass*)

SUGAR LOU  Honey, that's wonderful. I'll knock 'em dead at the dance
tonight.

TINY  You sure will. Who you goin' with, Sugar Lou?

SUGAR LOU  A new hot papa I just met down at the theatre—that is, if
I can sneak away from my butter and egg man.

TINY  What's his name?

SUGAR LOU  Which one, the young one or the old one?

TINY  I mean the one what pays your bills here, darling.

SUGAR LOU  You ought to know him—he's the biggest undertaker in
Harlem. Has three funeral parlors, and ten to twenty funerals a day.

TINY  You ain't talkin' 'bout old man Willis?

SUGAR LOU  That's him. He's my board and upkeep at the moment.

TINY  Why he's so old his features all run together!

SUGAR LOU  He's generous, though, honey. He says he's gonna gimme
a half-dozen more watches for this arm.

TINY  No, he ain't!

SUGAR LOU  Yes, he is, too.

TINY  Well, keep him, child, keep him, even if he is ninety! You
ain't met my sweet papa, though, has you? I mean my real one.

SUGAR LOU  Who is he?

TINY  (*Proudly*)  His name is Little Ham.

SUGAR LOU  Not little sporty Ham that shines shoes in the Paradise?

TINY   That's him! And believe me, he ain't shining shoes no more. Not after last night. He's gone into business.

SUGAR LOU   He has? What kind o' business?

TINY   Numbers. Them new racketeers is working him right in with them. They say he's got per-son-ality.

SUGAR LOU   He has that, all right. Smoothest little sawed-off pigmy this side of Abyssinia! He's got a way with the lady-folks, too.

TINY   He might-a had a way—but he belongs to Tiny now.

SUGAR LOU   Congratulations!

TINY   Thank you.

SUGAR LOU   But, say, where's Gilbert?

TINY   I done put that lounge-lizard out o' my life. Gilbert warn't no good for nothing but what my white actress lady where I used to work calls " horizontal refreshment."

SUGAR LOU   Gilbert always dresses nice.

TINY   Yes, but on my money. I want a man what gives *me* things, like Little Ham. Besides Gilbert's a married man.

MAMA   Speaking about men, you all heard about the run-in Geraldine had over her old used-to-be, ain't you?

TINY   Geraldine who?

MAMA   Geraldine Richards.

OPAL   Not that little old scrawny mud-colored girl what comes in here every Thursday afternoon from Long Island.

MAMA   That's her. She don't get off but once a week, but that day she wants to find her man ready and waiting just for her.

OPAL   I don't blame her.

MAMA   But this time she come in from her white-folks house and the man was nowhere to be found.

TINY   What you say?

MAMA   Nowhere to be found. She went to his rooming house, and she went to the pool hall where he usually hang out, and she went to the barbecue stand—but no George.

LULU   There now!

MAMA   Then she met Gussie. You know, Gussie Mae Lewis?

TINY   Gussie's a troublemaker. Always talking.

OPAL   For sure!

LULU   Yes, she's too broadcast.

MAMA   And Gussie say she has just seen George, about two hours before going down the street with Luella Johnson.

TINY   No, he wasn't!

MAMA   Yes, he was! Gussie seen him. So what did Geraldine do but take her little scrawny self right straight to the pawnshop and buy herself a gun!

LULU   Ay! Lawd! I know she was burnt!

MAMA   And went, just as straight as she knew how, up to where Luella rooms, and caught 'em red-handed on the settee.

TINY   Naw!

MAMA   Yes, sir!

OPAL   Huh!

SNOOKS   Mama, hurry up. I wanna go out o' here.

MAMA   Shut up, and wait for me. Play with that other little girl. (STAID LADY *gathers her child to her protectively, motioning* SNOOKS *away*) Yes, ma'am, Geraldine caught that huck right in the mood for love.

TINY   And what did she do to him?

MAMA   Wore his hips out with bullets, that's what she did.

LULU   There now!

MAMA   But seem like in her excitement, she couldn't shoot very straight, so ain't none o' the bullets proved fatal. But, anyhow, George is in the hospital this week end, and they say he can't set down.

OPAL   How about that hussy of a Johnson girl?

MAMA   They say Geraldine scared Luella so bad she jumped out the window. It was just the second floor, so I reckon it didn't hurt the hellion. And ain't nobody seen her since.

TINY   (*As* SUGAR LOU *leaves the chair*) Well, I'm a decent woman! I don't believe in no shootin' and cuttin'. When I gets mad, I just use the palm of my hand, that's all. And that's enough!

LULU   Believe me, it is! I seen Tiny slap a woman good in here one night, come startin' some stuff about she wasn't gonna pay no dollar-seventy-five—after she done had mighty nigh every treatment, shampoo, and process in the shop. She say back where she came from in North Carolina, she get all that for six bits.

TINY   Yes, child, and I say, well, in Harlem, New York, it cost just *one dollar more*. And she say, it do, huh? Well, I ain't gwine pay it! And I say, you'll pay it or else. And she say, I'll else then! And lift her dress in my face, and that is where I palmed her.

LULU   She was glad to pay to get out!

SUGAR LOU   Let me sign for my bill.

TINY   O.K., honey. (*Produces pad, and* SUGAR LOU *signs, and exits*)

SUGAR LOU   Goodbye, you all.  See you tonight at the Ball.

EVERYBODY   Goodbye!

TINY   (*To the* STAID LADY)   Now, I'll take you.

STAID LADY   (*To her child*)   You sit right here until they ready for you, too.

MISSOURI   *Yes'm.*   (*Her mother goes into* TINY'S *booth*)

SNOOKS   (*To the other child*)   My mama don't make me sit down. (*For the moment* MISSOURI *ignores her*)

STAID LADY   (*To Tiny*)   I wish there wasn't so much gossip and scandal and talk about numbers in these hairdressing parlors. It hurts my child's morals.

TINY   Your child's who?

STAID LADY   Her morals, to hear such stuff. She gets her mind full of sin.

TINY   Is that where her morals is, in her mind?

STAID LADY   I'm speaking of her soul. It's awful here in Harlem to raise a child.

TINY   I were raised here, myself.

STAID LADY   Yes, that's what I mean.

TINY   What *do* you mean?

STAID LADY   I'm sure you understand what I mean. Let's not discuss it further. And don't burn my head.

TINY   I hope not.

STAID LADY   Some of these hair shops is just terrible. One of 'em gave a brownskin friend of mine a bleaching treatment and just ruined her. When they got through, she looked like she were on her last round-up. Just took all the pigment out of her skin.

TINY   The pig-meat?

STAID LADY   Pigment! Color! Made her a deathly gray—all chalky. Her husband liked to whipped her when he saw her, he was so mad.

TINY   Some of them operators is terrible! They just dissects the hair from your scalp, their combs is so hot.

STAID LADY   And they're so careless. And so immoral. Why they raided a shop near me and confiscated the hair tonic.

TINY   I reckon it was licker.

STAID LADY   It probably was. That little she-woman that runs it is always drunk.

TINY   You don't say!

LULU   A girl was in here this morning says she know where you can buy the number.

OPAL   Where at?

LULU   She says she knows a man, what knows a man, that is a friend of the man that works at the track and can get the number an hour or more before it comes out in Harlem. And for fifty dollars he'll phone it to anybody that wants it, in time for them to play it before the books close.

STAID LADY   A racket, that's what it is.

TINY   I s'pect it is, 'cause can't nobody be sure about that number till it come out.

MAMA   Don't nobody know how them racing machines gonna add up.

LULU   I'm just tellin' you what the girl told me. But Lawd knows I ain't gonna try it, 'cause I ain't got no fifty dollars.

CUSTOMER   (*Rising*)   Thank you. (*Yelling*) And thank you, Tiny, for the Dream Book. I'll see you all sometime next week.

TINY   Thank you, and come back. I hope you hit on that *wash* number.

CUSTOMER   I'm gonna play *dress* and *wash*, too.

TINY   You doin' right. Good luck. Burn a black candle, and also play *green*.

OPAL   Be sure and box 'em.

LULU   And use lucky incense, child.

CUSTOMER   Goodbye, you all. (*Exits*)

EVERYBODY   Goodbye.

OPAL   Thank God for a minute to breathe. (*She goes to Ladies Room*)

MISSOURI   (*Fidgeting in chair, to* SNOOKS)   Do you know any bad words?

SNOOKS   I know two.

MISSOURI   Tell me one of 'em.

SNOOKS   Damn!

MISSOURI   Aw, I know a better one than that. (*Whispering*) . . . And I dare you to say it.

SNOOKS   I dare you to say this one. (*Whispers to* MISSOURI)
   (MAMA *gets out of chair and pays her bill*)

MISSOURI   'Tain't as bad as mine.

SNOOKS   Your word ain't as bad as mine, either.

MISSOURI   Yes, it is. Mine's badder.

SNOOKS   I'll be damned if it is!

STAID LADY   (*Shouting*)   Missouri, come here!

SNOOKS   I ain't gonna let her. (*Blocks other child's path*)

MISSOURI  Lemme by. (*Pushes* SNOOKS *and* SNOOKS *grabs her.* MIS-
SOURI *begins to cry.* MAMA *emerges from booth and shakes* SNOOKS)
MAMA  I told you to behave yourself. I won't take you to the Apollo
if you don't act right.
SNOOKS  Well, she started it.
STAID LADY  (*As* MISSOURI *comes sniffling into* TINY'S *booth*) Just
hush now. I tell you about fooling with strangers.
MAMA  Come on, Snooks. Goodbye all. (*Exits*)
EVERYBODY  Goodbye.
         (OPAL *returns to her table.* LULU *rearranges her tools.*
         MATTIE BEA *enters.* TINY *talks with the* STAID LADY)
MATTIE BEA  Howdy.
OPAL  Howdy-do!
MATTIE BEA  I had an appointment with Miss Lulu for two o'clock.
I'm just a little late.
LULU  Just waitin' for you. I said to myself, now I know she's gonna
be late.
MATTIE BEA  Yes, I had to stop by the Paradise Shine Parlors to look
up a friend o' mine, but he wasn't there. He's s'posed to pick me up
for the dance tonight.
LULU  Hello Club Ball?
MATTIE BEA  Uh-hum!
LULU  Everybody's going, ain't they? That Charleston Contest'll sure
be hot. Do you Charleston?
MATTIE BEA  Well, I ain't learned yet, but I'm gonna try. I never was
much of a dancer. You see, I was raised up in the Baptist Church
and didn't get away from it till I grewed up. My pa was a deacon.
LULU  Mine was too, child, but I didn't let that hold me back.
MATTIE BEA  I don't play cards till now.
LULU  You don't?
MATTIE BEA  Naw, child. I was taught that every card in the deck is
a devil, and the aces—they is Satan's claws.
LULU  Now, ain't that something? Do you play the numbers?
MATTIE BEA  Oh, yes! I wasn't taught nothing about numbers when
I was little.
LULU  They didn't have 'em then.
         (*Enter a large* BUXOM LADY *of commanding presence, a
         lodge ribbon across her breast*)
LODGE LADY  Can I get a 'pointment for this afternoon? I got to have

something done to this haid o' mine before tomorrow. The grand lodge's havin' a turn out, and I'm the High Grand Daughter Ruler.

OPAL   Certainly, we can find a place for you today. (*Looking at her appointment sheet*) How about four o'clock?

LODGE LADY   Which operator's that?

OPAL   Miss Tiny.

LODGE LADY   All right then! I likes Tiny cause she never yet has burnt a strand o' my hair. I'll be here at four.

OPAL   (*Writing in book*) I'm putting you down.

LODGE LADY   (*Exiting*) Thank you kindly.

MATTIE BEA   And they had a new shine boy at the Paradise, that's what worried me. Madam Bell say my fella's gone to writing numbers. Ain't shining shoes no more.

LULU   There's been a new pay-off down at city hall, and they say they changing lots o' writers up here. The new gang o' gangsters don't want the old crew no more. They all got bad reputations, them old writers. People would hit, then never see the runner. He'd collect the money, and keep it himself. It were awful!

MATTIE BEA   Yes, it were. And half the folks in Harlem on relief, too. Don't hardly get enough money to play one number a day, let alone eat.

(*They continue to talk between themselves.* OPAL *is busy polishing her own fingernails.* TINY *is working on the* STAID LADY'S *head*)

TINY   I been in this business for ten years now. And when I straighten a head, it's really straight. Wait till you see what I do to your daughter's head when I get round to it. I send anybody out o' here ready to put a man in the mood for love!

STAID LADY   I don't want no love for my daughter. I'm preparing her to be baptized tomorrow.

TINY   Then why straighten her hair out? It'll frizzle right up again. Ain't no kind o' treatment that's water proof.

STAID LADY   I want her to look her best when Reverend Hinds pushes her down in that pool to receive the spirit of the Lord.

MISSOURI   Do I have to go *all* the way down in the water, mama?

STAID LADY   Every inch of you's got to get wet, daughter, or you ain't baptized right. And I want *you right*. This Harlem's a place o' sin, child, and I want you protected.

TINY   Religion protected me, I know. I been a Baptist for years—and ain't sinned since I was seventeen.

STAID LADY  What did you do then?

TINY  Told a half-lie. I told a man that Lulu was my sister and 'twarn't so. She's my half-sister.

STAID LADY  Well, I ain't sinned since I were ten.

TINY  What did you do?

STAID LADY  Smoked a cigarette out in the barn with my brother, but the next month I was converted to Christ, and I ain't smoked since.

TINY  Hallelujah!

STAID LADY  Amen!

TINY  Religion is a wonderful thing!

STAID LADY  Yes, indeed it is! Bless God! (*A verse of " Old Time Religion " may be sung or hummed*)

TINY  (*Half-shouting*)  Oh my! My! My! Praise the Lawd!

LULU  Amen! Amen!

> (*Enter* LITTLE HAM. *He is very sportily dressed and wears the red muffler* MATTIE BEA *gave him*)

OPAL  Howdy-do!

HAM  How are you?

OPAL  Right well, I thank you. Did you wish to see someone?

HAM  Is this the shop o' Miss Tiny Lee?

OPAL  You ain't missed it.

HAM  Who is in charge?

OPAL  I make appointments.

HAM  Well, put me down for one.

OPAL  With me, or Miss Tiny?

HAM  (*Looking around*)  Where is Tiny at?

OPAL  Right there. (*Indicating booth at her right*)

HAM  Oh, then put me down for Tiny. And tell her I needs to see her bad.

OPAL  Shall I interrupt her work?

HAM  Sure, tell her Little Ham is here!

OPAL  O. K. (*Rises and goes to* TINY'S *booth*)  Here is Mr. Ham!

TINY  He is? Well, bless my soul! (*Leaves the hot comb in* STAID LADY'S *hair and comes out*)  Hello, there, darling! Sugar lump! Sweetness! This is the first time you been in my shop, ain't it? Well, it's full o' old ladies now! Come on back here where we can talk a minute. (*Takes* HAM *back to the sink and storage corner*) You little old Ham you! (*Kissing*)

HAM  How's tricks?

TINY  O.K., baby! I sent my new coat over to the seamster this

morning to be extended, and she say she'll have it all ready and bring
it back to me this afternoon, so I can wear it to the dance tonight. It
ought to be here most any time now. How's things by you?

HAM  I done wrote up most fifty dollars worth o' numbers today.

TINY  Naw you ain't.

HAM  Yes, I did, too! Folks just seem to take to me for a natural-
born number writer.

TINY  (*Worried*)  Honey, don't get pinched now.

HAM  Babe, I done been to headquarters! Them gangsters got a office
over yonder in East Harlem bigger'n ten shine parlors put together,
and seven hairdressing shops thrown in. And I seen the headman,
the big shot, the one the G-men even never seen. I seen him! And
he told me everything's all fixed with them that's in politics, and
if by accident a detective or a policeman should happen to nab me
by mistake, not knowin' I's one o' their men, all I got to do is say
that name his first lieutenant told me last night—and the turnkey, or
judge, or whoever got me locked up'll let me right out. He say
just say—what were it, darling?

TINY  Snizzle, or Snopple or something like that, weren't it? You
told me.

HAM  Supple, I believe.

TINY  It were something like that.

HAM  But, anyhow, I ain't gonna get locked up. I'm a fool-proof
number writer, anyhow. They can't ketch me in no trap. I'm just
gonna write for my friends and my friends' friends, and I got a
million friends in Harlem.

TINY  (*Coyly*)  And who is your best friend?

HAM  You, Tiny! (*They embrace fervently*)

TINY  Then make me know it!

STAID LADY  (*Yelling*)  Aw-ooo! My haid is burning up! (*Her hair
is smoking*)

MISSOURI  Aw-ooo! Mama's burning up!

TINY  I love you, Ham.

HAM  And me you, too.

TINY  You never gonna leave me?

HAM  Never!

TINY  And you takin' me to the Ball?

HAM  *Understood.*

TINY  We's gonna strut our stuff!

HAM  Gonna dance on down!

STAID LADY (*Loudly*) Yaw-oow!

TINY Oh, my lands! That woman's haid! (*Rushes to her booth*) Darling, is you burnt?

STAID LADY (*Angrily*) Lemme out of here! Just lemme out of here!

HAM (*Appearing in the door of the booth*) Don't you want to play a number today, lady? I can still get it in for you.

STAID LADY Jest lemme out of this place! It's possessed of the devil. (*Putting her hat on angrily over her uncombed hair*)

MISSOURI Let us out of this damn place!

TINY Well, go on then! A little thing like a burnt haid might happen any time, specially when it's tight and dry as yours is!

STAID LADY I thought you had religion! But I'll get back at you, Tiny Lee, don't worry! An eye for an eye and a tooth for a tooth.

TINY Yes, and a strand for a strand.

(*Enter a* FEMALE MEMBER *of Father Divine's cult*)

DIVINITE Peace, angel!

OPAL Peace!

DIVINITE All o' Father's beauty parlors is full to overflowin' this afternoon, so I come to you.

OPAL We'll take you on, sister.

DIVINITE I want my hair straightened.

OPAL Just have a seat. One o' our operators'll take you directly. (DIVINITE *sits down*)

DIVINITE It's truly wonderful!

STAID LADY (*Going toward door*) It's full of devils—that's what I say about Harlem. Why my head feels like I been in hell, it's so burnt up. (*Exits*)

DIVINITE Peace!

TINY That's what I say—Peace!

HAM Peace, sister! I'm selling the numbers! Who wants one?

DIVINITE I don't need no numbers, son. I got Father and he's truly wonderful! Peace, Little Ham!

HAM (*Surprised as he recognizes the* DIVINITE) Peace! Why, if it ain't Gertrude! Is you done got righteous?

DIVINITE Indeed I have, you devil you! And my name ain't Gertrude no mo'. I done took a new name in the Kingdom.

HAM What is it?

DIVINITE Sweet Delight! That's what they calls me now. Sweet Delight! (*She follows* TINY *into booth*)

HAM    (*To* OPAL)   I'm taking 'em down, girl, any number you want
to play.

OPAL    Well, put me down for—wait a minute. (*Looks in Dream
Book*) What's the number for *green?* Also *dress?* I wants to play
'em, boxed.

HAM    I drempt you was handlin' money last night.

OPAL    You drempt *I* was handlin' money last night? Why you didn't
even know me last night.

HAM    No, but I drempt I knowed you last night.

OPAL    Well, I want to play 448 for *green* and 006 for *dress.* Put me
down, papa.

HAM    I sho' will, sweet.

TINY    (*Calling*)   Opal, how many more appointments have I got
before suppertime?

OPAL    (*Looking at book*)   Four.

TINY    Oh, pshaw! I thought I might get a chance to run out and have
a beer or two with Little Ham. Say, Ham, what about that boy
Shingle, that you told me got arrested yesterday?

HAM    Aw, he's out. Five-dollar fine, that was all, for carrying con-
cealed slips.

TINY    And how about Boss LeRoy?

HAM    Don't know for sure, but I hear he's been put out o' the racket.
Madam's still in, though. The Shine Parlor's writing numbers today,
even if Madam do say her nerves can't go it.

TINY    She's just puttin' on—that old hardfisted woman! Baby, don't
you want a glass o' beer? I wish I could go out with you, Ham.
            (MATTIE BEA *in other booth pricks up her ears*)

HAM    I wish you could too, darling. But I know you got to work.
(*To* OPAL) How much you puttin' on these numbers?

OPAL    Box 'em, and put a nickel on each. That makes sixty cents,
don't it?

HAM    You are perzactly correct.

OPAL    (*Paying him*)   Come around every day.

HAM    As sure as the sun rises and sets and Roosevelt's a white man.

OPAL    I ain't never heard o' no black Roosevelt.

HAM    Neither's I. (*Going toward* LULU'S *booth*) Lemme see, is
there any business over here? (*Looks in and sees* MATTIE BEA, *and
is terribly embarrassed*) Howdy-do!

MATTIE BEA    (*Dryly*)   So you a number writer now.

HAM    I just started today!

MATTIE BEA   No wonder I couldn't find you at the Paradise! I been there three times lookin' for you today. I want to know what time you coming by to get me to go to the dance tonight?

HAM   That's pro-bli-ma-ti-cal.

MATTIE BEA   And what's that mean?

HAM   I mean—that's a problem.

MATTIE BEA   What kind o' problem? You see me settin' up here getting my hair all ready to go. Now, you don't mean to say you ain't gonna take me?

HAM   I mean to say that since I got to be a number writer, I works nights too. I got to count up all those numbers, and divide up all this change.

MATTIE BEA   You mean you ain't goin' to the Ball?

HAM   Honey, I don't see how I can.

MATTIE BEA   (*Leaning forward*) And me done spent *my* good money for tickets, too. And give 'em to you yesterday.

LULU   Keep still, please. You'll make me burn you.

MATTIE BEA   You ain't gonna pull no stuff on me, Ham!
                (TINY *comes out of her booth to listen*)

HAM   Shss! I ain't tryin' to pull no stuff on you. I'll take you, baby, but it can't be till late.

MATTIE BEA   (*Delighted*)   I knowed you'd take me, honey! You just wanted to tease me a little, didn't you?

HAM   That's all, darling.

MATTIE BEA   You little sweet ole devil you. Come here and hold my hand. I knowed you'd take me.

TINY   (*Approaching*)   Take *who* where?

MATTIE BEA   Take *me* to the Hello Club Ball.

TINY   Naw he don't! Ham's *my* man. He ain't takin you nowhere. What put that in your head? And who's you?

MATTIE BEA   Who *is* you, Jumbo?

TINY   (*Hands on hips*)   I'm a real good mama that can shake your peaches down!

MATTIE BEA   Sister, my tree's too tall for you! You'd have to climb and climb again.

TINY   (*Loudly*)   I hear you cluckin', hen, but your nest must be far away. Don't try to lay no eggs in here. (*Putting her arm around* HAM) This rooster belongs to me, Miss Tiny Lee! Don't you, little Ham?

MATTIE BEA  (*Rising*)  Take your hands off that man, you heifer, before I stomp your head!

LULU  Lawd have mercy!

TINY  Heifer ain't my name—but I'll take it in my left hand. If you give it to me in my right, it's your hips!

MATTIE BEA  (*Removing towel from neck*)  Yes, you's a heifer! No other she-varmint'd try to take a woman's man away from her right under her very nose. You'll never take Ham from me. Come on, Ham, let's get out of here.

HAM  Now don't act that way, Mattie Bea, you know I ain't nothin' to you.

TINY  (*To* HAM)  So you know the wench's name? Uh-hum! Well, I want you to forget it!

HAM  All right, darling.

DIVINITE  (*In* TINY's *booth*)  Peace, Father!

MATTIE BEA  This place's too small to whip a cat in, without getting fur in your mouth, but I'm gonna whip you, Tiny Lee.

LULU  Now here, woman, don't start no ruckus in my booth, knocking over my oils and things. If you want to fight—you, Tiny, or anybody, back on out of here.

> (*The belligerents back on toward the entrance.* OPAL *gathers up her manicure tools and retreats toward sink. The* DIVINITE *comes out to intercede*)

TINY  I'll whip you less you fly to Jesus!

DIVINITE  (*Touching* TINY's *sleeve*)  Peace, daughter!

TINY  Peace nothing! She says she's gonna take my Ham.

DIVINITE  (*Gently*)  You can buy mo' ham in the butcher shop.

TINY  But not this kind! Stand back you all.

MATTIE BEA  Little Ham, get out o' the way! Don't you get hurt.
> (*Just as they prepare to fight, in comes a* DELIVERY BOY *with a package*)

DELIVERY BOY  Coat for Miss Tiny Lee.

TINY  Lemme see if it's fixed right before I pay for it. Gimme it here.
> (*Opens the box.* MATTIE BEA *recognizes it as the same coat* HAM *promised to buy for her the day before from the Hot Stuff Man*)

MATTIE BEA  That's my coat, ain't it, Ham?

HAM  (*Disclaiming responsibility*)  It ain't none o' mine, I know that much.

TINY  (*Lifting out coat*)  It belongs to me. Ham bought it, and it belongs to me. I paid my own money to have this solid gold ex-

tension back put in it for the Hello Club Ball tonight. (*To* HAM)
And we gonna go, too, ain't we, papa? But first lemme attend to
this here she-dog! (*Putting down coat*)

MATTIE BEA   Oh! Ham, get out of the way! (MATTIE BEA *ups with
her purse and hits* TINY *on the head*)

TINY   That's a dying lick. I'll limb you, woman!

> (TINY *reaches for* MATTIE BEA. *The* DIVINITE *runs scream-
> ing,* "Peace," *through the door, and the* DELIVERY BOY
> *exits as the manicure table falls.* MATTIE BEA *grabs for and
> secures* TINY'S *hair. Just then the* LODGE LADY *enters, sees
> the turmoil, and rushes out calling,* "Police!")

LODGE LADY'S VOICE   Police! Police! Murder! Police!

LULU   Fight her to a finish, Tiny, before the cops come. Do it to
her, sister! You and me had the same mama, if not the same papa—
so I'm half with you.

TINY   Yes, indeedy! Just get back and gimme room.

OPAL   You all better stop!

HAM   Do it, Tiny, cause I know you can! I'm backing you up!

MATTIE BEA   Ham, you turn against me?

HAM   Mattie, you small potatoes and few in the pot to me now.

MATTIE BEA   After all I did for you? Take off my muffler! (*Reaches
out and grabs the muffler from* HAM'S *throat, then resumes her
struggle with* TINY)

TINY   Leave him, and everything he owns, alone.

MATTIE BEA   That little jiver don't own nothing. You Ham, take off
that overcoat I bought you last year.

HAM   What do you mean, woman?

MATTIE BEA   I'll show you what I mean, if I ever get loose here.

> (*She grabs the collar of* HAM'S *coat, and as she and* TINY
> *push and shove,* HAM *is almost choked. He has to struggle
> to get loose.* TINY *releases her grip to puff and blow a
> moment. And just as a* COP *comes in,* HAM *is pushing*
> MATTIE BEA *roughly away. It looks as if he has been beat-
> ing her, so the* COP *grabs him*)

COP   You dirty little woman-beater, you, come with me! You know
it's against the law to hit a lady.

HAM   She hit me.

COP   That's no difference. Come on, now.

TINY   But, officer . . .

COP   That's all right, Miss Lee. I know you run a decent place. I'll
take this little ruffian out of here.

TINY   But I don't want you to take him.

MATTIE BEA   Neither do I. He ain't done a thing.

HAM   I sho' ain't.

TINY   He sure ain't.

COP   I know you women's got good hearts. (*Loudly*) But I ain't got no heart for a brute that would hit a lady. (*Jerks him roughly*) Come on!

HAM   (*Rapidly*)   Shovel, Shrivel, Chapel! What's the word?

COP   Is he crazy?

HAM   (*Frantically*)   Tiny, what's the word? What's the word? What's the word?

TINY   Sappy, soopy, sippy . . . Oh, my God, I can't remember!

COP   Well, all of you all must be fools! I'm gonna call the wagon. (*Roughly*) Stand up! (*Drags* HAM *by the coat collar out into the street. The wails of the women follow him. At the door the* COP *turns and pushes the women back inside*) Don't bring that noise out here in the street, if you do, I'll arrest you all, too.

MATTIE BEA   He ain't done nothing! Not a thing!

TINY   Naw, he ain't. He's the sweetest little man in the world.

MATTIE BEA   And he belongs to me.

TINY   If he does, then go take him back from that cop, please.

MATTIE BEA   I'll take some of your hide first.

TINY   Then I'll give your collar bone a permanent wave!

MATTIE BEA   You mean you'll try. Well, come on to me. (*Reaches down in her stocking and produces a knife*)

TINY   Uck-oh! Lulu, hand me your hot comb. (LULU *hands* TINY *a red-hot straightening comb*)

LULU   (*To* MATTIE BEA)   Don't you cut my sister!

(MATTIE BEA *ups with the knife, but* TINY *waves the hot comb while* LULU *threatens her with a curling iron.* MATTIE BEA *shrieks and rises to run toward the door.* TINY *jabs the hot comb at her back as she escapes into the street*)

LULU   Now, maybe we can have some peace in here.

TINY   I hope we can. Is there anybody else wants some o' this comb? (*Looks pointedly at* OPAL) I heard you talkin' to Ham. Don't think I didn't. (*Mocking her*) " Come back again." Playin' numbers with my little Ham, heh?

OPAL   (*Pleading*)   That's all I was doin', Miss Tiny.

TINY   And that's all you'll ever do, too! Take yourself out of here now! Get! And take your tools. You don't work for me no more.

OPAL    (*Rushing into her coat*)   Yes, ma'am.

TINY    Anybody wants any of my Ham, they'll pay for it. Cause I'll put my brand on 'em.

OPAL    I'm goin', Miss Tiny. You won't have no trouble out o' me.

TINY    (*Swiping at her from a distance with the hot iron*)  Go!

OPAL    Ow-ooo! (*Exits*)

TINY    There ain't no woman faithful to you—where a man is concerned.

LULU    Nobody but your sister.

TINY    (*Bursting into tears*)  Now Ham is gone, locked up, and I couldn't think o' that word for to tell the judge! Snibble, Snozzle, Snozzle! Lulu, lock the door. I can't work no more today. And turn down the radio, sister, so I can cry out loud! (*Bawling*) Little Ham is gone! He's gone! Gone! (*She buries her face in the velvet coat with the gold brocaded back and weeps aloud*)  Hamlet is gone!

CURTAIN

# ACT THREE

## SCENE ONE

*That night.*

TINY'S *apartment in Harlem. Her boudoir, very silken and sleek, with soft lights and gay colors. Large shiny photos of Harlem theatrical celebrities all around. Big box of chocolates on the table. Radio going. Telephone by bed.*

*As the curtain rises,* TINY, en déshabillé, *and an illegitimate part-Pekinese, named Nelson, are running wildly about the room,* TINY *evidently is in great distress.*

TINY  (*To the dog*)  Nelson, why don't you lay down, gettin' right under my feet all the time! Can't you see worried as I is, I'm liable to step on you and mash your gizzard out? Get from under my feet! (*Goes to the telephone*) Lawd, I'm so nervous I can't hardly work this dial . . . Hello! Hello! That you, Lulu? . . . Honey, sister, I wish you'd come right on over here! . . . Naw, Ham ain't out yet. Leastwise, he ain't here . . . Naw . . . Yes, I been callin' and a-callin' up de jail. And he been a-callin' me from the police station. We been tryin' to remember that name. That name the white gangster told him to say last night, and they'd let him right out. I heard it, too, but I disremembers myself. Seem like it were Snopple . . . Heh? You say maybe it was Snozzel! Naw, that's Durante . . . It's a gangster's name. The name that works like magic down at City Hall . . . Aw, Lawd, I don't know what I'm gonna do, sister. Here 'tis long past time to go to the Hello Club affair, and my Ham's in jail . . . Naw, I can't get nobody on the phone now, since seven o'clock. They got him up in police court, I reckon. And if he could just tell the judge that name, I know they'd let him out . . . Sure, I called Boss LeRoy. But he ain't boss no more in Harlem. This new gang's got a new boss up here. Some Detroit Jigaboo they imported . . . Yes . . . Please do, Lulu. Come right over . . . I'm liable to faint before you get here. This thing's got me so worried it's gimme nervous prostitution . . . The first and only man I ever really loved, and he done gone and get locked up protecting me.

Honey, wasn't it marvelous the way he lit into that other woman?
Ham is a man, I'm tellin' you . . . yes, he is . . . Honey, bring me
a pint o' gin when you come. I don't know if I can keep my senses
or not till you get here . . . The dance? . . . Naw, I ain't goin' to
no dance by myself . . . Yes, I got my clothes all laid out, red gown
and velvet coat and all, but I ain't goin' nowhere without Ham . . .
Gilbert? Now, I ain't studyin' lettin' Gilbert take me . . . Should
you bring him along? Gilbert? Well, bring him if you want to,
but you and I know, *and he knows*, that he ain't my man no mo'.
He ought to stay home with his wife. I called him up and told him
so last night after Ham left here. I told him he were a good old
wagon, but he done broke down—far as I'm concerned. Gilbert
didn't care nothing about me no how . . . What you say? He
says he gonna shoot Ham? He'll have me to kill if he do . . .
Um-hum! You mean take Gilbert back just for tonight, so we can
all go to this Charleston Contest? . . . I tell you I can't dance, worried
as I is about my little, short, sweet, brand new papa . . . Well, yes,
tell Gilbert he can come up here, but to behave himself. You say
you're bringing your boy friend, too? . . . Well, hurry up, some o'
you all and come on, 'cause I'm just about to die o' worryment.
And I can't stand being alone with just a dog. Nelson ain't no
company. And my *heart* is in jail . . . Take a taxi . . . Goodbye.
(TINY *rises and goes to the mirror and begins to comb her hair.
She takes a chocolate from a box. To dog*) Nelson, I reckon if you
was a human, you'd be grayheaded by now, old as you is, and as
much worryment as they is in this world! But you ain't never been
in love with no man in jail, has you? . . . Huh? . . . I wonder did
you care much about that police dog you tried to reach up to last
month in the hall? She were too tall for you, werent' she? Po' boy!
I must take you out where some small dogs is, in the spring! Yes sir!
Lawd, if I could only think of that name, to phone Ham! Snapple,
snipple, snopple, skipple, bipple! Aw, hell! The devil! Shupple,
maybe that were it! Naw, more like Scrappel! Scrappel! That's
right, I think. Lemme see can I get the police station on the phone
. . . (*Dialing*) Plaza 3-9600 . . . Hello! The Captain? . . . Yes,
you all tell Hamlet Jones, *Scrappel* is the name . . . What? . . . Yes,
I'm the same woman done called six times, and I'll call six more
times if I want to. I pays taxes for you-all bulls to live on, and I
votes for aldermen, and I knows every ward boss in Harlem, knows
'em well! Was married to one of 'em—in name only—once. And

I'll tell him to take your job, if you gimme any rough talk . . . Sure, I'd be just as brave if I was down there as I am on the phone. I knows my politics—which is Tammany! . . . You tell my little Ham *Scrappel* was the name . . . My name? . . . Naw! *The* name . . . Huh? You say you ain't got no Ham nor no Scrappel neither there? . . . Then where is Ham? You all discharged him? . . . What? Yo don't know? I have to call the night court? And they ain't got no phone? Oh, Lawd! (*Hangs up receiver*) Oh, Lawd! Nelson, Ham is up before the Judge! (*Praying*) Oh, Lawd, give that Judge a kind heart. Ham weren't doin' a thing but defending me. I hope he et up all them policy slips on him before they got him down to the station! (*To the dog, as the doorbell rings*) Nelson, get out of my way! (*Goes to door and admits* LULU *and her boy friend*, JACK, *and also* GILBERT, *her own former flame*)

LULU　Girl, I'm sorry you feelin' so bad. Maybe this gin'll cheer you up a bit. We brought lemons and ice, too. Where's your shaker?

TINY　Nothin' could cheer me up tonight, Lulu. Hello, Jack. (*Coldly*) Hello, Gilbert.

GILBERT　Don't bass at me, woman. I ain't bit you.

TINY　Now, don't start no stuff, Gilbert. We's familiar no more.

LULU　Come on, Jack, let's go out in the kitchen and mix up a cocktail. We going on to the Ball, soon's we drink it. Let the other two of 'em stay here if they want to.

GILBERT　Naw, we ain't gonna stay neither. Tiny's going to that dance *with me*.

TINY　You got that wrong!

LULU　Come on, Jack. Let's go mix the drinks. (*They exit into kitchen*)

TINY　I ain't steppin' out with you *no more*, Gilbert. I done told you that by phone last night.

GILBERT　I know you weigh two tons more'n a switch engine, but you can't sidetrack me like that. I'm sweet papa Gilbert from Texas where even the rabbits are too tough for stew. And I don't let no woman quit me. I quit them. Women don't quit me.

TINY　Now, Gilbert, you know you ain't been a-near me for three days.

GILBERT　I come up here last night and wouldn't nobody open the door. Don't think I didn't see your light. I went out in the alley and looked. Not only saw the light, but I saw shadows, too—two shadows on that back window shade—and big as you are, even you can't cast but *one*.

TINY   Are you insinuating?

GILBERT   Then why didn't you answer the doorbell? Or at least answer the phone? Naw, you waited till one o'clock in the morning—and then called me up to tell me you didn't want me in your life no more.

TINY   And I sure don't.

GILBERT   But don't think I don't know who you've taken up with? A dumb little shoeshiner named Hamlet Jones.

TINY   He's no shoeshiner. Ham's a business man.

GILBERT   What kind o' business man?

TINY   He deals in figures.

GILBERT   So do I. I play numbers, too.

TINY   Well, he writes them.

GILBERT   No wonder he's in jail then.

TINY   He's in jail for defending me from attack.

GILBERT   Who'd attack you?

TINY   Don't call me out o' my name!

GILBERT   Then get your clothes on and come on let's go to the dance. We liable to win that cup, good as you and I can Charleston.

TINY   I'll never Charleston with you no more. Last time I went to a dance with you, you danced all night with some meriney hussy that looked like a faded-out jack-o-lantern.

GILBERT   (*Chucking her under the chin*)   Aw, come on, baby, be sociable. I'll dance with you tonight, Tiny.

TINY   After all I gived you, you come tellin' me I'm too stout to offer any competition. You wants a woman you can hold on your lap.

GILBERT   Aw, sweetness, I was just kiddin'. You never forgets, do you? Just like an elephant!

TINY   Naw, I don't forget! But I forgot you. Get out o' my life, Gilbert. I'm goin' and see about them cocktails. (*Starts into kitchen, but backs out suddenly*) Oh, excuse me! I didn't know you all was engaged yet.

GILBERT   (*Harshly*)   Tiny, I guess you realize I really don't give a damn about you, but I'm a man. And ain't no woman gonna quit me. When I get ready to leave you, then I leave. But you ain't gonna tell me *you* are through. No, indeed! You're gonna see plenty more of Gilbert, till *I* get good and ready to lay off.

TINY   There won't be no more of *you* to see if you fool with me!

GILBERT   You must forget that I carry a gun.

TINY   (*As* LULU *and* JACK *enter with the cocktail shaker and glasses*) I ain't forgot nothing.

LULU   Have somethin' coolin' and refreshin'.

TINY   (*Pointedly to her sister*)   You all need somethin' coolin. That's
what I say about love. Last week right on Lenox Avenue, I had to
throw water on Nelson—that dog were so excited.

JACK   Did you all decide to go to the dance?

TINY   You all dance on down—and take Gilbert with you. I'm
stayin' here.

GILBERT   We're taking Tiny too.

LULU   (*Pouring cocktails*)   I wish you'd come, sister.

TINY   Just wish right on, 'cause I ain't budging.

   (*A loud knock at the door combined with the ringing of
   the bell*)

LULU   What a racket!

TINY   (*Shouting*)   Who's there?

HAM   (*Voice without*)   Little Ham, that's who! Me, Ham!

LULU   Oh!

GILBERT   (*Sinisterly*)   Aw!

JACK   Who?

TINY   (*Jubilantly*)   Thank God-a-mighty! Nelson, your daddy's come
home!   (*Rushes toward the door, then turns suddenly, recalling
GILBERT. Whispering*)   Gilbert, he might have a gun, baby. (*Sweetly
to her old lover*)   Just step in my fur-coat closet a minute till I
find out.

   (*Sulkily* GILBERT *steps into a closet.* TINY *closes the door,
   locks it, and takes the key with her, as she goes to let
   HAM in*)

HAM   You took long enough to let me in! I just got out of jail, and
looks like you don't want me here. Ain't you glad to see me?

TINY   (*Ecstatically*)   Baby, I certainly are! (*Takes him in her arms*)
Lawd knows I are!

LULU   I'm so glad you're out, Ham.

JACK   What'd they fine you?

HAM   Not a dime.

TINY   Baby, did you ever think o' the magic name?

HAM   Never did.

LULU   Are you out on bail?

HAM   Naw, I'm freed, released, don't have to go back no more.

TINY   Ain't that wonderful! Tell us about it.

HAM   Well, as luck would have it, it were a woman judge.

LULU   A woman judge?

HAM  Yes, a woman judge! (*Conceitedly*) So I just conversationed her. And she being a lady . . .

JACK  Boy, ain't you something!

HAM  I just told her any man would defend a woman, and I was a man! She say, that's right! And I say, it sure is. And smiled at her— and that were my defense.

TINY  And they ain't found no numbers on you?

HAM  Sure they found some few little slips. But I just said, now, that one there, that's my mother's telephone number what just moved to Sugar Hill. And that other one, why that's my initiation number in the Elks. They just initiated me last night, so I had to write it down to remember it. And them other slips there, the last four they found, why, that's my horoscope. I paid a astrologer ten dollars to figger that out for me and he wrote it in four pieces, what time my star comes due—at 1:16 the third month of the 47th year plus one thousand, minus 2-9-2. And the lady judge says, did I ever read Evangeline Adams, who knew all about the heavens? And I said no, but that I follows Father Divine who knows more about Heaven than anybody. So the Judge says, Peace, Father! And I said, Peace, Angel. And she lemme out.

TINY  It's truly wonderful!

LULU  Amen!

JACK  Well, now that you're here, let's go to the Ball.

HAM  Let's go. I'm ready! Honey, put on your clothes.

TINY  Give Ham a drink first. You all just turn your backs while I dress.

> (HAM, LULU, *and* JACK *gather round the cocktail shaker while* TINY *slips off her negligee and puts on a red lace evening gown, red slippers, and a rhinestone tiara*)

LULU  (*While* TINY *dresses*) Well, that woman what dreamed about a *colored* woman washing a green dress in a white lady's back yard was right. One of her numbers come out this afternoon.

JACK  What number?

HAM  0-0-6. That's dress! It sho' come out.

LULU  If she really played it, she caught, too.

TINY  That's a lucky lady. She catch all the time. (*Pulls open drawer to get her jewels and six or eight men's pictures fall out. Looks around anxiously to see if* HAM *notices. Relieved, she picks them up quickly*)

LULU  I wish it'd been me that hit today.

TINY　(*Still dressing*)　I knowed a 6 was coming out somewhere. 0-0-6 come mighty near being our 1-1-6 again, didn't it, Ham?

HAM　It sho' did. But we can't catch every day, baby.

TINY　Sure can't. It's enough I caught you—and five hundred and forty dollars both—inside o' two days. (*Coming toward them, dressed*)

HAM　And I got you! Baby, how pretty you look! Be-ooo-ti-ful!

TINY　It's all for you, sugar!

JACK　Tons and tons of it, boy!

LULU　Drink up and let's go. (*They lift their glasses and drink*)

HAM　(*Looking at his wrist watch*)　Hurry up, and we'll be just in time for the Charleston Contest. It starts at midnight. Maybe I'll stop by my flat and put on my new suit. This one ain't been pressed today. It won't take but a minute.

TINY　Sure, if you want to. I want my papa lookin' hot. (*Takes her new coat and gives it to* HAM *to hold*)　Jack, you see this pretty coat Ham bought me yesterday. I didn't have to do a thing to it to make it fit, but put a new back in it, and believe me, it's solid gold-brocaded Cadillac.

JACK　You look like the Queen o' Sheba.

LULU　You certainly look sweet, sis. I'm proud of my relative.

TINY　Let's go! (*To dog*)　Nelson, you stay here now, and be a nice dog.

HAM　Come on.

LULU　Everybody truck on down! (*Opens exit door*)

GILBERT　(*Thumping in closet, in loud voice*)　Hey! Hey! Lemme out o' here!

HAM　(*Stopping dead still*)　What's that?

TINY　Aw, come on, honey! That's some old wild man in the next apartment who's always making a lot of noise.

HAM　(*Doubling up his fists*)　Well, if he just must get out, I'll take him on.

TINY　Have you got a gun with you, darling?

HAM　I ain't got no gun, but I'm *a man*.

GILBERT　I'm a man, too, and I'll take you on, Ham.

HAM　Sounds like he's talkin' to me.

TINY　Oh, no he ain't, darlin'. Come on.

LULU　Yes, for God's sake, come on.

JACK　I'm going myself. (*Pulls* LULU *by the arm, but she does not move from doorway*)

GILBERT  Hamlet Jones, I say lemme out, you son-of-a . . .

HAM  Well, hot-damn! Now, I know that's me he's calling. (*Approaching closet*) Which dark horse is you? You also-ran!

GILBERT  Unlock this door and you'll see! Tiny, come here and open this closet door! You know you got me locked up in here, smothered.

TINY  You'll stay there, too, far as I'm concerned. Come on, Ham, let's go.

HAM  Don't think I'm afraid, whoever you is. You might be bigger'n I am, but I'm every inch a man.

GILBERT  I got more feet than you got inches, runt. And if you all don't lemme out o' here, you'll know it.

HAM  Who you callin' runt?

GILBERT  You, you stunted cockroach!

HAM  (*To* TINY) Lemme at him, whoever he is!

TINY  (*Pleading*) Come on to the Ball, baby. We'll attend to him by and by. I don't want to get my clothes all mussed up now.

GILBERT  (*Angrily*) You all, none of you, didn't have no mammy!

LULU  Aw-ooo!

HAM  (*Stepping toward door*) Well, your'n must-a been a mole, what borned you in a coal mine, 'cause even your voice sounds caved in.

GILBERT  (*Shooting his pistol through the door*) Take that, you so-and-so-and-so. (*Fires five shots, one after another, through the door.* TINY, LULU, JACK *and* HAM *press back against the wall*) Take that! (*Bang!*) and that! (*Bang!*)

TINY  (*Calmly, after the shooting is over*) Well, now that's over! His kind o' gun don't carry but five bullets—and he ain't hit a thing but the other wall. Come on, you all, let's go! I don't let no Abyssinian spoil my evening. Come, Ham, let's win that Charleston cup, like we done said we would!

HAM  I'll give you a taste o' my forty-four when I come back, creeper. Just stay there and breathe through them holes you done shot in the door.

GILBERT  (*In closet*) Please lemme out! Tiny, please lemme out 'fore you go.

TINY  (*Yelling back from the doorway*) I want to spare your life, Gilbert—for your wife's sake. I can't have no murder here, no how, 'cause little Ham would tear you to pieces, wouldn't you, Ham?

HAM  I'd limb him—limb from limb! (*Taking empty gin bottle from tray and poking its neck through one of the bullet holes in the*

*closet door*)  Here, smell this through that bullet hole till I get back
with *my* pistol.  You might need something stronger than gin to
help you, by and by.
GILBERT  (*Moaning*)  Tiny, help me, baby!
TINY  Help you, hell!  Me and Ham's going to the Hello Club Ball.
    (*Turns out the light*)  Goodbye, Nelson, you is a sweet dog!
        (*All exit except the dog.  Nelson remains to bark loudly
        in the dark as* GILBERT *yells and pounds on the locked door*)
GILBERT  Lemme out!  Lemme out!  Lemme out!

CURTAIN


SCENE TWO

*Midnight.*

*The Savoy Ball Room in Harlem.  The orchestra may be in
sight or hidden (as producer chooses), but the front of the
platform should be seen.  The* MASTER OF CEREMONIES
*stands thereon, the Grand Silver Charleston Trophy in
hand, to be awarded to the winning couple of the contest
about to take place.  A brilliant crowd of Harlem's suavest
and sportiest set, boxers, number writers, theatrical folks,
hairdressers, maids, sports, and their ladies.  Women in
evening gowns, men in extravagantly cut suits from tuxedos
to pleated backs, hair lacquered, diamonds flashing.* MADAM
BELL *and* LEROY *are there together;* SUGAR LOU *and her
new boy friend;* SHINGLE, *out of jail, and his company;*
JASPER *and a fair young lady; the* WEST INDIAN *and a
Bahama dancer—but not yet* TINY *and* HAM, *nor* JACK
*and* LULU.

*As the curtain rises, the orchestra is just coming to the end
of a blues number to which everybody is dancing.  As the
piece cools off, the* M.C. *signals for a loud chord to indicate
that silence is desired.  Everybody stops dancing.*

M.C.  Ladies and gentlemen, Lad-dees and gentel-mun!  And gigolos!
I have in my hand the Grand Silver Charleston Trophy engraved with

the name of Harlem's most prominent, high-toned society institution, the Hello Club. Hello! Hello! Hello! (*Applause*) This club has been ruling supreme amongst the Harlem Four Thousand for many years, and is known from Central Park north to the Yankee Stadium, from the Harlem River to Sugar Hill, from the Cotton Club to the Silver Dollar.

VOICE    And from the police station to Harlem Hospital.

M.C.    Also! We are known everywhere! The Hello Club leads where others follow.

VOICES    Yeah, man! . . . Yes, indeedy! . . . True! True!

M.C.    And when we give a ball, we give a ball!

VOICE    Yes, sir!

> (*Enter* LULU *and* JACK, TINY *and* HAM, *pushing to the front*)

M.C.    And tonight we are presenting the Hello Club's First Annual Social Charleston Contest. This here cup I got in my hand is to be awarded to the couple that, in the opinion of the audience, and of the applause they receive, has done the best job of real righteous oh-my-soul dancing on the floor. Everybody starts at once, and the judges will go around and eliminate them that ain't got the right movements in they feet, nor Charleston in their souls. Now listen, when the man taps you on the shoulder, that means go off the floor and be audience. I don't want nobody to get bullheaded and not withdraw—'cause that would spoil the social part. (*Gaily*) Everybody, now, let your spirits go to your feet, let the rhythm go to your heads, let the music move your souls, and dance on down! (*Lifting his baton*) Orchestra, give it to me!

> (*The orchestra begins a ballroom Charleston piece, and* EVERYBODY *starts to prance, rocking and swaying in a carnival of joy. Two or three* GENTLEMEN, *committee members, with ribbons across their chests, the colors of the Hello Club, are tapping those couples on the back who are dancing with the least originality and abandon. They withdraw to the sidelines. As the music goes on, finally all but four couples are eliminated. Those remaining include two* UNKNOWN COUPLES, MADAM *and* LEROY, *and* LITTLE HAM *and* TINY.)

M.C.    (*Stopping the music*) Ladies and gentlemen! And dancers! The Contest is now reaching its final and most important stage! That of who shall win! Somebody gotta win. Now it's up to you to show, by your applause, just who deserves the cup. We'll take these last four couples in rotation, for the crowning feature of the Hello Club Ball! Couples, line up over yonder! As I give the signal, dance on out across the floor, then Charleston. First couple, let's go. (*The* FIRST COUPLE *come out and do their dance. They have probably been practicing nightly for the last three weeks at the Savoy. But it is obvious that they are trying too hard, although the crowd gives them a good hand as they finish on the opposite side of the floor*) Second couple, bring it to me! Let's go, band! (*The* SECOND COUPLE *come dancing out across the floor, bowing and tapping, parting and swaying, circling around one another like a rooster and hen, then going into the Charleston. They get a good hand, as they finish on the left in front of the* M.C.)

VOICES  Pretty good, Joe! Too tight! . . . Young stuff! . . . Oh, my!

M.C.  All right now, Madam Bell of the Paradise Shining Parlors and her partner, Big Boss LeRoy! Let's go! (LEROY *and the* MADAM *truck on out to the center of the floor and break*) Aw, Break! . . . Do it, Madam Lucille Bell!

MADAM  Let's go to town!

LEROY  How we gonna get there?

MADAM  Truckin' on down.

VOICES  (*And laughter*) Do it, old folks! . . . Lawd, look at Madam Bell! . . . Aw, strut it, Boss! . . . Oh, my, my, my, my! . . .

LEROY  Let's break!

MADAM  Hey! Hey! Charleston! (*They finish up to great applause just in front of the* M.C.)

M.C.  And now for the last roundup! Come on, Little Ham! (LITTLE HAM *and* TINY *take the floor*)

VOICES  Lawd! Lawd! Lawd! . . . Boy, haul that load! . . . Tons—and tons—and tons!

HAM  All the way to town!

TINY  (*Trucking*) I'm comin', baby!

M.C.  Rock, church, rock!

> (TINY *and* HAM *do the most exciting, original, and jazzy dance of the whole evening, Suzy-q-ing, Lindy-hopping, Camel-walking, breaking, clutching, parting, and dancing on a dime until the entire crowd rocks with laughter, cheers, and applause*)

VOICES  That's the best! . . . Two tons o' rhythm! . . . Look at that little boy go . . . My! My! O my! My!

> (*They finish, sweating and out of breath*)

HAM  Yes, Tiny!

TINY  Yeah, man!

M.C.  That sends me! (*Holding up the cup*) Now, all four couples truck around the hall, one at a time, and the applause will tell who gets the trophy. (*To the band*) Come on, boys. Let's go, truckers! (*The band strikes up again, and in turn, the* FOUR COUPLES *dance around the hall, ending all together in a Charleston at center.* LITTLE HAM *and* TINY *get the most applause, much to the chagrin of* BOSS LEROY)

VOICES  Give it to Ham! . . . Yeah, man! . . . Ham and Tiny! . . .

M.C.  You all must mean Tiny and Ham! Is that right? (*To* TINY *and* HAM) Step out here in the middle of the floor. (*As they do so*) Is this who the crowd wants?

VOICES  (*And applause*) Yes! . . . They get it! . . . Sure! . . . Little Ham's won! . . . You're right! . . . Give Tiny that cup! . . .

M.C.  They surely deserve it. My compliments! Quiet, please. (*Signals the orchestra for a chord*) Ladies and partners! On behalf of the Hello Club's social committee and the entire membership of our estimable organization, I am delighted and exuberated to present this Grand Solid Silver Charleston Trophy to the winners of our contest tonight, Mr. Hamlet H. Jones and Miss Tiny Lee!

VOICES  'Ray! . . . Good! . . . Yes! . . . That's right! . . . Hurray! (*TINY and* HAM *receive the cup amid much applause.* LULU *and* JACK *rush forward to shake their hands, also* JASPER *and* SHINGLE. LEROY *stands in a corner moping with* MADAM)

LEROY  Here I done lost my job with the numbers, and can't even win a dancing cup! When a man is down, he's down.

MADAM  Baby, you can have Little Ham's job, shining shoes. He's working in the field now.

LEROY  (*Incensed, raises his arm to hit* MADAM) Woman, don't tell me . . .

A COMMITTEE MEMBER  (*grabs him*) This here's a social, brother.

LEROY  Oh, all right! Then I won't fight. (*Mumbling*) Come offering *me* a job shining shoes. (*To* MADAM) Come on, Lucille, let's go!

MADAM  Yes, darling, let's go. (*They start toward door, but* MADAM BELL *suddenly pauses as* MATTIE BEA *enters. Excitedly*) Look, LeRoy, there's Ham's other woman! Uh-oh!

LEROY  Who? Where? Which one?

MADAM     (*Pointing*)   Mattie Bea!
LEROY   Uh-oh! Watch out!
MADAM     (*In anticipation*)   The fur'll fly now.
          (MATTIE BEA *pauses, looks around, clenches her fists, and
          advances toward the bandstand with venom in her eye.* HAM
          *and* TINY *do not see her. Suddenly, however, the door is
          flung open and* GILBERT *stalks in*)
GILBERT     (*Loudly*)   Everybody stand back. I'm here! (*Everybody
turns toward the door.* TINY *and* MATTIE BEA *both scream*)   I done
broke down one door tonight, and I'll turn this place out, too.
I'm mad!
TINY   Oh! The lion is loose!
HAM   Who? Where? What lion?
MATTIE BEA     (*Yells in astonishment*)   My husband! Gilbert!
HAM     (*Sees her for the first time and looks worried*)   Mattie Bea!
(*Hides behind* TINY)
GILBERT     (*Mollified*)   My wife! Mattie Bea, what you doin' here?
MATTIE BEA   How about you, Gilbert? I thought you said you had to
work tonight?
GILBERT   I did. I just got off, honey.
MATTIE BEA   Then who are you lookin' for here?
GILBERT   You, baby, you! (HAM *and* TINY *both seem much relieved*)
I thought you might be at this dance.
MATTIE BEA   Well, all right, then! I hate to be at a dance all by
myself, Gilbert. But what makes you come in so loud, honey?
GILBERT   I just want everybody to know we're here, that's all—me
and you. We ain't been to a dance together for so long, it's a shame,
Mattie Bea.
MATTIE BEA   Sure is! (*Sweetly*) But now we here, Gilbert, and you
look so nice tonight, I believe I'm in love with you all over again.
Take off your coat, and let's dance.
          (*The orchestra begins to play the* " St. Louis Blues ")
GILBERT   I always was in love with you, sweetheart, even since we
been married.
MATTIE BEA   Let's rest our wraps. This here's another honeymoon.
          (*They pull off their wraps to dance as the floor fills with dancers*)
MADAM BELL     (*To* LEROY)   Sugar, let's dance one more time.
LEROY   Why not?
M.C.   All right now, everybody rock!
          (*Entire crowd begins to dance.* TINY *places the cup in
          front of platform and embraces* HAM)

HAM  (*While dancing*)  Tiny, is you happy, baby?

TINY  Ham, I ain't nothin' else but!

HAM  You's a dancin' thing!

TINY  And so are you, darling!

HAM  What we gonna do with this cup?

TINY  Take it to my house, and keep it there—'cause, I'm gonna keep you there, too. We going get married.

HAM  What about that man in the closet?

TINY  Who? Oh, you mean Gilbert? Honey, yonder he is dancing with Mattie Bea. He's her husband, I reckon.

HAM  So that's her husband!

TINY  He never was no headache of mine, baby.

MATTIE BEA  (*Dancing with* GILBERT *at the other end of the stage*) The old love is always best, ain't it, honey?

GILBERT  Do you mean to say I'm old, darling?

MATTIE BEA  Just old enough to be sweet, that's all. Kiss me, sugar-pie. (*As they dance, they kiss. Meanwhile, the spotlight picks out the various couples dancing in the arms of love:* MADAM BELL *and* LEROY; SUGAR LOU *and her boy friend;* SHINGLE *and his lady;* JASPER *and his Harlem blonde; the* WEST INDIAN *and the Bahama girl;* JACK *and* LULU; *and at the end,* TINY *and* HAM)

TINY  (*Shyly, as they dance in the spotlight*)  You ain't mad about Gilbert, are you, Ham?

HAM  Naw, honey! I know things like that can happen. (*Pauses*) You ain't mad about nothin' I ever did, is you?

TINY  Naw, darling. The past is past, ain't it?

HAM  Long gone!

TINY  And I don't care nothing about nobody, no how, but you. I don't want to have no more trouble today, no ways. We ain't had nothing but trouble, since we got engaged yesterday.

HAM  Trouble and luck put together! Money from the numbers, and a cup from the Charleston.

TINY  That's what life is, ain't it, baby? Trouble and luck, put together.

HAM  I reckon it is, but it's more *luck* than trouble—when a man's got the woman he loves.

TINY  Ain't it the truth! That's the way I feel about you! And you know, Little Ham, I think you better put them numbers down. It's nothing but a racket for a good man. I'm thinking about opening a whole chain of beauty shops—and you can be my manager.

HAM    We're the same as in business together.

TINY   With my brains, and your personality——

HAM    We'll keep them shops full of women's all the time.
        (*The orchestra plays increasingly loud the sad-doleful strains
        of the " St. Louis Blues."* SHINGLE *and his lady friend
        dance near* TINY *and* HAM *as the lights go dim and soft
        colors begin to play over the dance floor*)

SHINGLE   (*Dancing past, yelling*)   Hello, boy! You lucky dog!

HAM    You see I got my arms full, don't you, Shingle? And, boy, we're
        dancing right on through life—happy—just like this!
        (*Music and rose-colored darkness as the curtain falls with
        the spotlight on* LITTLE HAM *and* TINY)

CURTAIN

# SIMPLY
# HEAVENLY
*A Comedy*

# CHARACTERS

JESSE B. SEMPLE   *Harlemite*
MADAM BUTLER   *Simple's landlady*
ANANIAS BOYD   *Simple's neighbor*
MRS. CADDY   *Joyce's landlady*
JOYCE LANE   *Simple's girl*
HOPINS   *A genial bartender*
PIANIST   *A barfly*
MISS MAMIE   *A plump domestic*
BODIDDLY   *A dock worker*
CHARACTER   *A snob*
MELON   *A fruit vendor*
GITFIDDLE   *A guitar player*
ZARITA   *A glamorous goodtimer*
ARCIE   *Bodiddly's wife*
JOHN JASPER   *Her son*
ALI BABA   *A root doctor*
A POLICEMAN
A NURSE

TIME: The present
PLACE: Harlem, U. S. A.
MOOD: Of the moment

## SCENES

## CHARACTER NOTES

GENERAL: The characters in "Simply Heavenly" are, on the whole, ordinary, hard-working lower-income bracket Harlemites. Paddy's Bar is like a neighborhood club, and most of its patrons are not drunkards or bums. Their small kitchenette rooms or overcrowded apartments cause them to seek the space and company of the bar. Just as others seek the church as a social center, or the poolhall, or dancehall, these talkative ones seek the bar.

SIMPLE: Simple is a Chaplinesque character, slight of build, awkwardly graceful, given to flights of fancy, and positive statements of opinion—stemming from a not so positive soul. He is dark with a likable smile, ordinarily dressed, except for rather flamboyant summer sport shirts. Simple tries hard to succeed, but the chips seldom fall just right. Yet he bounces like a rubber ball. He may go down, but he always bounds back up.

JOYCE: Joyce is a quiet girl more inclined toward club work than bars, toward "culture" rather than good-timing. But she is not snobbish or cold. She is tall, brownskin, given to longish ear-rings, beads, scarfs, and dangling things, very feminine, and cries easily. Her charm is her sincerity.

BOYD: Boyd has probably been half-way through college before his army service in Europe. Serious-minded, pleasant-looking, trying to be a writer, perhaps taking English courses at New York University on the last of his G. I. money. Almost every Harlem bar has such a fellow among its regular customers, who acts sometimes as a kind of arbiter when "intellectual" discussions come up.

ZARITA: Zarita is a lively bar-stool girl wearing life like a loose garment, but she is *not* a prostitute. Brassy-voiced, good-hearted, good-looking, playing the field for fun and drinks, she lives a come-day-go-day existence, generous in accepting or giving love, money, or drinks. A good dancer.

MISS MAMIE: Mamie is a hard-working domestic, using biting words to protect a soft heart and a need for love too often betrayed.

GITFIDDLE: Gitfiddle is a folk artist going to seed, unable to compete with the juke box, TV, and the radio, having only his guitar and his undisciplined talents. He furnishes all the music, with the Barfly pianist, for the songs and interludes.

MADAM BUTLER: Madame Butler has a bark that is worse than her bite—but her bark is bad enough. Large, fat, comical and terrible, she runs her rooming house as Hitler ran Germany.

## MUSICAL NUMBERS
### (*Music by David Martin*)

#### ACT ONE

| | | |
|---|---|---|
| *Scene Two*: | Simply Heavenly | Joyce and Simple |
| *Scene Five*: | Did You Ever Hear the Blues? | Mamie and Melon |
| *Scene Six*: | Deep in Love With You | Simple |
| *Scene Seven*: | I'm Gonna Be John Henry | Simple |

#### ACT TWO

| | | |
|---|---|---|
| *Scene One*: | When I'm in a Quiet Mood | Mamie and Melon |
| | Look for the Morning Star | Pianist and Joyce |
| *Scene Two*: | Look for the Morning Star | Joyce and Simple |
| | I Want Somebody To Come Home To | Joyce |
| *Scene Three*: | Let's Ball Awhile | Zarita and Guests |
| *Scene Nine*: | A Good Old Girl | Mamie |
| *Scene Eleven*: | Look for the Morning Star | Ensemble |

# ACT ONE

## SCENE ONE

*A lonely guitar is playing in the darkness—it's the Blues . . .*

SIMPLE'S *room. Early spring evening.* SIMPLE, *just coming home from work, removes his jacket as he enters, but before he can hang it up, the voice of* MADAM BUTLER, *his landlady, is heard calling up the stairs, through the half-open door.*

LANDLADY  Mr. Semple! Oh, Mr. Semple!

SIMPLE  Yes'm?

LANDLADY  I heard you come in! Mr. Semple, would you mind taking Trixie out for a walk? My arthritis is bothering me.

SIMPLE  Madam Butler, please! I've got no time to walk no dog tonight. Joyce is waiting for me.

LANDLADY  From all I've heard, that girl's been waiting for you to marry her for years! A few minutes of waiting for you to show up tonight won't hurt.

SIMPLE  Madam, my private affairs ain't none of your business.

LANDLADY  Um-hum! Well, you don't need to take Trixie to no tree—just the nearest fireplug. (*Boyd, a fellow-roomer, peers in*)

SIMPLE  Aw, I ain't hardly got home from work good, yet. . . Hello, Boyd. Come on in. Landladies is a bodiddling! How come she never make none of the other roomers—or you—to walk her dog?

BOYD  She knows I won't do it, that's why.

SIMPLE  Don't you ever get behind in your rent?

BOYD  Not to the point of walking dogs. But you seem to walk Trixie pretty often.

SIMPLE  Mostly always.

LANDLADY  Did you say you would take the dog?

SIMPLE  Oh, hell, lemme go walk the bitch.

LANDLADY  No profanity in my house.

SIMPLE  Madam, that's a perfectly good word meaning a fine girl dog —bitch—for female dog.

LANDLADY  There'll be no bitches in my house—and that goes for your girl friend, Zarita, too.

SIMPLE    I'll thank you to leave my friends out of this.

LANDLADY    I'll thank you to keep your profanity to yourself. This is a decent house. Now, come on and walk my dog—else pay me my rent.

SIMPLE    I'll walk your dog—because I love Trixie, though, that's what! If I had a dog, I wouldn't keep it penned up in the house all day neither. Poor old thing, airless as she is.

LANDLADY    She's not hairless.

SIMPLE    I said *airless*, Madam! Shut up airtight, wonder Trixie don't get arthritis, too. Dog and womens, dogs and womens! Damn! What am I gonna do?

BOYD    Good luck, pal. (*Simple and Boyd exit.* BLACKOUT. *In the darkness, Trixie's bark is heard. Auto horns, street noises.* SIMPLE'S *voice addresses the barking dog*)

SIMPLE    Now, Trixie, come on now. Come on, Trixie, do your duty. Leave that other dog alone, Trixie! Hound, get away from here! O.K., O.K., let's head on in the house. (*Bark*) Now, go on to your madam. I guess you love her. Well, I love somebody, too! My choice, Joyce! She's the one I found—and that's where I'm bound. Trixie, that's where I am bound. (*The music of " Simply Heavenly " rises happily as the* LIGHTS COME UP *to reveal* JOYCE'S *room*)


## SCENE TWO

JOYCE'S *room a bit later.* JOYCE *is singing as, in a frilly dressing gown, she is putting her clothes away.*

JOYCE    Love is simply heavenly!
What else could it be?
When love's made in heaven
And you are made for me.
Love is simply heavenly!
What else can I say?
When love sends an angel
To hold me close this way.
Love is like a dream
That's too good to be true,
But when your lips kiss mine

The dream turns into you.
Yes, it's simply heavenly!
Our love's just divine—
For love is made in heaven
And you, my love, are mine!

Love is simply heavenly——
(*Voice of her Landlady calls from below stairs*)
MRS. CADDY   Oo-oo-oo-oo! Miss Lane!
JOYCE   Yes?
MRS. CADDY.   I'm letting Mr. Semple come up. O.K.?
JOYCE.   Yes, indeed, Mrs. Caddy, I'm expecting him. (SIMPLE *knocks lightly and enters grinning*)
SIMPLE   Hey, Baby! (*He closes the door, to which* JOYCE *objects*)
JOYCE   Jess! No! Just a crack. . . .
SIMPLE   Aw, your old landlady's worse than mine. At least I can shut my door when I got company.
JOYCE   You're a man. I'm a —— (SIMPLE *bugs* JOYCE)
SIMPLE   Lady! Which is what I like about you. Joyce, morals is your middle name. But you can still be a lady behind closed doors.
JOYCE   I know, Jess, those are the landlady's rules. Besides, I respect Mrs. Caddy.
SIMPLE   She don't respect you if she thinks soon as the door is shut . . .
JOYCE   Sshhss! Come on, rest your jacket, honey. It's warm.
SIMPLE   I knowed there was something! I forgot to bring your ice cream! I passed right by the place, too!
JOYCE   We can walk out for a soda.
SIMPLE   Or a beer?
JOYCE   Tomorrow's communion Sunday, and I do not drink beer before communion.
SIMPLE   You just don't drink beer, period! Gimme a little sugar and we'll skip the beer.
JOYCE   Don't think I'll skip the ice cream.
SIMPLE   Let's set on the —— (*He dances toward the studio bed*)
JOYCE   There's a chair.
SIMPLE   Baby, what's the matter? Don't you trust me yet?
JOYCE   I don't mind you being close to me. But when you get close to a bed, too ——
SIMPLE   Then you don't trust yourself.
JOYCE   Have you ever known me to ——

SIMPLE   That's the trouble . . .

JOYCE   That goes with marriage, not courtship. And if you don't move on from courtship to engagement soon, Jess Semple, and do something about that woman in Baltimore.

SIMPLE   My wife! Isabel—she run me out—but she could claim I left her. She could find some grounds to get a divorce.

JOYCE   Since you're not together, why don't you get one?

SIMPLE   Joyce, I don't want to pay for no woman's divorce I don't love. And I do not love Isabel. Also, I ain't got the money.

JOYCE   I would help you pay for it.

SIMPLE   One thing I would not let you do, Joyce, is pay for no other woman's divorce. No!

JOYCE   Well, if you and I just paid for half of it, you'd only be paying for your part of the divorce.

SIMPLE   That woman wants me to pay for it all! And, Joyce, I don't love her. I love you. Joyce, do you want me to commit bigamy?

JOYCE   Five years you've been away from your wife—three years since you met me! In all that time you haven't reached a point yet where you can ask for my hand without committing bigamy. I don't know how my love holds out so long on promises. But now my friends are all asking when I'm going to get married. Even my landlady's saying it's a mighty long time for a man to just be " coming around calling," just sitting doing nothing.

SIMPLE   I agree, baby—when there ain't no action, I get kinder drowsy.

JOYCE   Well, to me, a nice conversation is action.

SIMPLE   Conversationing makes me sleepy.

JOYCE   Then you ought to go to bed early instead of hanging over Paddy's Bar until all hours. You have got to go to work just like I do.

SIMPLE   When I sleep, I sleep fast. Anyhow, I can't go to bed early just because you do, Joyce, until—unless ——

JOYCE   Until what?

SIMPLE   Until we're married.

JOYCE   Simple!

SIMPLE   But, listen! It's Saturday night, fine outside. Spring in Harlem! Come on, let's us get some ice cream.

JOYCE   O.K., but, Jess, are you coming to church in the morning to see me take communion?

SIMPLE   You know I'll be there. We'll just take a little stroll down Seventh Avenue now and catch some air, heh?

JOYCE   And you'll bring me home early, so we can both get our rest.

SIMPLE   In a jiffy, then I'll turn in, too.
JOYCE    You don't mean into a bar?
SIMPLE   Baby, one thing I *bar* is bars.
JOYCE    Turn your back so I can dress.
SIMPLE   Don't stand over there. Anybody could be looking in.
JOYCE    There are no peeping-toms in this house. (SIMPLE *turns his back as she dresses, but drops his pack of cigarettes on the floor, bends down to get it, then remains that way, looking at* JOYCE *from between his legs*) Baby, is your back turned?
SIMPLE   Yes'm. (JOYCE *glances his way, clutches her dress to her bosom and screams*)
JOYCE    Oh, Simple!
SIMPLE   I love it when you call me Simple. (*Head still down, he proceeds to turn a somersault, coming up seated on the floor with his back toward her*) Now say my back ain't turned.
JOYCE    I didn't mean you had to turn inside out.
SIMPLE   That's the way you've got my heart—turned in . . . (*He turns his eyes to look at her*)
JOYCE    Then turn your head so I can dress.
SIMPLE   O.K., Joyce. Now, is everything all right?
JOYCE    Everything is all right.
SIMPLE   So you feel O.K.?
JOYCE    Simply heavenly! Oh, Jess, it's wonderful to be in love.
SIMPLE   Just wonderful—wonderful—wonderful ——— (*As* JOYCE *dresses, they sing*)
BOTH

> Love is simply heavenly!
> What else could it be?
> When love's made in heaven
> And you are made for me.
> Love is simply heavenly!
> What else can I say?
> When love sends an angel
> To hold me close this way.
> Love is like a dream
> That's too good to be true,
> But when your lips kiss mine
> The dream turns into you.
> Yes, it's simply heavenly!
> Our love's just divine—

For love is made in heaven
And you, my love, are mine!

SIMPLE

Love is simply heavenly!
What else could it be?
When love is made in heaven
And you are made for me.

JOYCE

Love is simply heavenly!
What else can I say?
When love sends me an angel
To hold me close this way.

SIMPLE

Love is like a dream
That's too good to be true,
(*Dressed now,* JOYCE *emerges and* SIMPLE *rises to embrace
her*)

JOYCE

But when your lips kiss mine
The dream turns into you.

BOTH

Yes, it's simply heavenly!
Our love's just divine—
For love is made in heaven
And you, my love, are mine!

BLACKOUT


## SCENE THREE

*Paddy's Bar. Midnight.*

*At a battered old piano in the corner a roustabout* PIANIST
*is playing a syncopated melody while* HOPKINS, *the bartender, beats lightly on the bar with a couple of stirrers as
if playing drums. The music ceases as* MISS MAMIE, *a
large but shapely domestic servant, enters and sits at her
usual table.*

HOPKINS  Good evening, Miss Mamie. How's tricks?

MAMIE  Hopkins, them white folks over in Long Island done like to worked me to death. I'm just getting back to town.

PIANIST  You ought to have a good man to take care of you, Miss Mamie—like me.

MAMIE  Huh! Bill, from what I see of you, you can hardly take care of yourself. I got a mighty lot of flesh here to nourish.

PIANIST  Big woman, big appetite.

MAMIE  Right—which is why I like to work for rich folks. Poor folks ain't got enough to feed me.

PIANIST  I never eat much. But I sure am thirsty.

MAMIE  Stay that way! Hopkins, gimme a gin. (BODIDDLY, *a dock worker, leaps in shouting*)

BODIDDLY  Hey, now, anyhow!

MAMIE  Anyhow, what?

BODIDDLY  Anyhow, we's here! Who's setting up tonight? (*Dead silence. No one answers*) Well, Hop, I'll take a short beer.

MAMIE  It ain't nobody's payday in the middle of the week, Bodiddly. And the only man in this bar who manages to keep a little change in his pocket is Mr. Boyd here, drawing his G. I. pension.

BODIDDLY  (*Points at* BOYD *proudly*)  My boy!

BOYD  Hi, Bo!

MAMIE  Huh! There's as much difference between you and Ananias Boyd as between night and day.

BODIDDLY  Yeah, I know! His predilect's toward intellect—and mine's toward womens.

HOPKINS  And beer.

BODIDDLY  Boyd's the only man around here who's colleged.

BOYD  For all the good it does me. You dockworkers make more a week than I ever see writing these stories.

BODIDDLY  But none of us gets pensions.

MAMIE  None of you all in the war and got wounded neither. But if I was a man, I would have gone to war so I could get me a pension.

PIANIST  They had lady soldiers.

BODIDDLY  Whacks and Wavers.

MAMIE  By that time I were too big. (*A* LITTLE MAN *in nose glasses, carrying an umbrella, enters with an armful of highbrow papers and magazines. Noticing no one, he takes a table and begins to remove his gloves*) There comes that character trying to make people think he's educated. One thing I like about Boyd here, even if he is a writer, he ain't always trying to impress folks. Also he speaks when he comes in a public place. (*The Little Man sits at an empty table*)

CHARACTER   A thimble of Scotch, please.

BODIDDLY   A thimble of Scawtch! (*All laugh but Boyd*)

CHARACTER   And a tumbler of plain water, no ice.

HOPKINS   Right, sir! Like the English. (*As if to show her derision* MAMIE *orders loudly*)

MAMIE   Hopkins, gimme some more gin.

HOPKINS   Coming up, Miss Mamie! (*A Vendor's cry is heard outside. Carrying a watermelon, a jovial fellow,* WATERMELON JOE, *enters*)

MELON
>    Watermelons! Juicy sweet!
>    Watermelons! Good to eat!
>    Ripe and red—
>    That's what I said—
>    Watermelons!

MAMIE   Joe, you better shut up all that catterwalling! You ain't working this time o' night?

MELON   Yes I is. I done sold all but one watermelon. Who wants it? Sweet as pie! No lie! My, my, my!

MAMIE   (*Inspects the melon*) Hmmm! It do look good. Thumps good, too. Leave it for me behind the bar. I'll take it.

MELON   Thank you, Miss Mamie.

BODIDDLY   Better tie your pushcart to the curb 'fore somebody steals it.

MELON   I'm ahead of you, Diddly—got it locked to the lamp post. Boy, when I cry "Watermelons!" do you all know what happens to womens?

BODIDDLY   What?

MELON   Their blood turns to water and their knees start to shake— 'cause they know I'm a man, and no mistake! Why, I sold a woman a watermelon one day and moved in and stayed three years.

BODIDDLY   That's nothing. I just spoke to a strange lady once setting on a stoop—and went upstairs and ain't come down yet. That was in 1936.

MELON   Diddly, you lying. Your wife done run you out twice with a kitchen knife.

BODIDDLY   I mean, excusing temporary exits.

MAMIE   Well, I been buying watermelons, Joe, for two summers, and I finds your fruits sweeter than you.

MELON   That's because you don't know me well, baby. Besides, I do
not use my professional voice in your personal presence:
>Wa-ter—melons!
>Melons! Melons! Melons!
>Sweet as they can be!
>Sweet, good Lord!
>But they ain't as sweet as me!
>Watermelon Joe has got your
>Wa-ter—melons!
>(*He eases up to her cheek*)
>Me-lawns! ... Me-loans! ... Me-loons!

MAMIE   Man, you better get away from me! You know I got a
husband, Watermelon Joe.

MELON   Where's he at?

MAMIE   I don't know where he's at, but I got one. And if I ain't, I
don't want you.

MELON   (*Croons in her ear*)   Watermelons. Wa-ter-mel-ons. ...

MAMIE   I sure do like your watermelons, though.

MELON   Nice red melons . . .

CHARACTER   (*Rises indignantly*)   Stereotypes! That's all both of you
are. Disgraceful stereotypes!

MAMIE   (*Turns on him furiously*)   Mister, you better remove yourself
from my presence before I stereo your type! I like watermelons, and
I don't care who knows it. That's nothing to be ashamed of, like
some other colored folks are. Why, I knowed a woman once was so
ashamed of liking watermelons that she'd make the clerk wrap the
melon up before she'd carry it out of the store. I ain't no pretender,
myself, neither no passer.

BODDIDLY   What do you mean, passer?

MAMIE   Chitterling passer—passing up chitterlings and pretending I
don't like 'em when I do. I like watermelon and chitterlings both,
and I don't care who knows it.

CHARACTER   Just stereotypes, that's all. (*He shakes his head*)

MAMIE   Man, get out of my face!

CHARACTER   Stereotypes . . . stereotypes . . . stereo . . . (*He retreats
muttering*)

MAMIE   Why, its getting so colored folks can't do nothing no more
without some other Negro calling you a stereotype. Stereotype,
hah! If you like a little gin, you're a stereotype. You got to drink
Scotch. If you wear a red dress, you're a stereotype. You got to

wear beige or chartreuse. Lord have mercy, honey, do-don't like no blackeyed peas and rice! Then you're a down-home Negro for true— which I is—and proud of it! (MAMIE *glares around as if daring somebody to dispute her. Nobody does*) I didn't come here to Harlem to get away from my people. I come here because there's more of 'em. I loves my race. I loves my people. Stereotype!

CHARACTER   That's what I said, stereotypes!

MAMIE   You better remove yourself from my presence, calling me a stereotype.

CHARACTER   Tch-tch-tch! (*Clicking his tongue in disgust, the* LITTLE MAN *leaves the bar as* MAMIE *rises and threatens him with her purse. The* PIANIST *rushes over to congratulate her*)

PIANIST   Gimme five, Miss Mamie, gimme five! (*They shake hands*)

MAMIE   Solid!

PIANIST   You and me agreed! I could drink on that.

MAMIE   You go right back where you was and set down.

BODIDDLY   Who agrees is me! Bartender, set up the bar—this far— from Mamie to me. What'll you have, Cleopatra, a beer?

MAMIE   You know I drinks gin, Bodiddly. And I needs another one. That character done got me all upset. Where's all the decent peoples tonight? Where's Jess Simple?

BODIDDLY   I seen old Simp a couple of hours ago walking down Lenox Avenue with his girl. But Joyce turns in early. And when she turns in, she turns him out.

MAMIE   That's what I call a decent woman.

MELON   Damn if I do.

MAMIE   And that Simple is a good man. He needs himself a decent woman—instead of gallivanting around with chippies like Zarita that keeps a bar door flapping all night long. I never seen a woman could run in and out of a bar so much and so fast.

BODIDDLY   Ah, but that Zarita, she's sure a fine looking chick.

MAMIE   She wears her morals like a loose garment. Ain't no woman's man safe with her around.

MELON   She sure will drink a body up. Zarita damn near drunk me out of a whole car load of melons one night.

MAMIE   You sure is weak for young womens.

MELON   Miss Mamie, I could be weak for you.

MAMIE   Melon, scat! I done told you, get from over me! Scat!

(*The door flies open and a seedy looking fellow rushes in calling to the bartender*)

GITFIDDLE  Hey, Hop! Hey, Hop! Lend me my guitar from behind the bar there, please. Hurry up, man! I'll bring it back.

HOPKINS  What's the hurry?

GITFIDDLE  There's a big party of folks in the Wonder Bar down the street spending money like water.

HOPKINS  Here you are, Git.

GITFIDDLE  Thank you, man! (*He takes guitar and exits*)

HOPKINS  I sure hope he can play up a few dollars—that man has been broke so long, it just ain't fair.

MAMIE  A good musicianer—doing nothing but playing for quarters folks throw him!

MELON  They say a woman brought old Gitfiddle low.

MAMIE  Getting high brought him low! Womens helps more mens than they don't.

MELON  I sure wish you'd help me.

MAMIE  Wish again, honey, because I ain't coming. I likes a man who works in one place, with one job, not all up and down the streets where he's subject to temptation. And as for me, I don't need nobody to help me.

MELON  (*Shrugs*)  Well, so that's that!

SIMPLE  (*Entering*)  Good evening!

MAMIE  We been missing you. Excusing Boyd there, this bar's full of nothing but characters.

BOYD  Thank you, Miss Mamie.

MAMIE  Where you been, Simple?

SIMPLE  Eating ice cream.

CROWD  What?

SIMPLE  And I had my picture took.

BODIDDLY  With your lady fair.

SIMPLE  For my lady fair. All posed like this. (*He assumes an attitude*)

HOPKINS  She must've fell out laughing at that pose.

SIMPLE  She did not. That's one thing about Joyce. She never laughs at nothing about me, never does, which is why I loves that girl.

BOYD  You can find more reasons for liking a woman, Jess. Every time, a different woman, it's a different reason.

HOPKINS  Pay him no mind, Mr. Boyd. Zarita laughs with him and at him.

SIMPLE  Zarita's different. I do not, never will, can't—won't, and don't love no jumping jack of a Zarita. A man can't hardly keep Zarita in his arms, let alone in his heart.

HOPKINS   So we know, Jess Simple!

SIMPLE   But I have kept Joyce in my heart ever since I met her—and she is there to stay. Dog-gone it, I wish I had my divorce from Isabel. But at last, it looks like I am making some headway. They say a man's life changes every seven years. I sure hope I am going through the change.

HOPKINS   Mr. Change, what are you drinking?

SIMPLE   (*Takes an envelope from his pocket*)   Give me and Boyd a couple of beers. Then I want you to read something. Didn't even show it to Joyce yet—not to get her hopes up too high. It's from my wife.

BOYD   I don't want to read your personal letters, Jess.

SIMPLE   Here, pal, read it—because I can't believe my eyes.

BOYD   Um-mmmm! Well, here goes: " Dear Mr. Semple: Jess, at last I have found a man who loves me enough to pay for my divorce. This new man is a mail clerk, his first wife being dead, so he wants me for his second."

SIMPLE   Thank you, Father!

BOYD   " He knows I been married and am still married in name only to you, as you have not been willing to pay for the legal paper which grants freedom from our entanglement. This man is willing to pay for it. He says he will get a lawyer to furnish me grounds unless you want to contest. I do not want no contest, you hear me! All I want is my divorce. I am writing to find out if you will please not make no contest out of this. Let me hear from you tonight as my husband-to-be has already passed the point where he could wait. Once sincerely yours, but not now, Isabel."

SIMPLE   Sounds just like my wife!

HOPKINS   I suppose you've no intention of cross-filing.

SIMPLE   I would not cross that wife of mine no kind of way. My last contest with that woman was such that the police had to protect me. So that man can have her. I do not even want a copy of the diploma. I told Isabel when we busted up that she had shared my bed, my board, my licker, and my hair oil, but that I did not want to share another thing with her from that day to this, not even a divorce. Let that other man pay for it—they can share it together. Me, I'll be married again before the gold seal's hardly out from under the stamper.

HOPKINS   Good! Perhaps you'll settle down, stop running around, and stay home nights with Joyce.

SIMPLE   Married, I'll get somewhere in the world, too. Let's drink to it. And that man in Baltimore better pay for my wife's divorce! If he don't, I'll fix him. Here's my toast. (*He lifts his glass of beer*)

> In a horserace, Daddy-o,
> One thing you will find—
> There ain't NO way to be out in front.
> Without showing your tail
> To the horse behind. . . .
> (ZARITA *enters glittering*)

ZARITA   Hey now! Hi, all and sundry!

SIMPLE   Zarita!

ZARITA   Excuse me, folks, for being in a hurry.

MAMIE   I told you so!

ZARITA   Jess, I'm going to Jersey! Come on! Coleman and his girl've got their car outside.

SIMPLE   The one with the top down?

ZARITA   That's the chariot—and I got nobody to ride back there with me.

MAMIE   Don't that child just bring you to tears?

SIMPLE   Is Coleman sober?

ZARITA   Just feeling a little groovy that's all! Come on!

BODIDDLY   Woman, shut that outside door! It's chilly. You know it ain't official summer yet.

ZARITA   Your blood's thin. My, it's hot in here! Come on, Jess. The motor's running.

SIMPLE   The motor might be running, but I ain't. Come here, girl. I got somethings to say to you. Zarita, you know I'm almost engaged to be married. I can't be running around with you.

ZARITA   You really got yourself tangled up. Well, anyhow, we'll just ride over the bridge to a little after-hours spot in Jersey for a few drinks, and come right back. There's no harm in that.

SIMPLE   You sure you coming right back? And Coleman is gonna drive me right to my door?

ZARITA   Or mine! Your room is kinder little and small and cold. Sugar, is you is, or is you ain't? (*She moves toward the door*)

SIMPLE   Zarita, it's chilly out there and I ain't got my top coat.

ZARITA   Oh, Knuckle-Nose, we got a fifth of licker in the car to keep us warm. And there's some fine bars just across the George Washington bridge. You does or you don't?

SIMPLE   Aw, Zarita!

ZARITA   Old Simple Square, do I have to beg and plead with you?

Listen! I've got my own money. I'll even treat you to a couple of
drinks. Come on! Aw, come on! (*She entices him with a caress and
they exit*)

MAMIE   There goes a lamb to slaughter again. Ain't it a shame the
kind of a deal a good woman gets when she goes to bed early!

BODIDDLY   Huh?

MAMIE   I ain't talking about a man like you with 17 children. I'm
talking about Joyce.

BODIDDLY   Oh!

MAMIE   She goes to bed early, leaving Simple to yield to temptation.

MELON   I'd never yield, Miss Mamie. But if I did, I'd yield with you.

MAMIE   Melon, I say, get out of my face. It's mighty near midnight.
Lemme go home.

MELON   If I didn't have my pushcart to wheel, I would 'scort you,
Miss Mamie.

MAMIE   Watermelon Joe, with you at the handle, I might have to
jump out and walk—or roll out, one—wild as you is with womens.
Hopkins, hand me my watermelon and let me go to my virtuous
couch. Good night, all, good night! (*She exits with her watermelon
under her arm*)

MELON   Huh, so she don't trust me to 'scort her home. Anyhow, I
think I'll truck along after her and see can't I tote her melon to a taxi.
Watermelons! Nice red ones! (*He exits*)

BODIDDLY   Gimme a sherry, man. What'll you have, Boyd?

BOYD   Nothing, thanks.

(ARCIE *enters bustling*)

BODIDDLY   Arcie, my love, what you doing out this time of night?

ARCIE   I come out looking for you—and done looked in seven bars.
(HOPKINS *automatically pours* ARCIE *some sherry.*)

BODIDDLY   And had a drink in each and every one!

ARCIE   Naturally! A lady don't go in a bar and not buy nothing.
Diddly, lover, listen, there ain't but five of our children home—
which means an even dozen is still out in the streets.

BODIDDLY   The children's big enough to take care of themselves.

ARCIE   If you was any kind of a father —— If you was any kind
of . . .

BODIDDLY   Woman, hush! And put that sherry wine down—before
you be walking sidewise to keep from flying. Let's be getting upstairs—before some more of our children don't get home. Be seeing
you, folks!

ARCIE   That man! (ARCIE *and* BODIDDLY *go out. The bar is empty*
*except for* BOYD *who rises to leave*)
HOPKINS   Say, Boyd, as a writer, would you say them folks are
stereotypes?
BOYD   In the book I'm writing they're just folks. Good night, Hop.
GITFIDDLE   (*Comes reeling into the bar as* BOYD *exits*)   Got-dog it!
I done broke another string!
HOPKINS   Well, did you make any money?
GITFIDDLE   They paid me off in drinks. I had nothing to eat all day.
Here, Hop, lend me another half for a sandwich—and keep this for
security. (*He offers his guitar to* HOPKINS)
HOPKINS   You must think Paddy's Bar is a bank. I lent you two
dollars and a quarter already this week. Here's fifty cents more.
GITFIDDLE   Thanks, Hop! But wait a minute, Hop—lemme play you
just one more blues. (*The woebegone* GITFIDDLE *strums a lonesome*
*blues on his guitar as the lights fade to darkness*)

BLACKOUT


SCENE FOUR

*Hospital room. Next day. During* BLACKOUT *a bed backed*
*by a white screen already attached is wheeled* D. S. C. *with*
SIMPLE *already propped up in bed, very quiet. Both his*
*legs are up in traction. Near the head of his bed is a single*
*white chair. A* NURSE *all in white tiptoes in and calls*
*softly. He answers with a groan.*

NURSE   Mr. Semple.
SIMPLE   Aw-um-mmm-mm-m!
NURSE   Such groaning! You aren't that bad off.
SIMPLE   When I suffers, Nurse, I like to suffer loud.
NURSE   There's a gentleman to see you. (*She beckons the caller*)
Here he is, sir.
MELON   Thank you, Nurse. (MELON *enters. Nurse exits*)   Oh, man!
You're all packed for shipping!
SIMPLE   Strung, hung, and slung's what I am. Melon, this is the most!
Um-mmm-mm-m!
MELON   All I heard was, you was in an accident.

SIMPLE   It were an accident, all right. Got-dog that Zarita! My mind told me ——

MELON   Never mind what your mind told you, Daddy-o, just gimme the details. Here.

SIMPLE   What's that?

MELON   I brought you some books.

SIMPLE   I wish you'd of brought me a quart of beer and some pigs feet. I ain't much on books.

MELON   Comic books, man.

SIMPLE   Oh, *Horror in Hackensack. Terror in Trenton.*

MELON   Man, that's the crazy history of New Jersey.

SIMPLE   This makes me feel better already. Thanks, Melon.

MELON   Now, tell me what happened.

SIMPLE   The car tried to climb the George Washington Bridge, instead of going *across* it—turned half over—Coleman, his girl, and Zarita and me. But I was the *only* one that got throwed out, and on my—bohunkus. Melon, I'm all bruised up on my sit-downer.

MELON   I told you, you should stop balling, and take care of yourself.

SIMPLE   If I had took care of myself, I would not have these pretty nurses taking care of me now.

MELON   But look at the big hospital bill when you get out.

SIMPLE   Lemme hit one number, I'll settle it. But what worries me is when I'm going to get out.

MELON   You will never get out if you don't observe the rules and stop telling folks to bring you beer and pigs feet and things you are not supposed to have.

SIMPLE   But alcohol had nothing to do with it.

MELON   Oh, no?

SIMPLE   Womens aggravate a man, drunk or sober. Melon, I hope Joyce knows Zarita ain't nothing to me, even if I do accidentally go riding with her. But I don't want to discuss how come I'm in this hospital. You know, no matter what a man does, sick or well, something is always liable to happen—especially if he's colored. In this world, Melon, it's hard for a man to live until he dies.

             (NURSE *enters*)

MELON   I think you'll make it.

NURSE   There's a Miss Joyce Lane to see you. (*A look of great help-lessness comes over* SIMPLE. *He appeals to his friend*)

SIMPLE   Melon . . .

MELON   It's Joyce.

SIMPLE  Just like a man has to face his Maker alone, the same goes for facing a woman.

MELON  You want to see her, don't you?

SIMPLE  Worse than anything, I want to see Joyce, Melon. Also, I—I—I ——

MELON  Also, you don't want to see her. I know. Good luck, old man. (*The* NURSE *shows* MELON *out. As they exit,* JOYCE *enters*)

JOYCE  Jess! (*Tears come, and she takes out her handkerchief*)

SIMPLE  Baby, please don't cry. I'm all right.

JOYCE  But your legs! Are they broken?

SIMPLE  Doc says they ain't. But they sure are bent.

JOYCE  Then why are they all trussed up that way?

SIMPLE  Because I can't lay on my hine, that's why.

JOYCE  Your what?

SIMPLE  My hindparts is all skint up, Joyce. I hope that's a polite word for saying it.

JOYCE  But aren't you hurt badly?

SIMPLE  No.

JOYCE  I am.

SIMPLE  Baby, don't you want to set down? Here on the bed. Then pull your chair up close, please.

JOYCE  Oh, Jess!

SIMPLE  I know, Joyce, I know. I hadn't ought to done it.

JOYCE  With a drunken driver, too—and Zarita.

SIMPLE  You know I love you.

JOYCE  And that's the way you show it? With your legs tied up in the air—on account of a ——

SIMPLE  Auto wreck ——

JOYCE  Woman.

SIMPLE  Just a little old innocent joy ride.

JOYCE  Oh, stop it!

SIMPLE  Baby, did you take communion this morning?

JOYCE  Yes, Jess, I did. I was almost late. I waited for you to go with me.

SIMPLE  Did they sing, " Jesus Knows Just How Much I Can Bear "?

JOYCE  Not today.

SIMPLE  I used to like that song. You know how I feel now? Just like I felt the last time Aunt Lucy whipped me. Did I ever tell you about that, Joyce?

JOYCE  No.

SIMPLE  It were a girl caused that whipping.

JOYCE    I'm not surprised, Jess.

SIMPLE    Aunt Lucy is dead and gone to glory, Joyce. But it were Aunt
Lucy taught me right from wrong. When I were a little young child,
I didn't have much raising. I knocked around every-which-where,
pillar to post. But when Aunt Lucy took me, she did her best to
whip me and *raise* me, too—'cause Aunt Lucy really believed in her
Bible. "Spare the rod and spoil the child." I were *not* spoiled. But
that last whipping is what did it—made me the man I am today. . . .
I could see that whipping coming, Joyce, when I sneaked out of the
henhouse one of Aunt Lucy's best hens and give it to that girl to
roast for her Sunday School picnic, because that old girl said she
was aiming to picnic *me*—except that she didn't have nothing much
to put in her basket. I was trying to jive that girl, you know. Anyhow, Aunt Lucy found out about it and woke me up the next
morning with a switch in her hand. . . . But I got all mannish that
morning, Joyce. I said, "Aunt Lucy, you ain't gonna whip me no
more, I'se a man now—and you ain't gonna whip me." Aunt Lucy
said, "You know you had no business snatching my best laying hen
right off her nest." Aunt Lucy was angry. And big as I was, I was
scared. . . . Yet I was meaning not to let her whip me, Joyce. But,
just when I was aiming to snatch that switch out of her hand, I seed
Aunt Lucy was crying. I said, "What you crying for?" She said,
"I'm crying 'cause here you is a man and don't know how to act
right *yet*, and I done did my best to raise you so you'll grow up to
be a good man. I wore out so many switches on your back—still you
tries my soul. But it *ain't* my soul I'm thinking of, son, it's you. Jess,
I wants you to carry yourself right. You understand me? I'm getting too old to be using my strength up like this. Here!" Aunt
Lucy hollered, "Bend over and lemme whip you one more time!"
. . . Big as I was, Joyce, you know I bended. When I seen her
crying, I would have let Aunt Lucy kill me before I raised a hand.
When she got through, I said, "Aunt Lucy, you ain't gonna have
to whip me no more—I'm going to do my best to do right from
now on, and not try your soul. And I am sorry about that hen. . . ."
Joyce, from that day to this, I have tried to behave myself. Aunt
Lucy is gone to Glory, now, but if she's looking down, she knows
that's true. That was my last whipping. But it wasn't the whipping
that taught me what I needed to know. It was because she cried
and cried. When peoples care for you and cry for you—and *love*
you—Joyce, they can straighten out your soul. (SIMPLE, *lost in his
story, had not been looking at* JOYCE *Instead, as he finishes, he is*

*looking at the ceiling. Suddenly* JOYCE *turns to bury her hed on the back of her chair, sobbing aloud.* SIMPLE, *forgetting that his legs are tied and that he cannot get out of bed, tries to rise*) Joyce! . . . Joyce! . . . Joyce! (*If he could, he would go to her and take her in his arms*) Joyce you're crying for me!

JOYCE    I'm not! I'm crying for your grandmother.

SIMPLE    It wasn't my grandmother I was telling you about, Joyce, it were my Aunt Lucy.

JOYCE    Well, whoever it was, she had her hands full with you.

SIMPLE    She loved me, Joyce, just like I love you. . . . Come here, feel my heart—it's beating just for you. . . . Joyce, please come here. (*He reaches out his hand and* JOYCE *comes. She takes it, and he pulls her toward him*) Feel my heart. (*He puts her hand on his heart. But suddenly* JOYCE *buries her head on his chest and sobs violently.* SIMPLE *puts an arm about her and smiles, quietly happy*)

BLACKOUT

## SCENE FIVE

*Paddy's bar. Saturday night. The joint is jumping.* GIT-FIDDLE *is plunking his guitar.* BODIDDLY *is at the bar,* HOPKINS *behind it.* MAMIE *and* MELON *sit at a table.* ARCIE *is in the middle of the floor, cutting up as if she were a young woman.* JOHN JASPER, *one of her teen-age jitterbug sons, comes in, hits a few steps himself, whirls around, then taps her on the shoulder.*

JOHN JASPER    Mama! Hey, Mama!

ARCIE    (*Stops dancing*)    Get away from me, son! Can't you see your mama is having a good time and don't want to be bothered with no children? Stop that dancing! Where's all my children? Arcilee and Melinda and Mabel and Johnny and Little Bits and Cora? Also Lilac? Huh?

JOHN JASPER    They all in the street, gone to Saturday night parties and things. Mama, lend me a quarter. I want to take the bus down to 96th Street to the Swords and Sabres dance.

ARCIE    Ask your daddy. He ain't paid me off yet. (*She again continues dancing as the boy approaches* BODIDDLY *at the bar*)

JOHN JASPER   Hey, Daddy, gimme a quarter.

BODIDDLY   Scram! You too young to be in this bar, John Jasper. Here take this quarter, boy, and scram! Children all under a man's feet!

JOHN JASPER   Thanks, Dad! (*He skips off.* MISS MAMIE *and* MELON *do a slow Lindy hop to the music*)

BODIDDLY   Woman, you better stop spending my money before you get it. Is you done your Saturday night shopping yet?

ARCIE   Can I do it on credit? Hand it over, Diddly, lover!

BODIDDLY   Many mouths as you got to feed, you better get to the stores before they close.

ARCIE   Them's your children, too. Ain't you gonna help me carry the grits?

BODIDDLY   Woman, you know I'm tired. Go do your shopping.

ARCIE   Treat me first.

BODIDDLY   Hop, give this woman a glass of Domesticated Sherry. (HOPKINS *laughs and pours her another glass of sherry before she exits.* ZARITA *enters.* MELON *and* MAMIE *stop dancing*)

ZARITA   Simple hasn't been in yet tonight, has he, Hop?

HOPKINS   Not yet.

BODIDDLY   But if he's able to walk, he'll be here before it's over.

ZARITA   He's been back at work three or four days, and I haven't seen him. You know, Hop, when I went by Harlem Hospital, he acted like he was mad at me.

HOPKINS   No wonder—you took him riding and got him all banged up.

ZARITA   He didn't have to go. Nobody forced him. I just said, " Come on." Say, Hop, what you doing this morning when you get off from work?

HOPKINS   I'm going home, Zarita.

ZARITA   There's a nice new after-hours spot opened down on Seventh Avenue.

HOPKINS   I said, I am going home.

ZARITA   You didn't always go home so early after work, Mr. Hopkins.

HOPKINS   Do you call three o'clock in the morning early?

ZARITA   Real early! Don't you remember that night you drove me over to Newark?

HOPKINS   I remember.

ZARITA   And we didn't get back early either.

HOPKINS   Zarita, this is one morning I'm turning in. Maybe Simple'll take you to this new Bottle Club.

ZARITA  Maybe he will—if he ain't still mad. Anyhow, if you see him, tell him I'll be back. I will be back.

HOPKINS  Cool, Zarita, cool. (ZARITA *exits in rhythm to* GITFDDLE'S *guitar*)

MELON  Hey, Git, you sounds mighty good plunking over there in the corner. C'mon, Miss Mamie, let's dance some more.

MAMIE  Yes, you ought to be on the juke box.

GITFIDDLE  Juke boxes is the trouble now, Miss Mamie. Used to be, folks liked to hear a sure-enough live guitar player. Now, I start playing, somebody puts a nickel in the piccolo, drowns me out. No good for musicianers any more, but I got to make the rounds, try to hustle. See you later, Miss Mamie.

MAMIE  Git, I'd rather hear you than records any day. When you come back, I'm gonna throw you a dollar just to pick a blues for me.

GITFIDDLE  I won't be long, Miss Mamie, won't be long. (*He exits as* JOHN JASPER *runs in. At the piano the* BARFLY *continues to jazz*)

JOHN JASPER  Papa!

BODIDDLY  John Jasper, now what you want? A man can't . . .

JOHN JASPER  Ronnie Belle . . .

BODIDDLY  A man can't enjoy his self . . .

JOHN JASPER  Ronnie Belle . . .

BODIDDLY  . . . without some child stuck up in his face.

JOHN JASPER  (*Dances as he talks*)  Ronnie Belle says she won't stay home and mind the babies, and it's my turn to go out this Saturday night. She says if I go, she's going.

BODIDDLY  You tell Ronnie Belle I'll come up there and fan her good, if she don't do what she's supposed to. I declare to goodness, these young folks nowadays! You get upstairs, John Jasper, and tell your sister what I said.

JOHN JASPER  Yes, sir, Papa! (*He exits*)

MAMIE  Diddly, you sure got some fine children.

BODIDDLY  And every one of them born in New York City, Harlem. When I left the South, I never did go back. (JOHN JASPER *returns, dancing to the piano*)

BODIDDLY  Lord, that boy's back again. John Jasper, now what do you want?

JOHN JASPER  Mama says for you to come on upstairs and bring her a pint of cooking sherry.

BODIDDLY  You know your mama ain't gonna do no cooking this time of the night! Tell Arcie to come down here and get her own wine. Scat, boy, scat! (JOHN JASPER *dances out*)

MAMIE   Diddly, that's the cutest one of your children. I'll give him a dime myself.

BODIDDLY   Lemme get way back in the corner so's no more of my kin folks can find me—not even my wife. (*He goes into a corner as* SIMPLE *enters*)

MAMIE   Look who's coming there!

PIANIST   Hy, Jess!

MELON   Jess Semple!

HOPKINS   (*Lifting a bottle of beer*)   It's on the house!

MAMIE   Welcome home!

BODIDDLY   To the land of the living!

MAMIE   Amen! Bless Jess!

HOPKINS   Zarita was just looking for you. (*Happily the customers retire to tables with the drinks as* SIMPLE *remains leaning stiffly on the bar*)

SIMPLE   Don't mention Zarita, please, Hop! She's near about ruint me. Joyce is treating me cool, cool, cool, since I come out the hospital and I explained to her over and over I was just out riding. Hop, oh, Hop! Oh, man, have I got a worried mind! You know when I reached home my old landlady come handing me a Special Delivery from my wife which stated that the Negro in Baltimore has only made one payment on our divorce, leaving two payments to go. Hop, you're educated! How much is one payment on $400, leaving two payments to go?

HOPKINS   $133.33 and one-third cents.

SIMPLE   Now I could just about pay one-third cents.

HOPKINS   I thought you said that man in Baltimore loved your wife so much he was willing to pay for the whole divorce.

SIMPLE   Inflation's got him—so he just made one down payment. Isabel writ that if I would make one payment now, she would make one, then everybody could marry right away. But I cannot meet a payment now—with the hospital bill, rent up, food up, phones up, cigarettes up—everything up—but my salary. Divorces are liable to go up, too, if I don't hurry up and pay up. Lord! Women, women, women! (*He paces the floor*)

MELON   Don't let women get you excited, man! Set down and take it easy.

> (*Offered a seat,* SIMPLE *protects his haunches with his palms*)

SIMPLE   The last thing I want to do is set down!

MAMIE  Then stand up to it like a man! You made your own bed hard. What you drinking?

SIMPLE  Whiskey.

VOICES  Whiskey?

MELON  And you're usually a beer man!

SIMPLE  Tonight I want whiskey. Hop, I said, whiskey! I'm broke, busted, and disgusted. And just spent mighty near my last nickel for a paper—and there ain't no news in it about colored folks. Unless we commit murder, robbery or rape, or are being chased by a mob, do we get on the front page, or hardly on the back. Take flying saucers. For instance according to the *Daily News*, everybody has seen flying saucers in the sky. Everybody but a Negro. They probably won't even let flying saucers fly over Harlem, just to keep us from seeing one. Not long ago, I read where some Karl Krubelowski had seen a flying saucer, also Giovanni Battini saw one. And way out in Pennsylvania mountains some Dutchman named Heinrich Armpriester seen one. But did you read about Roosevelt Johnson or Ralph Butler or Henry Washington or anybody that sounded like a Negro seeing one? I did not. Has a flying saucer ever passed over Lenox Avenue yet? Nary one! Not even Daddy Grace has glimpsed one, nor Ralph Bunche. Negroes can't even get into the front page news no kind of way. I can't even see a flying saucer. When I do, that will be a great day.

HOPKINS  It would probably scare you to death—so you wouldn't live to see your name in the papers.

SIMPLE  Well, then—I could read about it in the other world then—and be just as proud—me, Jess Semple, kilt by a flying saucer.

ARCIE  (*Enters yelling tipsily*) Bodiddly! Bodiddly! Why don't you come on upstairs?

BODIDDLY  Aw, woman, hush! Every time I turn around there's families under my feet. Set down and leave me be.

ARCIE  I did not come to set down. It's past midnight. I come to get you to go to bed.

BODIDDLY  I know when to go to bed my own self.

ARCIE  Then come on, you great big no-good old bull-necked son-of-a-biscuit eater!

BODIDDLY  Sit down, I'll buy you a sherry wine. Hop!
(ZARITA *enters with* ALI BABA, *an enormous well-dressed fellow in a turban*)

ZARITA  Hello, you all! Hey, Jess Semple! Folks, dig this champion roots-herbs—and numbers-seller from south of the border. I just come by to show you my new man I met at the Baby Grand. Don't he look like a sultan? But we got business. Come on! We're gonna do the town, ain't we, Ali Baba?

MAMIE    Ali Baba?

ZARITA    Sugar Hill, Smalls, and every place! Come on, Texas Tarzan, come on! Jess, I'm glad you came out of that little accident O.K. 'Bye, all!

(ZARITA *kisses* ALI BABA. *He sneezes.* MELON *ducks. As* ZARITA *and her new man exit,* SIMPLE *looks sheepish*)

BODIDDLY    She don't need us tonight.

HOPKINS    She's got her a two-ton Sugar Daddy.

MELON    She's got her a human shower.

MAMIE    Paddy's Bar is small-time to Zarita this evening. She'll be in here Monday all beat out, though—and looking for Jess Semple.

SIMPLE    Or somebody else simple—but it won't be me.

MELON    Where have I heard that before?

SIMPLE    Where have I heard that before? (*They glare at each other*)

MELON    Where have I heard that before? (SIMPLE'S *feelings are hurt*)

SIMPLE    I'm going and see Joyce. I need to see somebody that loves me.

(*A Policeman's Voice is heard in the street*)

POLICEMAN    Hey, you! Stay off the street with that noise box. Don't you know it's against the law, out here hustling for dimes? Next time I hear that racket, I'll run you in.

GITFIDDLE    Yes, sir, Officer! (GITFIDDLE *enters crestfallen*) A man can't play music nowhere no more. Juke box drowns him out in the bars, cops run him off the streets, landlady won't let you play in your own room. I might as well break this damn box up!

MAMIE    Gitfiddle, I told you, you can play for me.

BODIDDLY    Me too.

ARCIE    Sure, Git.

MELON    And me, Git.

MAMIE    Come on, now! Let's have some music like you feels it, Gitfiddle.

MELON

Did you ever hear the Blues?
On a battered old guitar:
Did you ever hear the Blues
Over yonder, Lord, how far?
Did you ever hear the Blues

On a Saturday night?
Did you ever hear the Blues
About some chick ain't done you right?
Baby, did you ever hear the Blues?

MAMIE

Did you ever hear the Blues
On an old house-rent piano?
Did you ever hear the Blues
Like they play 'em in Savannah?
Did you ever hear the Blues
In the early, early morn?
Wondering, wondering, wondering
Why you was ever born?
Baby, did you ever hear the Blues?

MELON

When the bar is quiet
And the night is almost done,
Them old Blues overtake you
At the bottom of your fun.
Oh, Lord, them Blues!
Echo . . . echo . . . echo . . . of the Blues!

MAMIE

Good morning, Blues! Good morning!
Good morning, Blues, I say!
Good morning, Blues, good morning!
You done come back to stay?
You come back to bug me
Like you drug me yesterday?

MELON

Blues, I heard you knock last night,
But I would not let you in.
Knock, knock, knock, last night
But I would not let you in.
I tried to make believe
It weren't nothing but the wind.

ALL

Blues, Blues, Blues!
It were the Blues!
Maybe to some people
What the Blueses say is news
But to me it's an old, old story.

MAMIE

> Did you ever hear the Blues
> On a battered old guitar?
> Did you ever hear the Blues
> Over yonder, Lord, how far?
> Did you ever hear the Blues
> On a Saturday night?

BOTH

> Did you ever hear the Blues
> About some chick ain't done you right?

ALL

> Baby, did you ever hear the Blues?

BLACKOUT


## SCENE SIX

JOYCE'S *room. Sunday evening.*

JOYCE *is sewing. The bell rings seven times. The Landlady calls from offstage.*

MRS. CADDY   I'll answer it, Miss Lane. I'm right here in the hall.

JOYCE   Oh, thank you, Mrs. Caddy. You're about the nicest landlady I know.

MRS. CADDY   Are you decent? Do you want to see Mr. Semple? He's kinda cripple—so down here or up there?

JOYCE   I'm sewing, so let him come up here, please—if he can make it.

SIMPLE   (*Enters and closes the door*)   I've made it. Well, I'm back on my feet, up, out, and almost at it.

JOYCE   I see. You may come in. Remember the door—Mrs. Caddy's rules.

SIMPLE   (*Opens the door a crack*)   Dog-gone old landlady! Joyce, I know I'm a black sheep. But I explained it all to you the last time you come by the hospital.

JOYCE   I accepted your explanation.

SIMPLE   But you don't seem like you're glad to see me, now I'm out— the way you didn't say almost nothing when I come by Friday.

JOYCE   I'm glad to see you.

SIMPLE  Then lemme kiss you. Ouch! My back! (*He yells in pain as he bends over*)

JOYCE  Oh!

SIMPLE  I think my veterbrays is disconnected.

JOYCE  What did the X-rays show?

SIMPLE  Nothing but a black mark. The doctor says I'm O.K. Just can't set down too suddenly for a while.

JOYCE  Then have a slow seat.

SIMPLE  Joyce, is you my enemy? You sound so cool. Am I intruding?

JOYCE  Oh, no. I'm just having a nice peaceful Sunday evening at home—which I must say, I haven't had too often since I've been knowing you.

SIMPLE  Baby darling, I'm sorry if I'm disturbing you, but I hope you're glad to see me. What you making?

JOYCE  Just lingerie for a girl friend who's getting married.

SIMPLE  Step-ins or step-outs?

JOYCE  Slips, Jess, slips. Jess Semple, stop breathing down my neck. The way you say things sometimes, you think I'm going to melt again, don't you! Well, instead you might get stuck with this needle. Listen, hand me that pattern book over there. Let me see how I should insert this lace.

SIMPLE  What're you doing with all those timetables and travel books, baby?

JOYCE  Just in case we ever should get married, maybe I'm picking out a place to spend our honeymoon—Niagara Falls, the Grand Canyon, Plymouth Rock . . .

SIMPLE  I don't want to spend no honeymoon on no rock. These books is pretty, but, baby, we ain't ready to travel yet.

JOYCE  We can dream, can't we?

SIMPLE  Niagara Falls makes a mighty lot of noise falling down. I likes to sleep on holidays.

JOYCE  Oh, Jess! Then how about the far West? Were you ever at the Grand Canyon?

SIMPLE  I were. Fact is, I was also at Niagara Falls, after I were at Grand Canyon.

JOYCE  I do not wish to criticize your grammar, Mr. Semple, but as long as you have been around New York, I wonder why you continue to say, I were, and at other times, I was?

SIMPLE  Because sometimes I were, and sometimes I was, baby. I was at Niagara Falls and I were at the Grand Canyon—since that were in the far distant past when I were a coachboy on the Santa Fe. I was more recently at Niagara Falls.

JOYCE   I see. But you never were " I were " ! There is no " I were." In the past tense, there is only " I was." The verb *to be* is declined, " I am, I was, I have been."

SIMPLE   Joyce, baby, don't be so touchous about it. Do you want me to talk like Edward R. Murrow?

JOYCE   No! But when we go to formals I hate to hear you saying, for example, " I taken " instead of " I took." Why do colored people say, " I taken," so much?

SIMPLE   Because we are taken—taken until we are undertaken, and, Joyce, baby, funerals is high!

JOYCE   Funerals are high.

SIMPLE   Joyce, what difference do it make?

JOYCE   Jess! What difference does it make? Does is correct English.

SIMPLE   And do ain't?

JOYCE   Isn't—not ain't.

SIMPLE   Woman, don't tell me *ain't* ain't in the dictionary.

JOYCE   But it ain't—I mean—it isn't correct.

SIMPLE   Joyce, I gives less than a small damn! What if it aren't? (*In his excitement he attempts to sit down, but leaps up as soon as his seat touches the chair*)

JOYCE   You say what if things aren't. You give less than a damn. Well, I'm tired of a man who gives less than a damn about " What if things aren't." I'm tired! Tired! You hear me? Tired! I have never known any one man so long without having some kind of action out of him. You have not even formally proposed to me, let alone writing my father for my hand.

SIMPLE   I did not know I had to write your old man for your hand.

JOYCE   My father, Jess, not my old man. And don't let it be too long. After all, I might meet some other man.

SIMPLE   You better not meet no other man. You better not! Do and I will marry you right now this June in spite of my first wife, bigamy, your old man—I mean your father. Joyce, don't you know I am not to be trifled with? I'm Jesse B. Semple.

JOYCE   I know who you are. Now, just sit down and let's spend a nice Sunday evening conversing, heh?

SIMPLE   (*Sits down, but it hurts him*)   Ouch!

JOYCE   Oh, Sweety! Let me make you a nice cool drink. Lemonade?

SIMPLE   Yes, Joyce, lemonade. (JOYCE *exits. Suddenly* SIMPLE *realizes what he has agreed to drink and cries in despair*) Lemonade! (*He*

*sits dejected until* JOYCE *returns*) Baby, you ain't mad with me,
is you? (JOYCE *smiles and shakes her head, no*) Because I know
you know what I mean when I say, " I is "—or " I are " or " was "
or whatever it be. Listen, Joyce, honey, please. (*He sings*)
When I say " I were " believe me.
When I say " I was " believe me, too—
Because I were, and was, and I *am*
Deep in love with you.

If I say " You took " or " taken "
Just believe I have been taken, too,
Because I were, and am, and I *is*
Taken in by you.

If it *is* or it *ain't* well stated,
And it *ain't* or it *aren't* said right,
My love still must be rated
A love that don't fade over night.

When I say " I am " believe me.
When I say " I is " believe me, too—
Because I were, and was, and I *is*,
Deep in love with you.

Damn if I ain't!
JOYCE     A small damn? (*He grabs her.* JOYCE *screams*)

BLACKOUT

## SCENE SEVEN

SIMPLE'S *room. A month later.*

MR. BOYD *comes down the hall and sees* SIMPLE'S *door
ajar. He looks in.*

BOYD     Hey, fellow, what you doing home on Saturday night?
SIMPLE     Boyd, man, come on in. Joyce is gone to some gal's wedding
shower—and damn if I'm going out to any bar. Still and yet, Boyd,
I'm in a good mind to take that money I been saving and blow it all
in, every damn penny, because man, it looks hopeless. Push done

come to shove on that divorce, I got to pay for my part of it. So last month I started saving. But, damn, I got so far to go!

BOYD   How much do you have to save in all?

SIMPLE   One hundred thirty-three dollars and thirty-three cents. I'm as far as Leviticus.

BOYD   What do you mean, Leviticus?

SIMPLE   Aunt Lucy always said, " The Bible is the Rock: Put your trust therein." So that's where I'm putting my money. I got to save $133.33. If I put a ten dollar bill in each chapter every week from Genesis on, in eighteen and a half weeks I will have it—and I'll only have to go as far as Nahum.

BOYD   Nahum?

SIMPLE   That's a book in the Bible, somewhere down behind Ezekiel. If I ever get to Nahum that's it. I done put ten in Genesis, ten in Exodus, and five in Levi.

BOYD   I thought you said *ten* every week.

SIMPLE   I were a little short this past week. Anyhow, I got twenty-five.

BOYD   Come on, let's go around to Paddy's.

SIMPLE   Thanks, Daddy-o! I will not yield to temptation! No! Not especially since I done got another letter from that used-to-be wife of mine, Isabel. Sit down, Boyd. Listen. " Jesse B. Semple, you are less than a man. You marry a girl, neglect her, ignore her, and won't help her divorce herself, not even when your part ain't only but one-third of the payment. You can go to hell! You do not deserve no gold seal on your decree, because you have not put a cent into it. Therefore, since I am going to pay for this divorce myself, your paper may not be legal. From now on, you kiss my foot! Isabel Estherlee Jones. P.S. I have taken back my maiden name, as I wants no parts of you attached to me any longer. MISS JONES."

BOYD   She's angry.

SIMPLE   Seems like it. Boyd, I will not let Isabel get the last word on me. I'll send that lawyer my part of the money next week, even if I have to put my whole paycheck in to do it. Right now I got twenty-five in the Bible. When I add my old check, that won't leave but about ah—er—a sixty to go. I can pawn a suit, one overcoat, and my radio—which might still leave about fifty. Boyd, can you lend me fifty?

BOYD   Fellow, are you out of your mind?

SIMPLE   This is an emergency. I need a gold seal on my divorce, too— so I got to pay for it. I got to have that gold seal, Boyd! I got to have it! It's got to be legal for Joyce. But then it's up to me to get that money, ain't it, Boyd? It ain't up to you nor nobody else—it's just up to me.

BOYD  Yes, Simple, I'm afraid it is. Get hold of yourself, make a man of yourself. You got to live up to your obligations.

SIMPLE  You done said a big word, Boyd.

BOYD  And it's a big thing you've got to do, fellow, facing up to yourself. You're not the first man in the world to have problems. You've got to learn how to swim, Jess, in this great big ocean called the world.

SIMPLE  This great big old white ocean—and me a colored swimmer.

BOYD  Aw, stop feeling sorry for yourself just because you're colored. You can't use race as an excuse forever. All men have problems. And even if you are colored, you've got to swim beyond color, and get to that island that is you—the human you, the man you. You've got to face your obligations, and stand up on that island of *you*, and be a man.

SIMPLE  Obligations! That's a word for you, Boyd! Seems like to me obligations is just a big old rock standing in a man's way.

BOYD  Then you've got to break that rock, fellow. Or, maybe I should say rocks.

SIMPLE  I know what you mean—like the beer rock, huh, Boyd?

BOYD  Um-hum!

SIMPLE  And the licker-rock—only I don't drink much whiskey.

BOYD  Well, say the bar-rock in general.

SIMPLE  That night-owl rock.

BOYD  Out until four A.M.

SIMPLE  Yes, the chick-chasing rock.

BOYD  Zarita!

SIMPLE  Not mentioning no names! But, man, I done shook that chick. But then there's always that old trying-to-save-money rock.

BOYD  You mean putting-it-off-until tomorrow rock.

SIMPLE  Which has really been my stumbling rock.

BOYD  You got to bust it, man. You know about John Henry, don't you?

SIMPLE  Sure I do.

BOYD  He was the champion rock-buster of them all.

SIMPLE  My Uncle Tige used to sing about him. Boyd, I been making up my mind to break through my rocks, too. (BOYD *smiles*) Yes, I is, Boyd, I is.

BOYD  You just got to bust 'em, fellow, that's all. (*Boyd exits*)

SIMPLE   (*Takes off his shirt and changes into a ragged pajama top*)
Bust 'em! I got to bust 'em. Like that song of Uncle Tige's. That
old man sure could sing—made up songs, too. (SIMPLE *sits on bed
to take off his shoes*) Made his own about John Henry which went—
lemme see. (*He tries to remember*) How did it go? Something
about—
>    They say John Henry was a man.
>    And they say he took a hammer in his hand—
>    (*He uses one shoe as a hammer*)
That's it!
>    And busted a rock
>    So hard he gave the world a shock!
>    Yes, they say John Henry was a man.
>    (SIMPLE *rises*)
>    They say John Henry won a prize,
>    And they say he gave his life to win that prize.
>    (*He comes forward*)
>    Yes, they say he hammered on
>    Until his breath was gone!
>    (*As if speaking to himself*)
>    They say John Henry won a prize.
>    (*He reaches toward his back pocket*)
>    Well, there's a prize I'm gonna win,
>    And the time's long gone I should begin.
>    (*From his wallet he shakes his last five dollar bill, opens
>    the Bible, and puts it in between the pages*)
>    But it's better late than never,
>    And no time ain't forever.
>    (*He clasps the Bible to his chest*)
>    So right now, I'm gonna start to win.
>    (*He turns forward resolutely, putting Bible down*)
>    It takes a long haul to get there, so they say,
>    And there's great big mountains in the way.
>    But I'm gonna make it through
>    If it's the last damn thing I do.
>    (*He bangs his hand on the Bible*)
>    I'm gonna be John Henry, be John Henry,
>    I'm gonna be John Henry, too.

**CURTAIN**

# ACT TWO

*SCENE ONE*

*The music of the Blues on the guitar, slow, haunting, syncopated, precedes the rise of the curtain.*

*Paddy's Bar. A week later. Evening.*

ARCIE *is sitting alone at a table drinking sherry wine and working a crossword puzzle in the paper.* BOYD *is writing in a notebook at another table. The* PIANIST *lazily runs his fingers over the keys as* HOPKINS, *behind the bar, stifles a yawn.*

HOPKINS  Blue Monday night, no money, and I feel like hell. What you writing, Boyd?

BOYD  Just making some notes for a story I might write—after observing life in Harlem over the weekend.

HOPKINS  You didn't go to Philly Sunday to see that young lady?

BOYD  She's vacationing in Paris, which is O.K. by me, because when we get ready to honeymoon, I won't have to take her to Europe.

HOPKINS  Far as I could take a chick on a honeymoon would be the Theresa Hotel.

BOYD  That's about as far as I could take one, unless I sell some of this stuff I've been writing.

(MAMIE *enters, panting*)

HOPKINS  Hey, Mamie! What's the matter?

MAMIE  I'm seeking escape—that Melon—— (MELON *enters with a hangdog* air) Man, if you would just stop following me! Now that you're so bold as to call at my house every night, at least let me have a little peace when I take a walk, without you at my heels.

MELON  Aw, Miss Mamie, you know I'm drawn to you.

MAMIE  When I get home from work, man, *I am tired.* I just want to set down, and rest, and read my paper. But Tang-a-lang-lang! You ring the bell! It looks like here lately, at home, in the bar, anywhere, every time ——
        When I'm in a quiet mood, here you come.
        When I'm deep in solitude, here you come.
        When I feel like settling down—

MELON

There I are!

MAMIE

When I'm gazing at the moon—

MELON

In falls your star!

MAMIE

My dial is set, the tone is low,
There's nice sweet music on my radio.
I take a book, the story's fun—
But when you ring my bell, I never get my reading done.
When I'm in a quiet mood, up you pop.
When I'm playing solitaire, in you drop.

MELON

The way you upset me makes my heartstrings hum—

MAMIE

When I'm in a quiet mood

BOTH

Here you (I) come!

MAMIE

It's raining outside. It's nice in the house.
Everything is cool—quiet as a mouse.
The doorbell rings. Who can it be?
My solitude is ended, Lord, you're looking for me!
Slippers on my feet, in my boudoir chair,
F-M on the dial, " The Londonderry Air."
The telephone rings, you say you're coming by.
When you get to my door—

BOTH

My, Oh, my!
(MAMIE *walks away,* MELON *follows*)

MELON

Oh, you act so cute and you switch so coy—
Mamie, I was meant to be your playboy.
I dial your phone, hear you yell, " Damn Sam! "
Which means that you know I'm your honey lamb.
With hankering heart, I just follow you.
Your kisses are as sweet as sweet mountain dew.
I ring your bell, it's just old me.—
I come around to try to keep you company.

I've sampled lots of melons whose flavor's fine,
But you are the sweetest melon on my vine.
I know that you love me by the look in your eye.
When I knock at your door—

BOTH

My! Oh, my!

MAMIE

When I'm in a quiet mood, up you pop.
When I'm playing solitaire, in you drop.

MELON

The way you upset me makes my heartstrings hum.

MAMIE

When I'm in a quiet mood—

BOTH

Here you (I) come!

MAMIE

When the night is free to get my beauty sleep,
I cannot sleep, so I'm counting sheep.
The doorbell rings—I shoot the sheep—Bam! Bam!
'Cause there in the door stands some old moth-eaten lamb.
I could scream! It's not a dream—
Here you come—to upset me! . . . And, honey, I'm leaving.
Here I go! . . . And I mean it!

MELON    Well, I guess this time she really means it.

MAMIE    Well, if you're coming, come on!

MELON    I'm going to follow—here I come!

(MAMIE *and* MELON *exeunt*. SIMPLE *bursts in exuberantly*)

SIMPLE    Hey, now, moo-cow! Gimme a little milk. Barman, untap
your key. Suds us up! Let's drink to it, even if it is my last dollar.

HOPKINS    Your last dollar, didn't you get paid this week?

SIMPLE    I did, but I took that money—all of it—and added it to what
was in the Bible and sent it off to Baltimore—$133.34. Being last
on payments, I had to pay that extra penny to change Divorce
Pending to Divorce Ending!

HOPKINS    Congratulations!

SIMPLE    Joyce knows I love her. But to get a woman to make his
bed down, a man has to make his mind up. Joyce is sweet, I mean!
My queen—my desire, my fire, my honey—the only woman who
ever made me save my money!

ARCIE    Simple.

SIMPLE   Yes, ma'am?

ARCIE   What's a four-letter word for damn?

SIMPLE   Arcie, do you see that sign? (*He points to*: " NO PROFANITY IN HERE ") Well, I do not repeat no four-letter words in public.

ARCIE   Damn! (ZARITA *enters briskly switching*)

ZARITA   Hi, folks! I thought I'd stop by and have a quick one. Mr. Semple, how do you do? Set me up, Hop. (*She approaches* SIMPLE) How are you, Sugar?

SIMPLE   Zarita, could I have a word with you, private?

ZARITA   Of course! It won't be the first time.

ARCIE   Hummmmm-mm-m! I thought so. That girl is like a magnet to that man.

(HOPKINS *pours* ARCIE *a drink as* SIMPLE *and* ZARITA *go aside*)

HOPKINS   Stay out of other people's business, Arcie.

ARCIE   O.K! O.K!

ZARITA   So you're not even going to speak to me again?

SIMPLE   What I do say is, I ain't gonna talk to you. Good evening— and Good-bye! Excuse me.

ZARITA   Aw, not like that, Jess, listen . . . (ZARITA *puts an arm around* SIMPLE)

ARCIE   Hey there, you writer, Boyd. What is the path in the field which a plow makes called?

BOYD   Furrow.

ARCIE   Six letters, just right. Now, wait a minute. Tell me, what is a hole with just one opening?

BOYD   How many letters?

ARCIE   Six, starts with D.

HOPKINS   Dugout?

ARCIE   Just fits. A dead general. A God-damn dead general!

(SIMPLE *pulls away from* ZARITA)

ZARITA   But, Jess, you know you and me together always has fun.

SIMPLE   Zarita, I'm the same as about to get married. I got responsibilities.

ZARITA   I am a lady, Jess Semple. Don't worry, I'll stay out of your life. I'm tired of paying you a sometime call when I'm feeling lonely. Anyhow, I always did bring my own licker. You never had none.

SIMPLE   But I always treat you when I meet you—when I can. Zarita, you know I'd give you the shirt off my back.

ZARITA   And I'd gladly give you mine. Go on and get your rest, Jess.
You never turned in this early before.
SIMPLE   I still got to make a week's work before that lay-off comes.
ZARITA   I guess you'll say good night, even if you wouldn't say hello.
SIMPLE   Good night.
ZARITA   Good night.
(SIMPLE *expects* ZARITA *to leave. Instead she stands there
and smiles at him her sweetest smile.* SIMPLE *looks at the
bar as if he wants to sit down on the stool again, then looks
at* ZARITA. *Finally he decides to leave*)
SIMPLE   Going my way, Boyd?
BOYD   I might as well, it's getting late. So long, folks.
ARCIE   And I ain't finished this puzzle.
BOYD   Hop'll help you. Good night. (SIMPLE *and* BOYD *exeunt, as the
Pianist ripples the keys*)
ARCIE   It ain't but a quarter to twelve. What's happening to Simple?
ZARITA   He's getting domesticated. You know, Arcie, I wish someone
would feel about me the way Simple feels about Joyce, and she about
him, even if they do have their ups and downs. I guess a little
trouble now and then just helps to draw people together. But you
got to have somebody to come together with. (*The notes on the
piano rise hauntingly*) Gee, Bill, you play pretty sometimes.
PIANIST   I studied to be a concert pianist, but the concert never did
come off.
ZARITA   What's that you're playing now? Sounds familiar. (*She leans
on the piano*)
PIANIST   Some new piece a colored boy wrote, I heard it on the radio.
Let me croon it to you:
> Just a little shade and shadow
> Mixed in with the light
> Helps to make the sunshine brighter
> When things turn out right.

ZARITA
> Just a little pain and trouble
> Mixed in with the fair
> Helps to make your joys seem double
> When clouds are not there.
>
> Look for the morning star
> Shining in the dawn!

Look for the rainbow's arch
When the rain is gone!

Don't forget there're bluebirds
Somewhere in the blue.
Love will send a little bluebird
Flying straight to you.
(*The light fades as* JOYCE *is heard singing*)

Look for the morning star
Shine, shine, shining in the dawn!
Rainbow, rainbow, rainbow's arch
When the rain is gone.

Don't forget you'll find bluebirds
Somewhere in the blue.
Love will send a little bluebird
Flying straight to you. . . .

(BLACKOUT *as the melody continues into the next scene*)


## SCENE TWO

JOYCE'S *room. Two weeks later.*

JOYCE *is serving* SIMPLE *some sandwiches as she continues to sing.* SIMPLE *looks very serious.*

JOYCE
　　　. . . Love will send a little bluebird
　　　Flying straight to you . . .
　　　Just a little shade and shadow . . .
SIMPLE　. . . Shades and shadows, just like the song says. Listen, Joyce, you know when I first met you on that boatride, I said to myself, "That girl's too good for me. I can't make no headway with that kind of woman." Yes, I did! To tell the truth, Joyce, you gave me a kinder hard road to go—you know, with your morals and ——
JOYCE　And you already married.
SIMPLE　Yes, but not wedlocked. . . .

JOYCE  Still and yet there was a shadow between us. . . .

SIMPLE  Of bigamy,

JOYCE  And gossip,

SIMPLE  Old landladies,

JOYCE  Friends,

SIMPLE  And I run around a lot in them days, too. . . .

JOYCE  In shady places—speakeasies, and things, so you said . . .

SIMPLE  Shady nothing! Them places was really dark—after-hours spots, Joyce. Now I know better. I'm older! And when I look at you, oh, I can see the sun, Joyce! It was dark, but now the clouds are rolling by.

JOYCE

> Just a little shade and shadow
> Mixed in with the light
> Helps to make the sunshine brighter
> When things turn out right.

SIMPLE  True, so true!

JOYCE

> Just a little pain and trouble
> Mixed in with the fair
> Helps to make your joys double
> When clouds are not there.

SIMPLE

> Wonderful the morning star
> Shining in the dawn!

JOYCE

> Wonderful the rainbow's arch

BOTH

> When the rain is gone!

JOYCE

> Don't forget you'll find bluebirds
> Somewhere in the blue.
> Love will send a little bluebird
> Flying straight to you.

SIMPLE

> Sing about the morning star
> Shine-shine-shining in the dawn!
> Rainbow, rainbow, rainbow's arch

BOTH

> When the rain is gone.

JOYCE

I am sure we'll find bluebirds
Right here in the blue.

BOTH

Love has sent a singing bluebird
Straight to me and you.
(*They kiss as the music rises lyrically*)

JOYCE    Oh, Jess! Life is really wonderful!

SIMPLE    I wouldn't be caught dead without it. But—er—a ——

JOYCE    But what, Jess?

SIMPLE    It's wonderful. But, Joyce, baby, something is always happening to a Negro—just when everything is going right. Listen—I'm sorry, but there's something I got to tell you, much as I don't want to.

JOYCE    About your divorce?

SIMPLE    No, sugar, that's all filed, paid for, ought to be ready for the seal soon. Something else has come up. It's that—it's that—well, the notice come last week that it was coming. I just didn't tell you—I'm being laid off my job.

JOYCE    Oh, Jess! Not fired?

SIMPLE    No, not fired, just temporary, three or four months till after New Year's while they converts. Converting! And us planning to get married. Every time a Negro plans something ——

JOYCE    Aw, come now! We'll get married, Jess.

SIMPLE    I can't even get my laundry out—let alone put my dirty shirts in.

JOYCE    Jess, I'll do your laundry. Bring me a bundle tomorrow and I'll bring them back to you—rub-a-dub-dub—white as snow.

SIMPLE    You're a doll, Joyce, you almost never come to my room.

JOYCE    Well, this'll give me a chance to see the curtains I made for you.

SIMPLE    Come see.

JOYCE    I will—when I bring this laundry, and if you need it, Jess, I can let you have a little money.

SIMPLE    I couldn't take no money from you.

JOYCE    But you can have it.

SIMPLE    I'd be embarrassed.

JOYCE    Have you got enough to eat?

SIMPLE    Oh, sure, I'll make out.

JOYCE    Well, on the weekend, Mr. Semple, you're going to dine with me. Make up your mind to that. And don't say one word about being embarrassed. Everything is going to be all right, I know. I talk to the Lord every night on my knees and I know.

SIMPLE   How long exactly it'll be before that job opens up again, to tell the truth, I don't know. Joyce, what are we going to do? We wants to get married, and all these years I have not saved a thing. Baby, have you figured up how much our wedding is going to cost?

JOYCE   There's no need to worry about that now. You've got enough on your mind tonight, darling. I just want you to know that I'm behind you.

SIMPLE   But, Joyce, baby, look! I ain't got nothing put away. I don't know if our plans are gonna go through or not.

JOYCE   Look, Jess, don't worry. If you ain't got the money to buy no license, well, when we get ready to get married we gonna get that license.

SIMPLE   But, Joyce, honey, I don't want you to be building no castles in the sand.

JOYCE   Jess, I have built my castles in my heart. They're not in no sand. No waves is gonna beat them down. No wind is gonna blow them apart. Nothing can scatter my castles. I tell you, nothing! Their bricks are made out of love and their foundations are strong. And you, Jess Semple, you are the gate-keeper of my castle—which is in my heart. You are the gate-keeper of my castle. (JOYCE *sits on the floor at* SIMPLE's *feet and lays her head in his lap*) Oh, Jess, we'll have our own little place, our own little house, and at night we'll both be there after jobs are done. Oh, Jess, baby, you don't know how much—

> I want somebody to come home to
> When I come home at night.
> I want someone to depend upon
> I know will do right.
>
> I want somebody to come home to
> I'm sure will be at home.
> I want someone who is sweet and kind
> I know will not roam.
>
> I'm a homebody—and this homebody
> Wants somebody to share my share
> For each homebody needs somebody
> Who will always be right there.

I want somebody to come home to
Who'll make my dreams come true
A nice someone who'll be the one
I know will be you.
*(Repeating from release closing with this)*
A nice homebody who's just somebody
Lovely to come home to.

BLACKOUT


## SCENE THREE

SIMPLE'S *room. Early evening.*

SIMPLE *is lying on his bed, shoes off and shirt tail out, dozing. A doorbell is heard ringing madly. Commotion downstairs and in the hallway.* ZARITA *bursts in on a startled* SIMPLE. *A large red pocketbook swings from one of her arms.*

ZARITA   It's my birthday, Jess! And I brought my friends around to celebrate—since you're broke these days and don't come out no more.
         (SIMPLE *leaps up and begins to tuck his shirt in and put on a shoe. Voices are heard on the stairs*)
BODIDDLY   What floor is it on?
HOPKINS   You're sure he's expecting us?
MAMIE   We rung the bell.
MELON   I been here before.
ARCIE   I'm having trouble with these steps.
         (BOYD *is seen outside* SIMPLE'S *door*)
BOYD   Shsss-ss-sss! Be quiet. What the hell is going on? You want to get us in trouble with the landlady? (*By now the crowd—which includes all the bar customers and as many strangers as desired to make the staging lively—has pushed* BOYD *into the room*)
ZARITA   I tell you, it's my birthday, Jess! Come on in, everybody.
MELON   Happy birthday!
PIANIST   Happy birthday, Zarita!
         (GITFIDDLE *begins to play*)
SIMPLE   Zarita, your birthday ain't mine. And I don't want ——

ZARITA  But I want to share it with you, Daddy! We brought our
own liquor. When it runs out, we'll send and get some more. Won't
we, Melon?

MELON  Liquor's about gone now, Whoopee-ee-ee!

ARCIE  Have some o' my sherry, Simple. I got my own bottle.

ZARITA  Jess, honey, I forgot to tell you I'd be twenty-some odd
years old today. We started celebrating this morning and we're still
going strong.

BODIDDLY  The ball is on!

ZARITA  Let the good times roll!

BODIDDLY  Let the good times roll in " D " !

MELON  Whoopee!

    (ZARITA *begins to sing*)

ZARITA

    If you ain't got nothing
    And there's nothing to get,
    Who cares long as you're doing it?
    If you ain't got anything
    Better to do,
    Why not do what's good to do?

MELON  What's that?

ZARITA

    Ball, ball, let's ball awhile!
    Ball, ball, honey chile!
    Sing! Shout! Beat it out!

ALL

    Dance! Prance! Take a chance!
    Grab the blues and get them told—
    When you're happy in your soul.

ZARITA

    Start the music playing
    Let the good times roll.

ALL

    Whail! Sail! Let it fly!

ZARITA

    Cool fool: we're riding high!

ALL

    Ball, ball, let's ball awhile!
    (*Everybody dances wildly with a dazed* SIMPLE *in their
    midst, one shoe still off*)

ZARITA

> Ball, ball, let's ball awhile!
> Ball, ball, honey chile!
> Sing! Shout! Beat it out!
> Dance! Prance! Take a chance!
> Grab the blues and get them told—
> When you're happy in your soul.
>
> Start the music playing,
> Let the good times roll.
> Whail! Sail! Let it fly!
> Cool fool: We're riding high!
> Ball, ball, let's ball awhile!
> (ZARITA *forces* SIMPLE *to dance*)

ALL

> Ball, ball, let's ball awhile!
> Ball, ball, honey chile!
> Sing! Shout! Beat it out!
> Dance! Prance! Take a chance!
> Grab the blues and get them told—
> When you're happy in your soul.

ZARITA

> Start the music playing
> Let the good times roll!
> (*The whole room starts rocking*)

ALL

> Whail! Sail! Let it fly!
> Cool fool! We're riding high!
> Ball! Ball! Let's ball awhile!

BODIDDLY   Hey, now!

ZARITA   Ow! It's my birthday! We're balling!

HOPKINS   Happy birthday, Zarita!

MELON   Dog-gone it! This bottle is empty.

ARCIE   Mine, too. Diddly, go get some more.

BODIDDLY   Send Melon. Here's fifty cents. (*He tosses* MELON *a coin*)

ZARITA   Play that again, Git, " Let's Ball Awhile."

MAMIE

> Ball! Ball! Honey chile!
> Ball! Ball! Let's ball awhile!

ARCIE   Yippeee-ee-ee-e! Diddly, shake yourself! (ZARITA'S *big red pocketbook is swinging wildly on her arms as the crowd stops dancing and moves back to let her and* SIMPLE *cavort madly together in a fast and furious jitterbug, each trying to outdo the other in cutting capers)* Aw, do it, Zarita! (ZARITA *spins around and around with her purse in her hand swirling high above her head. Suddenly the clasp comes open—the innumerable and varied contents of her enormous pocketbook fly all over the room, cascading everywhere: compact, lipstick, handkerchief, pocket mirror, key ring with seven keys, scattered deck of cards, black lace gloves, bottle opener, cigarette case, chewing gum, bromo quinine box, small change, fountain pen, sunglasses, address books, fingernail file, blue poker chips, matches, flask and a shoe horn)*

ZARITA   Oh, ooo-oo-o! My bag! Stop the music! Stop, Git, stop!

ARCIE   Girl, your perfume done broke!

ZARITA   My *Night in Egypt!*

BODIDDLY   If you broke your mirror, it's seven years bad luck.

PIANIST   Help her pick her things up, man.

BODIDDLY   I'm helping. But what's this! (*Holding up a red brassiere*)

BOYD   Lord, women sure can have a lot of stuff in their pocketbooks!

MAMIE   She's even got poker chips!

ZARITA   Jess, you help me, baby. The rest of you all stay where you are. I don't know some of you folks, and I don't want to lose nothing valuable.

ARCIE   You ain't got nothing I want, child.

ZARITA   Where's my *China Girl* lipstick in the jade-studded holder? I don't want to lose that lipstick! Jess, you reckon it rolled outside?

SIMPLE   Might could be. Lemme look. (*Just then the doorbell rings nine times*) My ring!

ZARITA   My lipstick! Where's my lipstick? Help me, sugar. (ZARITA *pulls* SIMPLE *down with her on the floor to search for the lipstick in the doorway as the bell continues to ring*)

ARCIE   Somebody let Melon in with that licker.

BODIDDLY   Let that man in.

HOPKINS   The door's still open. He ought to have sense enough to come in.

BODIDDLY   I say to hell with the bell, and help Zarita find her stuff. Whee! Smell that " Night in Egypt " !

(SIMPLE *finds the lipstick and* ZARITA *kisses him*)

SIMPLE   Here it is!

ZARITA   Aw, goody! (GITFIDDLE *starts the music again and all dance*)

Aw, Simple, just because we're dancing, you don't have to keep on kissing me.

SIMPLE   Who's kissing who, Zarita? *You're* kissing me.

BODIDDLY   Come up for air, you two! Come up for air! Aw, play it, Git.

> (*The music soars. But suddenly the room becomes dead silent as everyone stops still, except* SIMPLE *and* ZARITA *who are embracing.* JOYCE *is standing in the doorway. Drunkenly* ARCIE *speaks*)

ARCIE   Come on in, girl, and join the fun!

PIANIST   Slappy Slirthday!

JOYCE   (*Hardly believing her eyes*)   This *is* Mr. Semple's room, isn't it?

PIANIST   Sure is. We're having a ball.

ZARITA   (*Back to the door, hollers*)   Play it again, Git! Come on—" Let's Ball a While!" Where's Melon with the licker? . . . Oh! (*Suddenly both she and* SIMPLE *see* JOYCE. SIMPLE *is astounded*)

SIMPLE   Joyce!

JOYCE   Jess, I brought your laundry I washed for you. I thought you might want to wear one of the shirts Sunday.

ZARITA   Tip on in, Joyce, and enjoin my birthday. We don't mind. I'm Zarita. Just excuse my stuff all over the place. We been having a ball, Simp and me and ——

JOYCE   I did not know you had company, Jess.

> (*Watermelon Joe arrives with his arms full of bottles and pushes past* JOYCE)

MELON   Gangway! The stuff is here and it's mellowed! Get out of the door, woman! Make room for Watermelon Joe—and the juice with the flow.

JOYCE   (*Hands* SIMPLE *his bundle as* MELON *distributes bottles*) Excuse me for being in your guests' way. Here, please take your laundry.

> (*The loud voice of* SIMPLE'S *landlady is heard calling angrily as she enters in kimono and curlers*)

LANDLADY   Wait a minute! I'm the landlady here, and what I want to know is, who is this strange man walking in my house with his arms full of bottles! And *who* left my front door open? Who? I want to know who? Did you, Jess Semple? This is a respectable house. What's going on here? Do you hear me, Mr. Semple?

SIMPLE   (*Meekly*)   Yes'm. These is just some guests, that's all.

LANDLADY  Well, get 'em out of here—raising sand in my house!
Get 'em out I say! (*She exits in a huff*)
JOYCE  I'm going—as quick as I can. (*She starts to pass* SIMPLE)
SIMPLE  Joyce! . . . Joyce! You know she don't mean you. I wants
a word with you, Joyce.
JOYCE  (*Turns on him furiously, fighting back her tears*)  With me?
You don't need to explain to me, Jess Semple. Now I have seen that
Zarita woman with my own eyes in your bedroom. No wonder
you're giving a birthday party to which I am not invited. I won't be
in your way tonight, Jess—nor ever—any more. (*She looks back
into the room as she leaves*)  Enjoy yourselves. Good night! (JOYCE
*rushes down the hall and out of the house*)
SIMPLE  Joyce! . . . Joyce! . . . Joyce! . . .
ZARITA  Huh! Who does that old landlady think she is? You pay
your rent, don't you, Simple? Come on, folks, let's ball awhile.
PIANIST  Happy slirthday!
SIMPLE  (*Stands holding his parcel of laundry*)  I'm sorry, Miss
Arcie, Boyd, Diddly! . . . *To hell with your birthday*, Zarita! . . .
Folks, I'm sorry. Will you all go?
          (ARCIE *scurries out. The others follow.* MELON *retrieves
          several of the bottles and takes them with him.* ZARITA
          *picks up her red bag and swaggers out with* MAMIE
          *behind her*)
ZARITA  I know where we can ball, folks—at my house! Come on!
MAMIE  I been throwed out of better places than this.
          (GITFIDDLE *turns at the door and looks at* SIMPLE *as if to
          say he's sorry, but* SIMPLE *does not look up.* BOYD, *the last
          to go, closes the door. All exit down the stairs leaving
          SIMPLE in the middle of the floor. He feels his cheek, looks
          in the mirror, then takes his handkerchief and violently
          tries to wipe* ZARITA'S *lipstick from his jaw. He throws the
          handkerchief on the dresser and sinks down on the bed, his
          head in his hands*)
SIMPLE  Oh, my God! (GITFIDDLE'S *guitar is heard going down the
          stairs*)  Oh, my God! . . . My God! . . . Oh, God! (THE LIGHTS
          DIM TO A SINGLE SPOT *on the forlorn figure. There is the snapping
          of a broken string on the distant guitar*)

          BLACKOUT

### SCENE FOUR

*Paddy's Bar. A quiet Sunday evening.*

SIMPLE *enters and gloomily begins taking articles from his pockets and putting them on the bar.*

SIMPLE   Hop, is you seen Zarita?

HOPKINS   Nope. Guess she's still recovering from her birthday.

SIMPLE   If you do see her, give her this junk.

HOPKINS   Looks like to me you've snatched her purse.

SIMPLE   I'd snatch her head if I could! That woman has ruint me now—Joyce is out of my life.

HOPKINS   Have a drink, fellow, on me.

SIMPLE   This is one time I do not want a drink, Hop. I feel too bad. I have phoned her seventeen times, and Joyce will not answer the phone. I rung her bell four nights straight. Nobody would let me in. I sent Joyce eight telegrams, which she do not answer.

HOPKINS   And Zarita?

SIMPLE   I don't never want to see Zarita no more. The smell of that "Night in Egypt" is still in my room.

HOPKINS   A man should not fool around with a bad woman when he's got a good woman to love.

SIMPLE   Don't I know that now!

HOPKINS   Have you tried to see Joyce today? Sunday, she might be home.

SIMPLE   Tried? Are you kidding? That's all I've done. These is my bitter days! Hop, what shall I do?

HOPKINS   I don't know, Jess.

SIMPLE   Negroes never know anything important when they need to. I'm going to walk by her house again now. I just want to know if Joyce got home safe from church.

HOPKINS   She's been getting home safe all these years.

SIMPLE   Hop, I'm nearly out of my head. I got to talk to her. I'll stand in front of her house all night if I have to.

(ZARITA *enters, cool, frisky, and pretty as ever*)

HOPKINS   Uh-oh!

ZARITA   Hel-lo! Jess, I'm glad I caught you. I was a little shy about coming around to your place for my things.

SIMPLE  I brought your things here, Zarita. (HOPKINS *puts them on the bar*)

ZARITA  I thought you might, you're so sweet, sugar. Lemme treat you to a drink, and you, too, Hop.

SIMPLE  No, thank you.

ZARITA  Don't be that way. Set us up, here, Hopkins.

SIMPLE  I'm not drinking no more myself.

ZARITA  What? Just because you're out of work, you don't have to put down all the pleasures. Say, listen, Jess, if you're broke, I can let you have a little money.

HOPKINS  Zarita!

ZARITA  But no jive, Jess. Because you're wifeless and workless, a nice little old guy like you don't have to go hungry, never. I cook string-beans and ham almost every day.

SIMPLE  I don't like stringbeans.

ZARITA  I'll fry you some chicken, then.

SIMPLE  Forget it, please!

ZARITA  O.K. If you're that proud. (*She opens her purse*) Anyhow, here honey-boy, take this ten—in case you need it.

SIMPLE  Um-um! NO! Thanks, Zarita, no! (*He backs away*)

ZARITA  I meant no harm. I'm just trying to cheer you up. Like that party which I brought around to your house. Knowing you wasn't working, thinking maybe you'd be kinder embarrassed to come to my place for my birthday and not bring a present, I brought the party to you. Meant no harm—just to cheer you up.

SIMPLE  Please don't try to cheer me up no more, Zarita. Hop, I'm cutting out. I'm going by—you know where I told you, one more time. (SIMPLE *starts out*)

HOPKINS  Don't try to break her door down.

SIMPLE  I'm just gonna stand on the sidewalk and look up at her window.

HOPKINS  I hope you see a light, pal.

> (SIMPLE *exits as the* PIANIST *begins to play softly, " Look for the Morning Star." He sings, starting with the release*)

PIANIST

> Look for the morning star
> Shining in the dawn.
> Look for the rainbow's arch
> When the rain is gone.
> (*The remainder of the song he hums.* ZARITA, *lonely, looks around at the quiet bar, then cries in desperation*)

ZARITA   I'm lonesome, Hop! I'm lonesome! I'm lonesome! (*She buries her head on the bar and weeps as the piano continues*) I'm lonesome. . . .

BLACKOUT

## SCENE FIVE

SIMPLE'S *room. Late evening.*

SIMPLE is lighting a cone of incense in a saucer on his *dresser as* BOYD *pokes his head in the door, sniffs, and enters.*

BOYD   Hy, fellow! What's that burning on the dresser?

SIMPLE   Incense. I lit it to keep warm. I really hates winter.

BOYD   Oh, man, cold weather makes you get up and go, gives you vim, vigor, vitality!

SIMPLE   It does not give me anything but a cold—and all that snow outside!

BOYD   Perhaps you are just not the right color for winter, being dark. In nature you know, animals have protective coloration to go with their environment. Desert toads are sand-colored. Tree lizards are green. Ermine, for example, is the color of the snow country in which it originates.

SIMPLE   Which accounts for me not having no business wading around in snow, then. It and my color do not match. But, please, let's stop talking about snow, Boyd.

BOYD   Agreed—as cold as it is in this icebox!

SIMPLE   Landladies has no respect for roomers a-tall, Boyd. In fact, ours cares less for her roomers than she does for her dog. She will put a roomer out—dead out in the street—when he does not pay his rent, but she does not put out that dog. Trixie is her heart! She keeps Trixie warm. But me, I has nothing to keep warm by, but incense. I'm sick of this kind of living, Boyd. Maybe if I just had a little something, a place to live, some money, I could win Joyce back. If I don't get her back, Boyd, I don't know! I just don't know!

BOYD   I can lend you a small amount, Jess, if you need it—you know, five or ten.

SIMPLE   But I borrows only when I *hope* I can pay back, Boyd. (*A creaking sound is heard on the steps. The* LANDLADY'S VOICE *is heard outside*)

LANDLADY   I do believes somebody's smoking marijuana in my house.

SIMPLE   Listen! Don't I hear a elephant walking? (*She knocks loudly on* SIMPLE'S *door*) Come in!

LANDLADY   Mr. Semple, I am forced to inform you that I allows no reefer smoking in my home.

SIMPLE   I allows none in my room, neither.

LANDLADY   Then what do I smell?

SIMPLE   Chinese incense from Japan.

LANDLADY   Is you running a fast house?

SIMPLE   Madam, you have give me a idea!

LANDLADY   I am not joking, Jess Semple. Tell me, how come you burning that stuff in my house? Is it for bad luck or good?

SIMPLE   I don't believe in no lucky scents. I am just burning this for fun. It also gives out heat. Here, I will give you a stick to perfume up your part of the house.

LANDLADY   Thank you, I'll take it, even if it do smell like a good-time house to me. And that nude naked calendar you got hanging on your wall ain't exactly what I'd call decent. Don't your licker store give out no respectable girls on their calendars?

SIMPLE   They do, but they got clothes on.

LANDLADY   Naturally! Never would I pose in a meadow without my clothes on.

SIMPLE   I hope not, Madam.

LANDLADY   Meaning by that . . . ?

SIMPLE   Meaning you have such a beautiful character you do not have to show your figure. There is sweetness in your face.

LANDLADY   I appreciates that, Mr. Semple. (*She shivers*) Whee! It *is right* chilly up here.

SIMPLE   It's a deep freeze.

LANDLADY   If you roomers would go to bed on time—and your guests would go home—including Mr. Boyd—I would not have to keep heat up until all hours of the night.

SIMPLE   Has the heat been up tonight?

LANDLADY   You know it were warm as toast in this house at seven P.M. Funny where *your* heat disappears to. Downstairs I fails to notice any change myself.

SIMPLE   Madam, science states that heat is tied in with fat.

LANDLADY   Meaning . . . ?

SIMPLE   You're protected.

LANDLADY   I don't study ways of insulting roomers, Jess Semple, and
that is the second sly remark you made about me tonight. I'll thank
you to regret it.

SIMPLE   Madam, I does regret it!

LANDLADY   To my face—fat! Huh! You heard him, Mr. Boyd. (*She
exits muttering*) Elephant, huh? Behind in your rent, huh!

BOYD   Now our landlady's angry.

SIMPLE   I tell you, something's always happening to a colored man!
Stormy weather! Boyd, I been caught in some kind of riffle ever since
I been black. All my life, if it ain't raining, its blowing. If it
ain't sleeting, it's snowing. Man, you try to be good, and what
happens? You just don't be good. You try to live right. What happens? You look back and find out you didn't live right. Even when
you're working, and you try to save money, what happens? Can't
do it. Your shoes is wore out. Or the dentist has got you. You try
to save again. What happens? You drunk it up. Try to save another
time. Some relative gets sick and needs it. What happens to money,
Boyd? What happens?

BOYD   Come on, man, snap out of it! Let's go down to Paddy's and
have a drink. At least we can sit up in the bar and get warm—and
not think about what happens.

SIMPLE   You go, Boyd. What happens has done already happened
to me.

> (*Slowly* BOYD *leaves. Half through the door suddenly a
> bright thought comes to him. He smiles and snaps his
> fingers, then exits closing the door, leaving* SIMPLE *alone
> as the* LIGHT FADES SLOWLY TO DARKNESS)

BLACKOUT


## SCENE SIX

*Sidewalk on Lenox Avenue,* D. S. *apron, with a sign* LENOX
AVENUE, *a let-down flap at* L. *Early evening.* BOYD *walks
briskly down the street as if on a mission, entering* R. *Exits*
L. *Following him,* JOHN JASPER *comes dancing along the
sidewalk* R. *selling papers and stopping to hit a step now
and then.*

JOHN JASPER   Paper! . . . Amsterdam News! . . . Read all about it!
Get your paper! (*He dances off* L. BODIDDLY *enters* R. *followed by*
ARCIE *hobbling along behind him.* BODIDDLY *turns, stops*)

BODIDDLY  Woman, you better stop tagging *behind* me on the street, and walk *beside* me, like a wife should—before I lose my impatience.
ARCIE  Diddly, these new shoes hurt my feet.
BODIDDLY  I paid $20 for them shoes for you! Arcie, ain't you read in the Bible where Moses walked for forty years in the wilderness *barefooted*? Now, here you can't walk a block without complaining!
ARCIE  But Diddly, lover, I ain't Moses.
BODIDDLY  Aw, come on, woman! (*Exeunt. Enter* MAMIE, *trailed by* MELON R.)
MAMIE  Melon, you got more nerve that Liberace's got sequins. You ain't gonna get nowhere, so there's no need of you trailing me through the streets like this.
MELON  I can't help it, Miss Mamie. I'm marked by a liking for you!
(*He addresses her in rhymed jive, spoken*)

> You're my sugar,
> You're my spice,
> You're my everything
> That's nice.

MAMIE

> Melon, I done told you—
> You *ain't* my sugar
> You *ain't* my spice.
> If you was a piece of cheese
> I'd throw you to the mice.
> (*She moves on with* MELON *in pursuit*)

MELON

> Miss Mamie—
> Your words are bitter
> But your lips are sweet.
> Lemme kiss you, baby—
> And give you a treat.

MAMIE

> Melon—
> When cows start playing numbers
> And canary birds sing bass,
> That is when you'll stick your
> Big mouth in my face.
> (MAMIE *exits indignantly with* MELON *pleading as he follows*)

MELON

    Aw, Miss Mamie, listen!
    Wait a minute now!
    I ain't no canary bird,
    And you *sure* ain't no cow.
    But . . .
    (*Exit* MELON)

    BLACKOUT


## SCENE SEVEN

JOYCE'S *room. Same evening.*

BOYD *stands at the door as* JOYCE *opens it.*

BOYD   I hope you'll pardon me, Miss Lane—and maybe it's none of my business at all—but I was just walking down Lenox Avenue when the idea came to me and I felt like I ought to come and talk to you. (*He stands awkwardly*)

JOYCE   You may sit, Mr. Boyd. (*She takes his hat*)

BOYD   Thank you. I—I ——

JOYCE   Yes?

BOYD   Well, it's about Simple. You know, I mean Jess Semple. He didn't ask me to come to see you. In fact, he doesn't know I'm here at all. But he's been rooming right next to me quite a while now, and I—well—well, I never saw him like he is before.

JOYCE   (*Begins to freeze*)   You know him well?

BOYD   Very well.

JOYCE   Are you one of his drinking buddies of the Paddy's Bar set?

BOYD   I'm not much of a drinking man, Miss Lane. I'm a writer.

JOYCE   A writer! What do you write?

BOYD   Books.

JOYCE   Books!

BOYD   About Harlem.

JOYCE   Harlem! I wish I could get away from Harlem.

BOYD   Miss Lane, I'm worried about Simple.

JOYCE   You're worried about Simple. He never seems to worry about himself.

BOYD  I think maybe you really don't know about that birthday party.

JOYCE  There's really nothing I want to learn.

BOYD  Except that it wasn't Simple's party. He didn't plan it, and didn't know anything about it until it descended on him.

JOYCE  Huh! Just like that—from above.

BOYD  They came to surprise us.

JOYCE  You too? You don't look like the type of man to attract that conglomeration of assorted humans. If you're going to tell me something, Mr. Boyd, tell me the truth.

BOYD  Well, everybody just likes Simple. That's his trouble. He likes people, so they like him. But he's not going with all those women. He wasn't even going with Zarita.

JOYCE  (*Does not believe him*)  You can have your hat, Mr. Boyd, if you will.

BOYD  (*Takes his hat and continues talking*)  I mean, not lately, not for two or three years, since he's met you—why, he doesn't talk about anybody but you, hasn't for a long time.—Joyce, Joyce, Joyce! Now, he's even talking to himself in the night, trying to explain to you. I room next door, and sometimes I can hear him crying late in the night. Nobody likes to hear a grown man crying, Miss Lane.

JOYCE  (*Sternly dismissing him*)  Thank you very much, Mr. Boyd.

BOYD  Miss Lane!

.  (*She closes the door as he backs out.* JOYCE *comes toward the center of the room, stops, thinks, then rushes to the closet and begins to put on her coat*)

BLACKOUT

## SCENE EIGHT

SIMPLE'S *room. Same evening.*

SIMPLE *is alone, standing beside his dresser turning the pages of the Bible.*

SIMPLE  My old Aunt Lucy always said, " The Bible is the Rock, and the Rock is the Truth, and the Truth is the Light." Lemme see. (*He reads from Job*) It says here, " Let thy day be darkness. Let no God regard it from above, neither let the light shine upon it. . . . Man is born unto trouble." Lemme turn over! (*He tries the next page*) Uh-huh! This is just as bad. " They meet with darkness in the daytime and grope in the noonday like as in the night." Great Gordon Gin! What part of the Bible am I reading out of? *Job!* No wonder! He's the one what suffered everything from boils to blindness. But it says here the Lord answered Job. Looks like don't nobody answer me. Nobody! (*He shuts the Bible and goes to the window.* JOYCE *comes up the stairs and down the hall. Outside his door she calls*)

JOYCE   Jess! (*His body stiffens*)

SIMPLE   Am I hearing things?

JOYCE   Jess!

SIMPLE   I must be going crazy! Can't be that voice.

JOYCE   (*Knocks softly and enters*)   Jess!

SIMPLE   Joyce! Why are you here?

JOYCE   To see you, Jess. There's something maybe I ought to tell you.

SIMPLE   There's nothing for you to tell me, Joyce.

JOYCE   But, Jess —— (*After a long silence he speaks*)

SIMPLE   You've come to *me*, Joyce.

JOYCE   Yes, Jess.

SIMPLE   Every time something's happened between us, in the end you come to me. It's my turn to come to you now.

JOYCE   You tried. I wouldn't let you in. I got those messages. I heard you ringing my bell. It's my fault, Jess.

SIMPLE   It's not your fault, Joyce. I had no business trying to see you *then*. But I wasn't man enough not to try.

JOYCE   Jess, you were at my door and I wouldn't let you in.

SIMPLE   All my life I been looking for a door that will be just mine— and the one I love. Joyce, I been looking for *your* door. But sometimes you let the wrong *me* in, not the me I want to be. This time, when I come through your door again, it's gonna be the *me* I ought to be.

JOYCE   I know, Jess—we've had problems to solve. But ——

SIMPLE   The problem to solve is me, Joyce—and can't no one solve that problem but me. Until I get out of this mud and muck and mire I been dancing in half my life, don't you open your door to the *wrong* me no more. *Don't open your door.* And don't say nothing good to me, Joyce. Don't tell me nothing a-tall. (*He has already risen. Now she rises, embracing him, but he pushes her away*) Joyce, baby, darling, no. . . . (*He wants to call her all the sweet names he knows, to take her in his arms, to keep her then and there and always. But instead he speaks almost harshly*) No! Don't say nothing—to me—Joyce. (*He opens the door. As* JOYCE *turns to go, she looks at* JESS, *lifts her head, and smiles the most beautiful smile a man has ever seen—a smile serene and calm and full of faith.* THE LIGHTS DIM TO A SPOT *on her face as she turns and leaves without a word. Suddenly there is a great burst of music, wild, triumphant, wonderful, and happy*)

BLACKOUT


SCENE NINE

*Paddy's Bar on a winter night.*

BODIDDLY, BOYD, GITFIDDLE, *and the* PIANIST *are scattered about.* MELON *leans over* MISS MAMIE'S *table and emits a playful howl.*

MELON    Ow-ooo-oo-o! Miss Mamie, you're a killer, that you is! Sweet my lands! You-oo-O!
MAMIE    Melon, I don't want no wolf-howling compliments. I just come here to set in peace. I don't want to be bothered with you drunken Negroes.
MELON    Who is drunk?
MAMIE    You!
BODIDDLY.    She's right, you is.
MELON    Listen here! Diddly and Mamie, both you all belong to my church—the Upstairs Baptist—yet you go around talking about me like a dirty dog.
MAMIE    Well, you do drink—guzzle, guzzle, guzzle!
MELON    I don't get drunk!
MAMIE    I say you do!
MELON    Woman, listen! Miss Mamie, I respects you too much to dispute your word. If you say I do, I does.
MAMIE    Now that that's settled, come and have a drink on me. A little eye-opener in the morning, a bracer at noon, and a nightcap at night, never hurt nobody.
MELON    Mamie, you got money?
MAMIE    I always got me some money, been had money, and always will

have money. And one reason I do is, I'm a lone wolf, I runs with no pack.

MELON    I would pack you on my back if you would let me.

MAMIE    I don't intend to let you. To tell the truth, I doubt your intentions. And, Melon, I wants you to know: (*She sings*)
I been making my way for a long, long time,
I been making my way through this world.
I keep on trying to be good
'Cause I'm a good old girl.
I been making my way with a boot and a shoe.
In no oyster have I found a pearl.
I trust myself—so I've got luck
'Cause I'm a good old girl.
Sometimes the devil beckons
I look at the devil and say, (MELON *touches her hand*)
Stop that!
Devil, devil, devil—
Devil, be on your way!
I been making my way through thick and thin
'Spite o' devilish men in this world.
There ain't no man can get me down
Not even Harry Belafonte,
'Cause I'm a good old girl.
(MAMIE *rises and addresses the entire bar*)
I make five or ten dollars, sometimes more a day.
You men what ain't working know that that ain't hay.
Don't let no strange man get his hand on you—
There's no telling, baby, what a strange cat will do.
It takes all kinds of folks to spin this globe around,
But *one* bad actor tears your playhouse down.
Don't ever let no bad actor come around—
There's no telling, Baby, what that cat's trying to lay down!
Sometimes the devil beckons.
I look at the devil and say, (MELON *approaches*)
Devil, devil, devil—
Ain't you got enough trouble?
Devil, be on your way!
I been making my way through thick and thin
'Spite o' devilish men in this world.
There's no man can get me down

'Cause I'm a good old girl.
My name is Mamie—
I'm a good old girl!
Like Mamie Eisenhower,
I'm a good old gal!
(*To shouts of approval from the bar crowd, she continues*)
I been making my way for a long, long time!
Now listen, Punchy: I've been making my way:
I've been making my very own way for a long, long time.
I don't need you, Melon.
I've been making my way through this world.
Who needs that face?
I keep on trying to be good.
You think I'm a doll?
I'm a good old girl—
Might be a human doll! Anyhow—
I been making my way through thick and thin
'Spite o' devilish men in this world, (MELON *grins*)
You always been this ugly, Melon?
There ain't no man can get me down—
'Cause I'm a good old girl!
I keep repeating—I'm a good old girl!

Now, what's the sense of going on with this?

BODIDDLY. Melon, I guess you realize there's nothing more independent than an independent woman. You's better stop worrying Miss Mamie or she'll floor you and stomp on your carcass.

MELON  Diddly, if you don't have some respect for my personal conversation, I'm going to bust a watermelon over your head.

BODIDDLY  Take it easy, man. See you later. Hi, Simp! (*Simple enters shivering, passing* BODIDDLY *as he exits*)

SIMPLE  Hi, Bo! Hop! Man, this bar is the warmest place I know in winter. At least you keep steam up here.

HOPKINS  Cold as it is, do you mean to tell me you haven't got any steam in your room?

SIMPLE  I done beated on my radiator pipe six times today to let my old landlady know I was home—freezing.

HOPKINS  And what happened?

SIMPLE  Nothing—she just beat back on the pipes at me. Which is why I come down here, to get warm, just like Boyd.

HOPKINS  Want a drink?

SIMPLE   I sure could use one.

HOPKINS   Coming up.

SIMPLE   Hey Boyd! I got something to tell you. I'm working part-time, back down at the plant as a helper—helping reconvert.

BOYD   That's wonderful!

SIMPLE   With a good job and a good wife, man, it'll be like Joyce used to say when I kissed her—"Simply Heavenly." And when we get married, Boyd, you're gonna be standing there beside me at my wedding. You're gonna hand me the ring. Ain't that what the best man does?

MAMIE   Yeah, that's right. (MELON *approaches*) Melon, ain't you got no home?

BOYD   Hey, this is the first time you've sprung this on me, about being your best man. After all we've only known each other for a few years. A best man is usually somebody you grew up with, or something.

SIMPLE   I didn't grow up with nobody, Boyd. So I don't know anybody very well. So, will you please be my best man?

BOYD   Best man, eh? Then I'll have to start buying me a brand new suit. And a best man is due to give a bachelor's party for the groom a night or two before the ceremony. Your wedding's going to cost me a lot of dough, Jess.

SIMPLE   Just a keg of beer. I mean a private one—with my name on it.

BOYD   You got it, lad. I live to see the day! (*He rises*)

SIMPLE   Where you going, Boyd?

BOYD   Listen, Jess! Hot or cold. I've got to bust that book-writing rock and I've got to get home to my typewriter. Good night, all.

SIMPLE   Well, that's settled. Thank God, I don't have to worry about Zarita. I ain't seen her for months.

HOPKINS   Zarita's getting ready to fly to Arizona for Christmas. That Big Boy, Ali Baba, sent her a ticket. She's all set to go. I think they're going to get married.

SIMPLE   I wishes her all the luck in the world. But I sure wish I could understand a woman.

HOPKINS   Socrates tried, he couldn't. What makes you hold such hopes?

SIMPLE   Long as I live, Hop, I lives in hopes. (*Loud weeping is heard outside*) Damn, there's some woman hollering now.

HOPKINS   I wonder what's wrong. (ARCIE *enters crying and sinks at a table*) What's wrong, Arcie?

ARCIE    Gimme a sherry, Hopkins, quick! Gimme a sherry.

HOPKINS    What's the matter, Arcie?

ARCIE    Abe Lincoln is going to the army.

SIMPLE    The army?

ARCIE    My oldest son, Abraham Lincoln Jones.

SIMPLE    Well, why didn't you say so?

ARCIE    I'm trying to! Abe got his draft call.

SIMPLE    Don't cry, Arcie. The army'll do the boy no harm. He'll get to travel, see the world.

ARCIE    The first one of my children to leave home!

SIMPLE    As many as you got, you shouldn't mind *one* going somewhere.

ARCIE    I does mind. Abe is my oldest, and I does mind. Fill it up again, Hop.

SIMPLE    That boy Abe is smart, Arcie. You'll be proud of him. He's liable to get to be an officer.

HOPKINS    At least a sergeant—and come back here with stripes on his sleeve.

SIMPLE    Else medals on his chest. Now, me, if I was to go in the army today—now that we's integrated—I would come back a general.

HOPKINS    Quit your kidding.

SIMPLE    I would rise right to the top today and be a general—and be in charge of white troops.

MELON    Colored generals never command white troops.

SIMPLE    The next war will be integrated. In fact, I'd like to command a regiment from Mississippi.

HOPKINS    Are you drunk?

SIMPLE    No, sir.

MELON    Then why on earth would you want to be in charge of a white regiment from Mississippi?

SIMPLE    In the last war, they had white officers in charge of Negroes. So why shouldn't I be in charge of whites? Huh? General Simple! I would really make 'em toe the line. I know some of them Dixie-crats would rather die than left face for a colored man, but they would left face for me.

MELON    Man, you got a great imagination.

SIMPLE    I can see myself now, in World War III, leading white Mississippi troops into action. Hop, I would do like all the other generals do, and stand way back on a hill somewhere and look through my spy-glasses and say, " Charge on! Mens, charge on! " Then I would watch them Dixiecrats boys go—like true sons of the

Old South, mowing down the enemy. When my young white lieutenants from Vicksburg jeeped back to headquarters to deliver their reports in person to me, they would say, " Captain General, sir, we have taken two more enemy positions." I would say, " Mens, return to your companies—and tell 'em to keep on charging on! " Next day, when I caught up to 'em, I would pin medals on their chest for bravery. Then I would have my picture taken in front of all my fine white troops—me—the first *black* American general to pin medals on white soldiers from Mississippi. Then, Hop—man, oh, man—then when the war be's over, I would line my companies up for the last time and I would say, " Mens, at ease. Gentlemen of the Old South, relax. Put down your fighting arms and lend me your ears—because I am one of you, too, borned and bred in Dixie. (*Gitfiddle begins to play a syncopated march—a blend of " Dixie," " Swanee River," and " Yankee Doodle "*) And I'm willing to let bygones be bygones, and forget how you failed to obey my orders in the old days and right faced-ted when I said, " Left," because you thought I was colored. Well, I is colored. I'll forget that. You are me—and I am you—and we are one. And now that our fighting is done, let's be Americans for once, for fun. Colonels, captains, majors, lieutenants, sergeants, and, Hopkins, open up a keg of nails for the men—let's all drink to you, brave sons of the South! Drink, mens, drink! And when we all stagger back to peace together, let there be peace—between you, Mississippi, and me! Company—'tention! Right shoulder arms! . . . Forward, march! . . . Come on, boys, I'm leading you! Come on! By the left flank march! " (SIMPLE *proudly inspects his troops as they pass in review. Others in the bar, except* MISS MAMIE, *applaud and cheer*)

HOPKINS  March, fellows, march!

SIMPLE  By the right flank, march!

HOPKINS  March, fellows, march!

ARCIE  Ain't that fine!

HOPKINS  March, march, march!

SIMPLE  Forward! March!

HOPKINS  March! March! March! (SIMPLE *exits as if leading an army with banners. The music rises to a climax, then suddenly ends. In the silence* MISS MAMIE *speaks*)

MAMIE  You know something—that boy is sick!

BLACKOUT

### SCENE TEN

*A phone booth. Christmas Eve.*

*Chimes are softly tolling " Jingle Bells " as* SIMPLE *speaks excitedly into the phone.*

SIMPLE   Joyce? . . . Joyce? . . . Is this Joyce? . . . Yes, it's Jesse B. . . . It's Simple, honey! . . . What? You say I sound like a new man? I *am* a new man! And I got something for you, Joyce. It's Christmas Eve and, you know, well—like it says in the Bible, " Wise men came bringing gifts." . . . Joyce, I got a few little gifts for you on my Christmas tree. . . . Sure, I got a tree! What's on it for you? . . . I don't want to tell you, Joyce. I want to show you. You say you're coming right over? . . . Oh, baby! (*With the receiver still in his hand, he rises excitedly and starts out, but is jerked back by the cord. Quickly he hangs up and leaves as the music of " Jingle Bells " fills the air*)

BLACKOUT

### SCENE ELEVEN

SCENE: SIMPLE'S *room.*

TIME: *Christmas Eve.*

AT RISE: *A star shines in the darkness. The lights come up revealing* SIMPLE *and* JOYCE *standing before a tiny Christmas tree. The star glows atop this tree hung with tinsel and little balls of colored glass. On the tree there are four gifts tied with ribbons: one is a letter, one a roll of paper, one a long parchment, and one is a tiny box.* JOYCE *has just entered the room.*

JOYCE   Jess!
SIMPLE   Look. (*He shows her the tree*)
JOYCE   Oh! It's beautiful!
SIMPLE   May I take your coat? Won't you sit down? (*He hands her the parchment as* JOYCE *perches on the edge of a chair*)

JOYCE    Jess, what is it? A picture of some kind? Maybe a map?
Why, it's all in Roman letters. It's a divorce!

SIMPLE    With a gold seal on it, too.

JOYCE    Free! Jess, you're free! Like in Uncle Tom's Cabin!

SIMPLE    Yes, baby, I'm free. That's the paper.

JOYCE    It's dated a whole month ago. Jess, why didn't you tell me
you had your divorce?

SIMPLE    I was waiting for something else to go with it. Here, this
is for you, too. (*He hands her an envelope*)

JOYCE    My father's writing!

SIMPLE    Read it. You see, your ole—your father—gimme your hand.
(*While she reads the letter,* SIMPLE *opens the little box on the
tree and polishes a ring on his coat lapel.*) Now, can I take your
hand? (*He slips the ring on her finger*) For you—if you'll wear it?

JOYCE    Forever! *She starts to rise, but gently he pushes her down and
returns to the tree*)

SIMPLE    This is something only married people can have. And it's
not ready, yet, either. They just about now digging the first hole in
the ground—busting that first rock. We both got to sign our names
—if you're willing.

JOYCE    An apartment! Oh, Jess! A place to live! An apartment!

SIMPLE    Can we both sign our names, Joyce?

JOYCE    Yes, Jess (JOYCE *rises, scattering papers, and flings her arms
about him*)

SIMPLE    Now we can get ready for that wedding in June.

JOYCE    Oh, Jess! Jess, baby! Jess! (*Singing, they embrace*)

SIMPLE
               Just for you these Christmas tokens
               On our Christmas tree—

JOYCE
               Help to make me know that you are
               Santa Claus to me.

SIMPLE
               Just a little pain and trouble
               Mixed in with the past

BOTH
               Help to make our joys double
               When we're sure they'll last.

JOYCE
               Wonderful the morning star
               Shining in the dawn!

BOTH

Wonderful the rainbow's arch
When the rain is gone.
(*The bar is revealed as the entire company enters singing
and form tableaux, some around the piano,* MAMIE *at her
table with* MELON, BODIDDLY, ARCIE, *and* JOHN JASPER
*making a family group at another table. The entire chorus
of " Look for the Morning Star " is repeated as all come
forward for bows*)

ALL

Don't forget there's bluebirds
Somewhere in the blue.
Love will send a little bluebird
Flying straight to you.
(*Repeat chorus on bows*)

CURTAIN

# TAMBOURINES TO GLORY

## A Comedy

## AUTHOR'S NOTE

*Tambourines to Glory* is, in play form, a dramatization of a very old problem—that of good versus evil, God slightly plagued by the Devil, but with God—as He always intends—winning in the end.

*Tambourines to Glory* is a fable, a folk ballad in stage form, told in broad and very simple terms—if you will, a comic strip, a cartoon—about problems which can only convincingly be reduced to a comic strip if presented very cleanly, clearly, sharply, precisely, and with humor.

*Tambourines to Glory* is, on the surface, a simple play about very simple people. Therefore, all of its performers should be sensitive enough to appreciate the complexities of simplicity. All of them should be lovable, except BUDDY—whom one should love, too, in spite of one's better self.

The role of LAURA should be performed by a compelling personality, one not merely pretty, but capable of projecting sunlight, laughter, easy-going summer, and careless love. In contrast, the role of ESSIE is that of the good old earth, solid, *always* there come sun or rain, laughter or tears, the eternal mother image.

Much of the meaning of *Tambourines to Glory* lies in its songs, so both LAURA and ESSIE should be actresses who can sing. As if it were a rhythmic ballad, the overall conception of *Tambourines* must have rhythm—as " John Henry," " Casey Jones," " Stackolee," " Lord Randall," and " Mack the Knife" have rhythm. This the staging must achieve. When the curtain falls, the final effect must be that of having heard a song—a melodic, likable, dramatic song.

At certain points in the show audience participation might be encouraged—singing, foot-patting, hand-clapping, and in the program the lyrics of some of the songs might be printed with an invitation to sing the refrains along with the chorus of Tambourine Temple.

# CHARACTERS

LAURA WRIGHT REED  *A home relief client*
ESSIE BELLE JOHNSON  *An evicted tenant*
MARIETTA JOHNSON  *Essie's daughter*
BIG-EYED BUDDY LOMAX  *A handsome hustler*
GLORIA DAWN  *A glamour girl*
C. J. MOORE  *A young saint*
BIRDIE LEE  *A lady drummer*
CHICKEN-CROW-FOR-DAY  *A sinner saved*
MATTIE MORNINGSIDE  *Mistress of the robes*
LUCY MAE HOBBS  *Head deaconess*
BROTHER BUD  *A poor old man*
CHARLIE WINDUS  *Laura's chauffeur*
JOE GREEN  *A chump*
MINISTERS OF MUSIC  *Temple pianist*
*Temple organist*

DEACONS
BARTENDER
WAITER
PRISON WARDEN
POLICEMEN
THE GLORIETTAS
TAMBOURINE CHOIR
CABARET PATRONS
PASSERS-BY

## SCENES

PROLOGUE        Shadows of a street

### ACT ONE

*Scene One*:    Sidewalk before tenement
*Scene Two*:    A street corner
*Scene Three*:  A night club
*Scene Four*:   Shadows of a street
*Scene Five*:   A store-front church
*Scene Six*:    A living room
*Scene Seven*:  Tambourine Temple

### ACT TWO

PROLOGUE        Shadows of a street
*Scene One*:    Living room
*Scene Two*:    Robing room
*Scene Three*:  Tambourine Temple
*Scene Four*:   Robing room
*Scene Five*:   A jail cell
*Scene Six*:    Tambourine Temple

## MUSICAL NUMBERS

*Prologue*:     TAMBOURINES TO GLORY   Buddy and Ensemble
                Copyright © 1958 by Langston Hughes and Jobe Huntley

### ACT ONE

*Scene One*:    LORD ABOVE   Essie and Laura
                Copyright © 1959 by Langston Hughes and Jobe Huntley
                UPON THIS ROCK   Essie and Laura
                Copyright © 1959 by Langston Hughes and Jobe Huntley
*Scene Two*:    WHEN THE SAINTS GO MARCHING IN *   Birdie Lee
*Scene Three*:  SCAT CAT!   Gloriettas
                Copyright © 1959 by Langston Hughes and Jobe Huntley
                HAND ME DOWN MY WALKING CANE *   Gloria and
                                                 Gloriettas
                NEW YORK BLUES   Pianist
                Copyright © 1959 by Langston Hughes and Jobe Huntley

## PROLOGUE

*As lights dim half-way the leading man enters, spotlighted,
and smiles before a scrim of Harlem.*

BUDDY   You think I'm who you see, don't you? Well, I'm not. I'm
the Devil. . . . In this play, according to the program, you might
thing I'm Big-Eyed Buddy Lomax—if I didn't tell you in front, no,
I'm not. Big-Eyed Buddy is just *one* of my million and one names.
I've got plenty of names, had plenty—some pretty big ones—Hitler,
for example. *Yes, Hitler was me!* Mack-the-Knife, Gyp-the-Blood,
Don Juan among the covers. Oh, yes! Henry the Eighth. Katherine
the Great—I put on drag sometimes. Iago. Brutus—*et tu, Brute*—
right on back to Cain. Little names, big names—I'm liable to have
*your name* . . . The Devil comes in various guises—and disguises.
I'm disguised now. I am not the *me* you see here—tall, handsome,
brownskin. I am not always dark—sometimes I'm white. Sometimes
yellow, sometimes Khrushchev. I speak all tongues—*tovarish, mon
cher, kamerad, baby, daddy-o, amada, dulcissima*—all languages are
mine. *Mais, oui! Si, señor!* In Harlem I'm cool, in Spain I'm hot.
In Katanga I'm Tshombe. Sure, I have my troubles, get shot up
once in a while, ambushed, assassinated. But, quiet as it's kept, I love
being the Devil because I raise so much hell! Watch me this evening. I'll find work for idle hands—stage hands—to do. Unemployed
actors, too. The Theatre Guild put me up to this. On with the
show . . . Laura, are you in the wings?
LAURA   (*Answering offstage*)   I'm here, Buddy.
BUDDY   Essie, you old character actress, are you setting where you
ought to be, in place?
ESSIE   I'm setting.
BUDDY   Choir Director, you've got your pitch pipe?
CHOIR DIRECTOR   I got my pitch pipe.
BUDDY   Choir, are you ready to sing?
CHOIR   We're ready to sing!
BUDDY   Then, ladies and gentlemen—good folks and devils—the play
will begin. On this stage you'll see sin and salvation, me and God,
Beelzebub and Jehovah wrestling one more time. The old struggle
between sanctity and Satan, the Christians and the damned! The

damned, that's me. I never win—but I have a hell of a good time trying. And I'm generous. I'll even let the good church folks have a head start. Let's go! Come on! Sing, you Christians, sing!

(*Lights come up behind scrim to reveal the massed choir in a burst of song as they advance*)

CHOIR

If you've got a tambourine,
Shake it to the Glory of God.
Glory! Glory! Glory!
Shake it to the glory of God! . . . (etc.)

(*As the song ends and* CHOIR *exits,* ACT ONE *begins*)

# ACT ONE

## SCENE ONE

*A Harlem street on a night in spring.* ESSIE *has been evicted from her tenement room and her few belongings are piled on the curb. She is sitting on one of her suitcases as* PASSERS-BY *turn around to look at her plight. A* TEEN-AGER *stops.*

YOUTH   Lady, what happened to you?

ESSIE   Evicted, that's all.

YOUTH   Damn! Ain't that enough?

ESSIE   No need to use profanity, son.

YOUTH   Excuse me, ma'am. (*As he exits he turns*) But I still say, damn!

WOMAN   (*Stops and speaks kindly*) Poor soul! Even though it is May, it's not warm yet. I hope you don't have to sit out here all night.

ESSIE   I reckon God'll provide for me. My credit's run out.

WOMAN   Don't you have any relatives?

ESSIE   Not a soul in New York.

WOMAN   Not even a husband?

ESSIE   When I had one he warn't much good.

WOMAN   You can say that again! Neither was mine.
                (*She exits. Suddenly* ESSIE'S *face brightens as* LAURA *and* JOE, *a middle-aged man, enter slightly tipsy, with a wine bottle in a paper bag*)

ESSIE   Laura!

LAURA   What in God's name has happened to you?

ESSIE   Landlord finally put me out. But I warn't but three months behind on my rent.

LAURA   I'll move you back in.

ESSIE   You can't. The marshals put a padlock on my door.

LAURA   Bastards!

ESSIE   Laura!

LAURA   That's what they are. Joe Green, start lugging her things upstairs. Essie's my favorite neighbor. Treats me like a mother.

JOE   I didn't walk you all the way from Lenox Avenue to become a moving man, baby.

LAURA   Then be on your way, daddy! Thank you for the drinks you bought. Skeedaddle!

JOE   What? I thought we was gonna finish that bottle upstairs.

LAURA   You heard me! Beat it! And don't come back till pay day.

JOE   So that's the way you feel?

LAURA   That's the way I feel, chump. If you don't believe it— Essie, lend me that old knife you always keep in your pocket. (LAURA *reaches in* ESSIE'S *coat pocket herself and comes out with a pearl-handled switchblade*)

JOE   (*Steps back*) Woman, I ain't for no playing.

LAURA   Neither am I! Goodnight.

JOE   Don't look for another drink on me soon. (*He exits*)

LAURA   Aw, you'll be back. Cheapskate! Just because he buys me a bottle of wine ——

ESSIE   Laura, are you high again?

LAURA   Not high, just a little groovy, that's all. Essie, you can move in with me for the night. But, you know, I got too many boy friends to be having a permanent guest. I told you, you ought to get on Relief—like me. Else get yourself a man.

ESSIE   A man—to beat me all over the head? I'm old. I'm cranky. Besides, I'm disgusted with 'em. Lowdown no good men!

LAURA   (*Takes her bottle from the bag*) Here, take a taste of wine and get your spirits up.

ESSIE   No, thanks! I hate the stuff. Makes me sick at the stomach.

LAURA   You never do nothing but just set, like you're setting now— throwed out of your place, yet setting looking peaceful. Me, I'd be raising hell.

ESSIE   About all I can do, Laura, is ask the Lord to take my hand.

LAURA   Why don't you do that then? Get holy, sanctify yourself— since we're setting out here on the curb discussing ways and means. The Lord is no respecter of persons—if He takes the pimp's hand and makes a bishop out of him. You know Bishop Longjohn right over there on Lenox Avenue? That saint had three whores on the block ten years ago. He's got a better racket now—the gospel! And a rock and roll band in front of the pulpit.

ESSIE   Religion don't have to be a racket, Laura. Do it? Maybe he's converted.

LAURA   All the money he takes in every Sunday would convert me. Say, I got an idea! Why don't you and me start a church?

ESSIE   What denomination?

LAURA   Our *own*—then we won't be beholding to nobody else. You
know my grandpa was a jackleg preacher, so I can rock a church
as good as anybody.

ESSIE   Did you ever preach?

LAURA   No, but I've got the nerve to try. Let's start a church. Huh?

ESSIE   Where?

LAURA   On the street where the Bishop started his—outdoors—rent
free—on the corner.

ESSIE   You mean down here in the gutter where I am.

LAURA   On the curb—*above* the gutter. We'll save them lower down
than us.

ESSIE   Who could that be?

LAURA   The ones that do what you can't do—drink without getting
sick. Gamble away their rent. Cheat the Welfare Department—
more'n I do. Lay with each other without getting disgusted—no
matter how many unwanted kids they produce. Blow gauge, sup-
port the dope trade. Hustle. Them's the ones we'll set out to convert.

ESSIE   With what?

LAURA   The Lord Jesus—He comes free. Just look up at the Lord
above and the squares will think God is staring you dead in the face.
Dig? We'll make money's mammy!

ESSIE   It ain't that easy to make money. Lord knows, I tried all last
year to get enough money to send for my daughter. Marietta's sixteen and ain't been with me—her mama—not two years hand-
running since she was born. I always wanted that child with me.
Never had her. Laura, I were born to bad luck.

LAURA   Essie, raise your fat disgusted self up off that suitcase you're
setting on and let's go make our fortune saving souls. Remember
that white woman, that Aimee Semple McPherson what put herself
on some wings, opened up a temple, and made a million dollars?
Girl, we'll call ourselves sisters—use my name—the Reed Sisters—
even if we ain't no relation—sisters in God. I preach and you sing.
We'll let the sinners in the gutter come to us. Listen to my spiel.
I can whoop and holler real good. (*She mounts a pile of furniture
imagining herself a preacher*) I'll tell them Lenox Avenue sinners:
You all better come to Jesus! The atom bomb's about to destroy
this world and you ain't ready. Get ready! Get ready!

> Lord above, I am lost
> I have strayed from the cross
> And I cry, Yes, I cry, save me now!

ESSIE

>Lord above, hear my plea
>And from sin set me free.
>Fill my heart with righteousness right now!

BOTH

>Lord above, you I seek
>And I pray, humble, meek,
>That you'll help me on my way.
>Lord above, let your light
>Be my guide through the night.
>Hear, oh, hear me, Lord, as I pray.

LAURA  Step right up, join us, all you hellions of sin! Join our gospel band and live in grace. (*Descends from pile of furniture*) Essie, broke as we are, we *better* start a church.

ESSIE  But with what, Laura?

LAURA  Whilst taking my afternoon nap, today, I dreampt about fish. I'm gonna look *fish* up in my Dream Book. I think it's 782 and that's a good number. Lend me fifty cents so I can put it in early tomorrow morning.

ESSIE  Girl, you need to be thinking about praying, not playing. Here, I ain't got but a quarter.

LAURA  If 782 comes out, I'll put half of what I win down on a Bible.

ESSIE  We'll buy no Bibles with ill-gotten gains.

LAURA  Well, then, they got Bibles in the credit store for $18.50, $2 down. With a Bible you can read God's word—and with God's word you can save souls. Let's get a Bible on credit.

ESSIE  I'm kinder lacking in credit, honey.

LAURA  Then you tell me, with what are we gonna found our church?

ESSIE  (*Suddenly rises, looking upward*) With faith! And I mean that! Right now, tonight! Laura, I just got a vision. A voice tells me to take you up on this—and try to save *you*, too.

LAURA  What? . . . Essie . . .

>(*As* LAURA *stares in amazement,* ESSIE, *her face flooded with radiance, mounts her pile of furniture and sings*)

ESSIE

>Upon this rock I build my church.
>The gates of hell shall not prevail.
>Upon this rock I build my church.
>With strength from God I shall not fail.
>(ESSIE *snatches* LAURA'S *wine bottle and throws it away.* LAURA, *falling into the spirit of the thing, cries out dramatically*)

LAURA

    The call has come and I have heard!

BOTH

    The Gates of hell shall not prevail!

ESSIE

    I shall not doubt His holy word.

BOTH

    With strength from God I shall not fail.
    (*Gradually as they sing, windows open and heads pop out.
    Two or three* PASSERS-BY *stop to watch and listen. Then
    a few more gather on the street*)

BOTH

    I say, oh yes, I build my church.
    The gates of hell shall not prevail.
    Upon this rock I build my church.
    In God's own grace, I shall not fail.

LAURA

    Upon this rock I build my church.
    I shall not walk the devil's way.

ESSIE

    Upon this rock I build my church.
    God's blessed hand will guide my way.
    (*The* PASSERS-BY *cry approval and join in their song. The
    street is filled with music*)

CROWD    Amen! Hallelujah! Bless God! Yes! Amen! Amen!
    I say, oh, yes! I build my church!
    The gates of hell shall not prevail.
    Upon this rock I build my church!
    In God's own grace, I shall not fail!
    (*The light fades to pinpoint* ESSIE *alone upon her pile of
    furniture ecstatic*)
    In God's own grace, I shall not fail!
    In God's own grace, I shall . . . not . . . fail!

    BLACKOUT

MUSICAL BRIDGE:

    *Continuation of* CROWD *singing* "Upon this Rock" *into
    next scene.*

## SCENE TWO

*A Lenox Avenue Corner. Evening in late summer. There is a grocery store, and next to it a cleaners with a sign:*
WE SPECIALIZE IN REMOVING STAINS: GREASE, PAINT, INK, BLOOD, NAIL POLISH. ONE DAY SERVICE. *Auto horns honk and sirens scream.* STROLLERS *pass. Before the lights come up, we hear the shaking of a tambourine and a guitar playing softly as the song, "Upon This Rock," continues. A young man,* C. J., *sits on a camp stool with his guitar. On a second stool rests an enormous gilt-edged Bible. Some* FOLKS *stand talking at one side as* ESSIE *finishes her prayer which* LAURA *punctuates with loud Amens as the* CROWD *hums "Upon this Rock."*

CROWD   Upon this rock . . . umm-umm-umm . . . (etc.)

ESSIE   . . . Grant us your grace, Jesus! Fill us with Thy word, Lord, and bless this corner on which we, Your humble servants, stand tonight. Hear us, Lord, I pray Thee! Amen!

LAURA   We got to get an audience, Essie. Ain't nobody paying you no attention. (*She shakes her tambourine violently*) Hallelujah! Bless God! Amen! Hey, you talking over there, come here! I say, come here! I got something to say to you.

YOUTH   Well, if you say so, ma'am—but after all, our conversation was private.

LAURA   Son, mine is for the world. Come here and hear me. (A TEEN-AGE BOY *blowing a mouth organ dances by*) Hey, you, boy! Stop rocking and rolling and listen to me.

BOY   Aw, lady, hush!

LAURA   (*Points at a* LOITERER *against a post*) And you, too. (*And at still* ANOTHER) You're a sinner, too! We're all sinners out here on this corner this evening.

ESSIE   Sinners! Sinners! Sinners!

LAURA   Yes, you sinners, I say, *Stop!* Stop in your tracks now and listen to my words. (*As she speaks gradually a* CROWD *gathers*) Lemme tell you how I got the call. It was one night last spring with Sister Essie here, right on the street, I saw a flash, I heard a roll of thunder, I felt a breeze and I seen a light and a voice exploding out of heaven cried, "Laura Wright Reed," it said, "Take up the Cross and follow Me!" Oh, yes, that voice said, told me to come out on this corner tonight and save you! You young man laughing and about to pass on by. Stop! Stop and listen to my word. " Take up the Cross," it said, " and follow Me. Go out into the highways and byways and save souls. Go to the curbstones and gutters," it said, " rescue the lost. Approach," I was told, " approach the river of sin and pull out the drowning." Oh, I were drowning, brothers and sisters, just like you, until I got saved. I were down there too, in sin's gutter, lower than a snake's belly—now look at me up here on the curbstone of life reaching out to you to come and be saved.

ESSIE   Come and accept His salvation. Come, come!

LAURA   Yes, because time is a candle—and everybody's burning time. Don't let your candle burn down before your soul gets right. Time is your electric light bill. Everybody is burning lights. Pay your bill before your lights is turned off and your soul left in darkness.

ESSIE   Pay your bill! Pay your bill!

LAURA   Sinner, don't let your lights go out before your soul gets right. I'm gonna pay my bill tomorrow, yes! And you pay yours—take care of Con Edison. But let your soul get right tonight . . . Listen to Sister and me, folks, listen. We're the Reed Sisters, friends. Our Church is this corner—our roof is God's sky—there is no doors. No place in our church not open to you, because there is no doors. Everybody's welcome, black, green, grizzly, and gray, because there is no doors. Speak Spanish, speak English, speak Pig-Latin, join with us because there is no doors. So come, be one with Sister Essie and me, one with God, and be saved. Babes and boys, draw nigh! Men and women, come! Approach! Children, stand near! Young and old, everybody, drop a nickel, dime, quarter in this tambourine as we sing:

> Lord above, look you down
> On this poor soul who's found
> No help, no friends on the way.

Sing, Sister Essie, while I pass this tambourine.

CROWD

> Lord above, let your light
> Be a guide through the night.
> Hear me, hear me, Lord, as I pray.

LAURA   Everybody! Sing with us as you put your contributions in our tambourine. Better than in some juke box for the devil to get.

CROWD

> Lord above, I was lost
> I have strayed from the cross.

And I cry, yes, I cry, save me now.
Lord above, hear my plea.
And from sin set me free.
Fill my heart with righteousness right now.
(*As* CROWD *hums a verse,* LAURA *shakes her tambourine before a* MAN *who does not seem inclined to put his hand in his pocket*)

LAURA  Brother you can't get saved for nothing.
(*Embarrassed, the* MAN *drops a coin in as the* CROWD *continues singing*)

ESSIE  The Lord thanks you.

LAURA  And I do, too. Everybody help me stay on the right road. Put your money here. Help in the Lord's work. (*Almost* EVERY-ONE *in the Crowd contributes as* LAURA *moves among them*) That's right, Sister! . . . Thank you, folks! . . . Thanks, honey! . . . Thank you, sir! Good child, good, give your pennies for Jesus! "Suffer little children to come unto me."

ESSIE  Amen! Amen!
(C. J. *leads the* CROWD *in a verse of the song sung softly as* LAURA *speaks*)

LAURA  Hear that beautiful guitar, folks, to warm our hearts this evening! The Lord sent C. J. to us! Last week this young man stepped right out of the crowd on this corner and began playing the gospels, making up his own songs, not rocking and rolling in sin!

ESSIE  Amen! Thank God! Folks, lemme tell you—
Upon this rock I build my church.

CROWD

The gates of hell shall not prevail.
Upon this rock I build my church.
With strength from God I shall not fail . . .
(*Singing continues softly under dialogue as a* POLICEMAN *saunters up to* LAURA *swinging his billy*)

COP  Say, listen, you women . . .

LAURA  I'll see you later, Mister Law. Let us sing God's songs.
(*Aside,* LAURA *whispers*) Don't worry, man, just be cool. Be cool.
(*The* COP *stands aside until the verse ends.* ESSIE *and the* CROWD *continue to hum chorus after chorus as* LAURA *comes over to the* POLICEMAN *away from the* CROWD)

COP  How about it?

LAURA  As long as you let us get ours, baby, you'll get yours. (LAURA *slips a greenback to the* COP)

COP   You gals really ought to get a license to sing on the street every night.

LAURA   We're getting money. Don't that do you?

COP   That does me. But the big brass downtown——

LAURA   Aw, they can be had, too, can't they?

COP   Not for ten bucks. So, divvy.

(*The* COP *puts out his hand again but from the edge of the* CROWD *a solidly built, good-looking* YOUNG MAN *appears casually at his side*)

BUDDY   Say, Copper, let's take this thing step by step. The big brass ——

COP   (*Growling at the intruder*)   What? Who in the hell are you?

BUDDY   (*Jerks his head toward the next corner, as if someone of importance is standing there. He lowers his voice*)   I work for Marty. (*Immediately the* COP *calms down*)

COP   Oh, I see. Well, let's keep this thing friendly—between the three of us. Go ahead with your singing, Sister.

CROWD
> Upon this rock I build my church.
> I shall not walk the devil's way.
> Upon this rock I build my church.
> His blessed hand will guide my way.

(*The* POLICEMAN *walks away to exit.* LAURA *looks at the strange young man in astonishment*)

LAURA   Won't you come and join our meeting?

BUDDY   Don't worry about me. I'll be around when the fun is done.

LAURA   I beg your pardon?

BUDDY   I mean when the services are over. You go ahead back to your chores.

LAURA   Excuse me, then—for the moment. (LAURA *returns to the* CROWD *as* BUDDY *backs away into the shadows*) Ah, folks, miracles do happen! It's God's doing, so help me stay in His footsteps. When I pass this tambourine again, put a dime, a quarter, a dollar in.

(*A wrinkled little* OLD WOMAN *in the crowd speaks up*)

BIRDIE   I done put a dollar in once tonight. Now, I wants to testify.

ESSIE   Speak, Sister, speak!

BIRDIE   I done put a dollar in once tonight. Now, I wants to testify. backslid, backslid, backslid! Well, tonight I'm coming home—for which, Sister Essie I thank you! Sister Laura, I thank you, too! And this evening I'll tell the world, I makes my determination to stay on God's side from here on in—I mean to the Kingdom. *I've got a*

*hold of God, and I'm gonna hold my holt.* Sister Laura, lend me
your tambourine. Lemme shake it a mite to His glory—because I'm
a sinner determined to be a saint. I'm gonna join up with you all
in your holy work—now—and sing and shout out here on God's
corner till winter comes, and nobody's gonna stop me, because I
intends to be in that number when the saints go marching in. (*She
lifts her tambourine and her voice*)
> Oh, when the saints go marching in!
> When the saints go marching in.
> I want to be in that number
> When the saints go maching in . . . (etc.)

> (BIRDIE LEE *and* ESSIE *shake their tambourines to* LAURA'S
> *exasperation and jealousy. As a wave of song sweeps over
> the* CROWD, *she withdraws frowning from the circle and
> finds herself standing beside the handsome, brownskin,
> solidly built* YOUNG MAN. CROWD *hums* "Saints" *as
> they talk*)

BUDDY Don't worry about that little old dried-up singing lady, baby.

LAURA What?

BUDDY She can't steal your thunder. You're still the *most* on this
corner. You send me, Sister.

LAURA And who might you be?

BUDDY Buddy—Buddy Lomax—Big-Eyed Buddy. (*The music rises
again to drown the conversation between* LAURA *and* BUDDY *but it is
obvious he is making a play for her, and she is enjoying it*)

LAURA Big-Eyed Buddy, I thank you for your favor. Have I observed
you at services before?

BUDDY I've observed *you*. How about a little refreshments when you
get through tonight?

LAURA A drink?

BUDDY You're my kind of woman. I'll be leaning on the mailbox
yonder when your work is done.

CROWD Oh, when the saints go marching in! . . . (etc.)

> (LAURA *prances ecstatically back into the circle, snatches
> the tambourine from* BIRDIE LEE *and joins loudly in singing
> herself, soon bringing the song to a close*)

LAURA And now, friends, that is all for this evening. Goodnight!
God bless everyone.

> (LAURA *looks toward the corner to see if* BUDDY *is still
> there. He is coolly smoking a cigarette, his elbow resting
> on the mailbox. The* CROWD *begins to break up*)

ESSIE   Laura, you ended mighty short this evening. Are we through?

LAURA   Girl, I got business to attend to. Collection is took. Let's go.

ESSIE   I hates to just run off in a hurry. Sometimes peoples like to talk to me—they think I can help them.

LAURA   Maybe you *can* help them, but why bother tonight? We've helped ourselves.

ESSIE   Laura!

LAURA   Don't look so shocked. You're out here hustling just like I am—in God's name. (LAURA *transfers the greenbacks from the tambourine to her bosom, pours the coins into a bag and calls to the* GUITARIST *who is putting his instrument in its case*) C. J., help Sister Essie carry her Bible home.

C.J.    I will, Sister Laura. (C.J. *folds the camp stools and picks up Bible*)

LAURA   Essie, you carry the rest of the money home, except for these few bills I might need. Don't let nobody rob you on the way upstairs.

ESSIE   I got the same knife in my pocket I been had for twenty years, so I don't worry about being robbed, Laura. I worry about what we're doing, taking so much of these poor souls' money.

LAURA   As soon as we start doing right by us, you start worring about doing wrong. Essie, is your wig gone?

ESSIE   Laura, I'm going home and pray.

(LAURA *shrugs as* ESSIE *and* C.J. *exit.* LAURA *turns.* BUDDY *is coming halfway to meet her. Together they exit arm in arm as* BUDDY *gives his devil's cackle. There is a blare of night club music as the light fades*)

BUDDY   Ha! Ha!... Ha!...


BLACKOUT


MUSICAL BRIDGE:

A jazz piano plays " Scat, Cat! " *very loud and lively. Before the curtain* JITTERBUG DANCERS *cavort, merging as the curtain rises into the next scene.*

## SCENE THREE

*The Roamer Club whose motto on the wall is:*
WHEN YOU ROAM AWAY FROM HOME, ROAMER'S IS
THE PLACE TO ROAM.
*There is a small bar, a piano, booths, and a cozy atmosphere.*
*It is midnight and a* TRIO *of* GIRLS *about the piano are*
*finishing a scat song as* BUDDY *and* LAURA *enter and head*
*for a booth.*

TRIO

Skee-daddle-dee-dee-dee!
Skee-daddle-dee-dow!
Ha-ha-ha—ha-ha!
Let's scat it now!
Skee-daddle-dee—da-da!
Lee-lee-lee-lee—lee!
Hey-hey-hey-hey—hey-hey!
Aw, scat with me!

GLORIA

Oooo-ooo-oo-o——ya-koo!
Bee-ba-ba-bee—be-be—Boo!
Scat, cat! Scat, cat! Scat!
Skee-daddle-dee-dee dee!
Lay—lay-lay-lay—lay!
La—la-la—la-la!
Oh, scat today! Today! Today!
(*Applause as* GLORIA *rushes up to* BUDDY *effusively*)

GLORIA  Buddy! Welcome! Haven't seen you for a week, Kid Big-
Eyes.
BUDDY  I been around.
GLORIA  At Sugar Ray's maybe, the Shalimar, but not here.
BUDDY  I can't spend my life with you chicks. Laura, meet Gloria.
GLORIA  Hello, Laura.
LAURA  I'm Laura Reed.
BUDDY  Sister Laura. She can sing, too, believe you me.
LAURA  I'm a gospel singer.
GLORIA  Oh, I just love gospel songs. I grew up in the church.
LAURA  So did we all—but sometimes we stray.

BUDDY   Gloria's a stray—but we'll get her back. Heh, Laura? Come
on, let's sit down. What are you drinking?
  (GLORIA *joins some of the other* GIRLS *and* FELLOWS *as the*
  BARMAN *comes to serve* BUDDY)
LAURA   Vat 69.
BUDDY   (*Puts one hand on* LAURA'S *across the table*)   What chaser?
LAURA   Ginger ale.
BUDDY   Only squares drink ginger ale with scotch, sugar.
LAURA   Oh! I just lately turned to whisky.
BUDDY   Two scotch and sodas, waiter.
BARMAN   Okey dokey, Big Eye.
LAURA   Everybody seems to know your name.
BUDDY   I get around—like I make the scene. Everybody's gonna know
*your* name in a little while, too. You've got something on the ball—
what I'd call personality.
LAURA   Aw, Buddy! (*This time* LAURA *puts her hand on his*)
BUDDY   You're forty!
LAURA   What? (*For a moment* LAURA *looks startled*)
BUDDY   You know, forty means fine, O.K., great. And you're great
with me.
  (*They kiss. The music starts and among those rising is*
  GLORIA, *who addresses* BUDDY *as she dances by*)
GLORIA   You all are not dancing?
BUDDY   (*Frowns and answers abruptly*)   No, but I see you are.
LAURA   Why do you look at Gloria that way?
BUDDY   Oh, I just like to look at a good-looking chick. But you're
the most.
LAURA   Guess I'll have to get me a spangled gown to put on, too.
BUDDY   Baby, you'll have everything in due time—spangled gowns,
diamonds, ermine coats. We gonna get there.
LAURA   We—?
BUDDY   Sure! I'm gonna help you. Listen. You want to know how to
make some money out of this religious jive?
LAURA   I'm making money.
BUDDY   I mean a lot, baby, not peanuts.
LAURA   How?
BUDDY   I guess you know with cold weather coming, you have to get
off the street or freeze your knees. Your crowd's getting too big
anyhow. You got to get a church.
LAURA   A church?
BUDDY   A store front, or something, to start with.

LAURA  You know how hard it is to rent anything in Harlem.

BUDDY  Marty can fix that.

LAURA  Who's Marty?

BUDDY  Shss-ss-s! Once you got your own place, you can do anything —sell Holy Water from the Jordan, for instance.

LAURA  The Jordan? That's across the ocean, ain't it? How much does imported water cost?

BUDDY  Imported? Turn on the tap, that's all. For little or nothing I can get you a hundred gross of empty bottles with labels on them— HOLY WATER—a green river and some palms, you know, about the size of a dime store Listerine. Just take them to the sink.

LAURA  You mean the water ain't really holy?

BUDDY  It's holy if you bless it, Sister Laura.

LAURA  (*Laughs*)  Holy if *I* bless it—ha-ha! Ain't that a gas! How much would I sell it for?

BUDDY  A dollar a bottle. The bottle and the label cost about two cents. The water's free. Figure the profit? See a Cadillac by Christmas? Humm-mm-m! (BUDDY *takes a long look at* LAURA) Baby, you're built—no false brassieres.

LAURA  Thank the Lord, He made me a high-breasted woman.

BUDDY  I'll say He did! A good-looking chick like you should be riding on rubber. You don't have to go to bed early, do you?

LAURA  What I really want is an apartment, Buddy.

BUDDY  I'll call up Marty.

LAURA  Just who *is* Marty?

BUDDY  The fixer—the man behind the men behind the men. He can get you anything.

LAURA  Is he colored?

BUDDY  You know he *can't* be colored.

GLORIA  Ladies and Gentlemen, this number is especially for Big-Eyed Buddy and the lady he is escorting this evening who is, I understand, an old gospel songstress.

> Oh, hand me down, hand me down,
> Hand me down my silver trumpet, Gabriel,
> Hand it down, throw it down,
> Any old way to get it down
> Hand me down my silver trumpet, Lord!
> I haven't been to heaven but I've been told
> Hand me down my silver trumpet, Gabriel,
> That the gates are pearl and the streets are gold.
> Hand me down my silver trumpet, Lord.

Oh, hand me down, hand me down.
Hand me down my walking cane, Gabriel,
Hand it down, throw it down,
Any old way to get it down
Hand me down my walking cane, Lord.
("Walking Cane" *refrain repeated by the* TRIO *as* GLORIA
*does a dancing strut. Applause. Bows. Then the* PIANIST
*begins to play the* "New York Blues" *for general dancing*)

BUDDY    Baby, are we together?
LAURA    Daddy, we *are* together!
BUDDY    Then let's demonstrate.
(BUDDY *rises, pulls* LAURA *up, and the two dance slowly*)
LAURA    You're holding me so tight, you're hurting me.
BUDDY    But it hurts so good, don't it, kid?
LAURA    You're strong! . . . Buddy, something's happening to me.
BUDDY    Something's happening to me, too, baby.
LAURA    Do you think it could be the same thing?
BUDDY    Could be! But you've got to tell me what's on your mind.
LAURA    Couldn't we sit down?
BUDDY    Sure. (*Music dies as they go to their table*) What's happening?
LAURA    Listen, I don't want you to think it's my likker talking, Buddy,
but—let's get out of here. I want to sing just to you.
When you hold me in your arms
All other arms I ever knew I just forget.
BUDDY    Give her a little backing there, piano man, to waft us on
our way.
(*The* PIANIST *picks up the melody as the lights fade, the
scrim falls, and a spot picks up* BUDDY *and* LAURA *in the
street*)


## SCENE FOUR

*Shadows of a Harlem Street. Very close to* BUDDY, LAURA
*looks up into his eyes as she sings.*

LAURA

I say, when you hold me in your arms,
All other arms I ever knew, I just forget.
When I look into your eyes

Somehow I know, I just know that's it.
I know yesterday is gone
And tomorrow is a brand new day
Put those mean old blues in pawn
Lover, love is on the way!
Oh, what blessings to receive!
Oh, what joy I know is mine!
Forever and always I'll believe
Love is waiting down the line.
So glad stormy weather's gone.
We'll make tomorrow bright and gay.
My heart sings to a new dawn.
Lover, love is on the way!
All my loneliness is gone
And happiness has come to stay,
Put those mean old blues in pawn—
Lover, love is on the way.
(*They dance down the street together as the melody continues in up tempo.* BUDDY *turns his head to whisper an aside to the world as they exit*)

BUDDY   She don't know she's with the devil. Ha! Ha! . . .

BLACKOUT

MUSICAL BRIDGE

*Two* VOICES *are heard humming* "Upon This Rock" *behind the scrim.*

## SCENE FIVE

*The interior of a store-front church with, behind the rostrum, a large mural of the Garden of Eden in which a brownskin Adam strongly resembles Joe Louis and Eve looks just like a chocolate Sarah Vaughn. Only the Devil is white. At a small table in front of the rostrum on which rests the collection tambourines, sits* ESSIE *in her ministerial robe of black, a ledger before her. A gray-haired man,* BROTHER BUD, *is putting the front row of folding chairs away as he sings and* ESSIE *hums behind him.*

BUD
Upon this rock we build our church.
The gates of hell shall not prevail.
Upon this rock we build our church
With strength from God we shall not fail
Upon this rock we build our church.
The devil's wrath shall not avail.
On solid rock we build our church.
In God's sweet grace, I shall not fail.
Um-ummm-um-um! Um-ummmm-ummm-umm-um! . . .

ESSIE   Our little church is certainly growing, Brother Bud. All these extra chairs tonight.

BUD   Busting out at the seams—and it ain't been a month since we come with our mops and pails to clean and fix-up this old place.

ESSIE   Birdie Lee sure was a help. That little woman can scrub!

BUD   That soul's got spirit—when it comes to slinging water.

ESSIE   A willing worker!

(BROTHER BUD *continues to sing until* LAURA *enters and shoos him out*)

LAURA   Listen, we're trying to have a meeting of the Board of Trustees, Brother Bud. This is it. I'm Secretary, Essie's Treasurer.

ESSIE   And God is President.

LAURA   Now, what's your mission?

BUD   I kind of stuck around to see if you can help me. My wife is sick, I'm out of work, and my grandchildren is hungry.

(ESSIE *immediately puts her hand in her tote-bag*)

LAURA   Essie! . . . Brother Bud, Jesus will help you.

BUD   He don't come to earth very often.

ESSIE   Meanwhile, here, brother, here!

(ESSIE *hands him some money.* LAURA *shrugs*)

BUD   Thank you, Sister Essie! Thank God! And bless you both! (*He exits*)

LAURA   Let's go on with the meeting. Now, as you were saying——
(LAURA *flings one shapely leg over the arm of her chair and we see that she is wearing toreador pants beneath her churchly robe. As she turns, she glances at the mural behind her*) Just look at Joe Louis peeping out from behind that bush—Adam. That artist sure painted us a pretty Garden of Eden. I told him to make Eve look just like Sarah Vaughn—and he did.

ESSIE   Who told him to make the Devil white?

LAURA   Me—also to put a real diamond in the snake's head.

ESSIE   That snake should've been named Buddy.

LAURA   All right, Essie! Come on, let's hear the Treasurer's report.

ESSIE   I got two thousand dollars in my spice jar in the cupboard at home which I think we better take to the bank. Who'd ever thought you and me would be banking money?

LAURA   I've made another payment on my mink coat—gonna get it out for Christmas.

ESSIE   You deserves a nice Christmas present, Laura. But I wonder will I have my daughter with me by then?

LAURA   You said you wanted a nice place to bring Marietta to. Essie, suppose we take this two thousand dollars and move, instead of putting it in the bank?

ESSIE   No. Laura. The church needs a nest egg. We'll put it away.

LAURA   O.K., as you say. I'm happy—I got my man to keep me warm. Let's get done with this business so——(*There is a sound of a door slamming and a* WOMAN'S VOICE *is heard.* BIRDIE LEE *enters*) Uh-oh! Another worriation!

BIRDIE   My goodness! It sure is snowing. Sisters, I just can't walk another step without going to the bathroom. I was passing by and seed the lights still on. You know, I drunk so much beer when I was a sinner I'm still going to the bathroom, now that I'm a saint.

(LAURA *frowns,* ESSIE *smiles, as* BIRDIE LEE *rushes to a sign pointing to Rest Rooms*)

LAURA   Can we finish our Treasurer's report?

ESSIE   To printer, $22.55, for new Sunday School cards, with black angels.

LAURA   I second everything black.

ESSIE   New tambourines—the old ones wore out—$17.50.

LAURA   We really work them tambourines.

ESSIE   To ward boss, $50, to keep from putting in fire extinguishers.

LAURA   That bald-headed politicianer!

ESSIE   And to C. J. for guitar strings, $1.00. Loan also to C. J. $44.00 for his schooling.

LAURA   All right, bleeding heart! What else? I wish you'd get yourself some new clothes.

(BIRDIE LEE *re-enters to cross toward exit*)

BIRDIE   Bless God! I guess I'll try and make it home now. Services sure were fine this evening. See you tomorrow. Hold your holt! (BIRDIE *exits*)

ESSIE   Good night, Birdie! Oh, but there's so much our church can do in Harlem—make a playground for the neighborhood kids, establish an employment office, set up a day nursery for children of mothers what works. I'll get me some new clothes in due time. But first I wants to make our church a *good* church, Laura. The needs is so big up here in Harlem, we have to do all we can, me and you—and you're God's handmaiden, even if you don't always act like a holy maiden do.

LAURA    Just how does a holy maiden act?

ESSIE    They be's not so bold with their sinning.

LAURA    There you go! Buddy again: (LAURA *rises and removes her robe*) I might convert that stud yet, who knows?

ESSIE    Looks like he's converting you—to sin—selling Holy Water from the sink.

LAURA    *I am*—as soon as the bottles come.

ESSIE    You'll never fill them from my faucet.

LAURA    I got a sink in my room. And I sure hope Buddy's there when I get home tonight.

ESSIE    You gave him a key?

LAURA    Of course! That locksmith around the corner's made so many keys to my keyhole he ought to know the shape of it by heart.

ESSIE    That's no way for a lady minister to do. And I don't like that holy water neither.

LAURA    Well, if you don't like it, just walk off the rostrum, go pray in the anteroom, but leave me be. I'm gonna live fine, and look fine.

ESSIE    Laura, one of these days the Spirit is going to strike vanity from your heart, lust from your body, and——

LAURA    And make me as stupid as you are, heh? Without an idea in your head until I put one there! Without me you'd still be on relief. Yet you want to cramp my style. Well, you won't. I'll tell you now, Essie, I'm getting a fur coat, a Cadillac, and buying a hi-fi set—for Buddy.

ESSIE    Do Jesus! All of that out of this poor little church!

LAURA    Poor? Running five nights a week and taking in two hundred dollars a night? Overflowing! We gonna have to move soon. All these old theatres in Harlem they're turning into churches. Maybe Marty can rent us one.

ESSIE    Marty? Who's Marty?

LAURA    Whoever he is, you'd think he was the devil—and Buddy his shadow in the form of a snake. Well, I'm not afraid of devils myself. I've wrestled with them all my life—and some devils have got diamonds in their heads. Look! My idea! (LAURA *switches out the lights. In the mural of the Garden of Eden the diamond in the snake's head glows brilliantly*) It was my idea to buy that light bulb in the wall behind that snake. My idea to paint black saints. Everything people are talking about around here was my idea. But what do you do? Criticize, criticize, criticize! Come on, Trustees' meeting is over, let's get the hell out of here. (*But* ESSIE, *head in hands, begins to cry.* LAURA *pauses, turns, regrets her anger, then comes back*) Essie, I'm sorry I blew my top. Look! Give away as much of that money as you want, lend it out, put that two thousand in the bank for the church, like you said. We'll take up more collections next week, and week after. If they're as big as they were this week, you take next week's money and send for your daughter. (LAURA *puts her arm about* ESSIE'S *shoulders*) Essie, I want you to have something, too, out of this deal.

> (ESSIE'S *sobs are like a prayer as the diamond in the serpent's head glitters in the darkness*)

ESSIE    My God! . . . Oh, my God, Laura! My God!
> (*Raucous jazz is heard on a hi-fi set far away*)

BLACKOUT

MUSICAL BRIDGE:
> *Modern jazz.*

## SCENE SIX

> *Living room of an expensively furnished apartment, rather on the showy side, but* ESSIE'S *large old-fashioned motto:* GOD BLESS OUR HOME *on the wall. There is a glowing electric cross in the panel between the two windows.* BUDDY *reclines on a long silken lounge reading "Playboy" and listening to jazz on the hi-fi.* LAURA *enters in a stylish negligee, trailing perfume. From behind, she puts her arms around* BUDDY *and caresses him.*

BUDDY    Relax, woman, and let me listen to these fine sounds.
LAURA    Big-eyed Buddy! You sweet old joker, you!
BUDDY    Stop calling me them cute names—I'm no poodle puppy. Grrr-rr-r! (*Growling, he pulls her toward him and bites her sharply on the neck*)

LAURA   Oh, Don't bite so hard, Buddy!
BUDDY   Tastes good, baby.
LAURA   Tom cat! Billy goat! You big brown bar stud!
BUDDY   All right now, Laura! Don't get me roused up *again* this
early in the evening.
LAURA   Chocolate daddy with coconut eyes! Want a little Scotch?
BUDDY   (*Shaking his head*)   No.
LAURA   I do. Say, I love that old theatre we moved into! No more
store fronts, thanks to you—and Marty.
BUDDY   Um-hum!
LAURA   I love my name up on the canopy—THE REED SISTERS TAM-
BOURINE TEMPLE—in lights where it used to say: *Lana Turner.*
BUDDY   You look good up on the stage, baby——
LAURA   Rostrum, honey.
         (LAURA *laughs, pours herself a drink and returns to Buddy*
         *on the sofa as the record on the hi-fi runs out*)
BUDDY   This church racket's got show business beat to hell. But some
churches don't have sense enough to be crooked. They really try to
be holy—and holiness don't make money. By the way, baby, I
could do with a little change myself tonight. I might take a hand of
stud at Shoofly's. How about table stakes?
LAURA   Table stakes?
BUDDY   Say, fifty simoleons.
LAURA   Aw, honey! That's a lot to gamble away.
BUDDY   I can't sleep here tonight, so Essie informs me, with that young
girl coming. Something tells me that kid's going to be in our way,
Laura.
LAURA   Essie's daughter is no kid, Buddy. She's sixteen.
BUDDY   Sweet sixteen—but I expect she's *been* kissed.
LAURA   Wonder if the girl'll get off the bus hungry?
BUDDY   I don't know about that girl, but me, I could give a steak
hell right now—I like them rare, with the blood oozing out.
LAURA   They ought to be here soon, then me and Essie'll fix dinner.
I told her to bring in some groceries. Meanwhile, I better get
decent and put on a dress, heh? Also put this likker away (LAURA
*takes glass from* BUDDY) That child might think something. After
all, I'm gonna be her " Aunt Laura " so no bad examples the first day.
BUDDY   Do I look like a bad example?
         (BUDDY *slaps* LAURA *resoundingly on the fanny as he pulls*
         *her down on the couch*)

LAURA  Ouch!

BUDDY  The hot half of the Reed Sisters!

LAURA  If I'm the body, Essie's the soul.

BUDDY  And I'm your stick man—with the extra dice up my sleeve. Holy Water from the Jordan at a buck a bottle! How simple can people get. Always looking for some kind of lucky stuff. I depend on myself, myself.

LAURA  Me too, Buddy.

BUDDY  Marty gave me a new idea the other day for you.

LAURA  What?

BUDDY  Numbers.

LAURA  Numbers? We can't play no numbers in the church.

BUDDY  Not play 'em, baby. No gambling. Just pronounce 'em.

LAURA  Pronounce them?

BUDDY  Give 'em out in service. You know, you all got a mighty big theatre now——

LAURA  Church.

BUDDY  Church there to fill. Let the word get around that you give out lucky numbers every Sunday—and it will be packed and jammed —Holy hymns from the pulpit of Bible texts with three numbers, that's all, and let people write them numbers down.

LAURA  Buddy, you got an idea!

(*She kisses him square on the mouth then offers him a puff from her cigarette*)

BUDDY  Marty's idea. His syndicate backs the biggest numbers bank in Manhattan.

LAURA  Lucky Texts! Each time I give out a text, I'll pass the tambourines for a quarter.

BUDDY  We'll add a few more hundreds to the bank account every week. And the government can't tax that church money.

LAURA  Amen!

BUDDY  Amen is right, baby. I want you to get me a red Cadillac— sport model—convertible.

LAURA  Ain't one Cadillac in the family enough?

BUDDY  You know I got a birthday next month.

LAURA  Well, maybe—but there's one little thing you could do for me, too.

BUDDY  What's that?

LAURA  Join the church.

BUDDY  Aw, there you go *again*!

LAURA  But, honey, you're in and out of the temple so much, lots of the saints are wondering how come you don't belong—why you're not converted.

BUDDY  Well, since nothing exciting happens in the middle of the week, I'll get converted next Wednesday.

LAURA  That might cool Essie down a little, she still thinks you're Satan. But listen, Daddy, after you get converted, don't go getting *too* holy. Just keep on being nice to me.

BUDDY  Don't give me no *do's* and *don'ts*! I know how far to go, up, down, right, left, or in between.

(VOICES *are heard in the hall.* LAURA *runs to hide glasses and whisky in the cabinet*)

LAURA  Oh, here comes Essie. I'm gonna run and change.

(LAURA *hurries off to exit, leaving* BUDDY *on the couch as* ESSIE *enters with a valise and a very pretty* GIRL)

ESSIE  Why, good evening! I didn't know you'd still be here, Buddy. Marietta, this is Mr. Lomax.

BUDDY  Pleased to know you, Marietta. Essie, you've got a be-*ooo*-ti-ful daughter!

ESSIE  I'm blessed, Buddy.

(BUDDY *holds* MARIETTA'S *hand longer than necessary, squeezing it tightly until she jerks away*)

MARIETTA  Oh, that hurts!

BUDDY  Just my way of welcoming you to Harlem. Hope you like it.

MARIETTA  Mama, it's so pretty in here! Oh, Mama, what a nice place, so modernistic. And a lighted cross on the wall!

ESSIE  We're all blessed, honey! But just wait till you see our new church. All of this is the Lord's own miracle, Marietta. Laura, where are you?

LAURA  I'm coming, Essie, coming. (LAURA *enters freshly dressed*) Child, I'm your Aunt Laura.

ESSIE  Marietta, this is my old friend, who's stuck by me through thick and thin.

LAURA  I'm glad you're here, Marietta, so glad! This is your home. (LAURA *embraces* MARIETTA)

ESSIE  Thank God! I just thank God for all.

BUDDY  God—and your tambourines! Marietta, can you play a tambourine?

MARIETTA  I used to try sometimes in church down home.

BUDDY  Then you'll fit.

MARIETTA  Are you in the choir?

BUDDY  No, baby, I'm just a backstage man.

LAURA  Buddy, her name's Marietta, not *baby*.

BUDDY  She's a baby to me. And I'm sure glad you got here, kid, so we can eat.

ESSIE  Oh, Laura! Meeting Marietta, I got so excited, I clean forgot to bring the chops. Ain't that awful?

BUDDY  My mouth's set on steaks, anyhow, so I'll go get 'em. Come on, Marietta, lemme show you where the butcher shops are in this neighborhood, since you'll be living here. We'll get some sirloin, ice cream, and beer. What else you need, Laura?

LAURA  Potatoes.

ESSIE  Marietta, ain't you kind of tired?

MARIETTA  Not really, Mama.

BUDDY  Oh, let the girl see what our block looks like—take a squint at Harlem. Come on, kid.

MARIETTA  (*Looking at her mother*)  All right, Mama?

ESSIE  You all come directly back, then. Meanwhile, we'll set the table—soon's I catch my breath.

(BUDDY *and* MARIETTA *exit*)

LAURA  She's a mighty pretty girl, Essie—for this city of sin. Don't you think maybe Marietta should stay for a *little* visit, then go on back to her grandma down in the simple South? (LAURA *goes to cabinet and pours a drink*)

ESSIE  After all these years, I just got my child with me. I want to keep her with me now, Laura, keep her here with her Mama.

LAURA  She's at the age, you know——

ESSIE  There's some mighty nice young mens in Harlem—in our church, in fact. I told C. J. my daughter was coming, and to drop around tonight.

LAURA  I hope C. J. don't bring that guitar of his, because the *last* thing I want is gospel music on my night off. Saturday night, I feel like letting my hair down.

ESSIE  Laura, I hope you don't drink so much no more, now that my daughter is here.

LAURA  Essie, I'll do my damnedest to respect your child. But you know, I ain't no saint. You just naturally got goodness in you. Me, I have to wrestle with temptation. You just take whatever comes.

ESSIE  I wrestle with temptation, too, Laura, in my heart. But somehow or another, I always did want to *try* to be good. Once I thought being good was doing nothing, like you said, I guess, so I done nothing for half my life. Now I'm trying to do *something*—and be good, too. It's harder.

LAURA   Um-hum!

ESSIE   What I'm trying to do, now that I got the time——

LAURA   And *money*——

ESSIE   —to set down and meditate, is to try to unscramble the good from the bad—in myself and others. If I can just separate the good, maybe I can hold on to it. I found a verse in the Bible I been studying over and over, says: "Canst thou by searching find out God?" (ESSIE *repeats it slowly*) "Canst thou by searching find out God?"

LAURA   What verse is that? Where is it?

ESSIE   Job 11:7.

LAURA   What a number! 11-7—wow! Rolled up in luck. That's gonna be one of my texts, too.

ESSIE   Laura, you thinking about numbers, and I'm thinking about God, finding out what *is* God in terms of what *we* is—us—on this earth. I'm just discovering there's so many ways to do good and be good I ain't found yet.

LAURA   Listen, you've been good ever since I've known you, Essie. But how good do you want to be—so good you ain't got a dime? I'm trying to figure how we can make *plenty* of money. You got a daughter up here in New York to educate—and that takes cash.

ESSIE   I want other people's daughters to get through school, too. There ain't no being good and keeping it to yourself. Is there, Laura?

LAURA   It's good to me when it's just *all* mine, Essie—like love—like Buddy. I don't want to share Buddy with nobody.

ESSIE   You talking about flesh-kind of love, not spirit.

LAURA   The spirit can't do a woman like me no good in bed.

ESSIE   Laura!

LAURA   Eat, drink, and love, that's what I live for!
          (*The buzzer sounds*)

ESSIE   Laura, I want you to find a good man and get married.

LAURA   Good men are usually poor—and I never did like to be poor, Essie. Did you? But I always was poor until I hit on shaking a tambourine—and met Buddy. He'll do for me.
          (ESSIE *exits to answer door as buzzer sounds again*)

ESSIE   Lemme see who's ringing.

LAURA   I want a man who knows all the angles! To get along in this world—*all the angles!*
          (VOICES *are heard in the hall*)

ESSIE   Hello, C. J. Come in.

C.J.   Howdy, Miss Essie! Did your daughter come?

ESSIE   Yes, son, thank God, safely! Come in. (ESSIE *returns with the* YOUNG MAN) Marietta'll be here in a minute. I see you brought your guitar.

LAURA   Dear God!

C.J.   How are you, Sister Reed? I've been practicing all evening on that new song I made up for our church. Want to hear it?

LAURA   Some saints can over-do, C.J. Serenade the young lady when she comes. (*Buzzer sounds*) Must be them.

(LAURA *exits into hall and* VOICES *are heard as* BUDDY *and* MARIETTA *enter with groceries*)

BUDDY   We are loaded down.

LAURA   Looks like you tried to buy out the store.

BUDDY   Well, since I had such a swinging little helper . . .

LAURA   Come on to the kitchen with the stuff, Buddy. Marietta, you've got company already.

(LAURA *takes bags from* MARIETTA *and exits to kitchen as* BUDDY *sits down to remove his shoes*)

BUDDY   Let me cool my feet here! Holy mackerel, Sapphire!

LAURA   Buddy!

BUDDY   I'm coming! (*He exits in his stocking feet with groceries*)

ESSIE   Daughter here's one of the young men of our church, C.J. meet Miss Johnson, Mr. Moore—Marietta, C.J. Now excuse me, children. I'm gonna help Laura get a quick dinner. I'll drop your bag in your room, Marietta. (ESSIE *exits*)

MARIETTA   Thank you, Mama! Mr. Moore, I——

C.J.   You can call me C.J.

MARIETTA   What does C.J. stand for?

C.J.   Just C.J., that's all. I only got initials for a first name—C.J.

BUDDY   (*Enters with three cans of beer and interrupts*) Certified jerk, consecrated jackass—that's what C.J. stands for—one of them holy and sanctified boys, baby. Probably won't even take a chick to the movies on Sundays.

C.J.   Sure I will.

BUDDY   Never see you around the pool halls.

C.J.   Well, with school work and all——

BUDDY   Square! Here, have a snizzle.

(*He hands* C.J. *a can of beer. The* BOY *takes it with hesitation.* BUDDY *gets a glass for Marietta*)

Marietta, would you like a cool one?

MARIETTA   Not beer, sir. I don't . . .

BUDDY   Sir? I'm not your father, baby.

MARIETTA    I don't drink, Mr. Buddy.

BUDDY    Just *Buddy*. Well, I'll drink yours, Marietta. Drink up, C.J., and get ready for the weekend. Let's see your guitar, boy. I used to beat out a mean blues before I left Savannah. (BUDDY *picks up the guitar*)

C.J.    A blues? Sure, if the Sisters don't mind.

BUDDY    A little blues won't hurt the Reed Sisters. Hum-mmm, you got a pretty gitfiddle, boy.

C.J.    I play in the college orchestra sometimes.

(*As* BUDDY *strums a soft slow blues, the two* YOUNG PEOPLE *talk as* C.J.—*afraid not to be a man—drinks his beer*)

MARIETTA    You go to college?

C.J.    Um-hum! I'm working my way.

MARIETTA    What are you taking?

C.J.    Chemistry. I can analyze that Holy Water they're gonna sell in church. I wish Sister Laura would give me a bottle tonight so I can tell what makes Jordan water different from what we have in New York City.

BUDDY    That water costs a dollar a bottle, boy, so they are not giving none away.

C.J.    Well, maybe I'll buy a bottle tomorrow.

BUDDY    I would advise you to leave that water alone.

C.J.    Why?

BUDDY    Just advice, that's all.

(*There is a puzzled silence on* C.J.'S *part as* BUDDY *strikes a series of loud chords*)

C.J.    Marietta, where are you in school—still high school, or what?

MARIETTA    High school, but you know, down South, the schools aren't very good, especially for colored, and I'm afraid——(BUDDY *plays louder and louder as if trying to drown out their conversation.* MARIETTA *shouts*)—afraid I won't match up to the girls up North here.

C.J.    Oh, yes you will. You look real smart to me, Marietta. Besides, you're so pretty you scare me.

MARIETTA    C.J.!

C.J.    Like I'm trying to tell you!

(BUDDY *turns on radio,* "New York Blues" *is playing*)

BUDDY    Hey, Marietta, listen to this! Did you ever dig the "New York Blues"? I guess not, down in the sticks where you've been. But after you're in Harlem for a couple of weeks, you'll understand. (BUDDY *sings*)

When you hear the motors purring
On the avenue
And you see the hep cats tipping
Through the evening dew,
You think about that dot-on-the-map
That once you knew—
And you love New York!
Baby, you love New York!
You've got the New York Blues!

When you're in a little jazz club
Where the cool cats strum,
Stashed in a cozy nook
Where all the cute chicks come,
You think about old squareville
Where you hail from—
And you love New York!
Baby, you love New York!
You've got the New York Blues!

When you hear a blues that's got
A Charlie Mingus chord
And it reaches down inside you,
Makes you holler, Lord!
You know down home you'd never hear no
Such cool chord—
Then you love New York!
Baby, you love New York!
Baby, you love New York!
You've got those New York Blues!

Oh, if I was the devil and didn't have hell for my base, I'd choose
New York. It's an ace-town—so many beautiful women in it for a
devil to tempt.

When you get the blues-for-going
And you get the blues-to-stay
You've got the blues-for-leaving
But you cannot get away—
You think about that sleepy town
That you left flat one day
And you love New York!
Baby, you love New York!

You've got those New York Blues!
Those real c-ooo-oo-l New York Blues!

(*During the song,* C.J. *holds* MARIETTA'S *hand. As* BUDDY
*ends the song,* ESSIE *enters with a kitchen apron on*)

ESSIE   Buddy! Cut this thing off. The neighbors'll hear all them blues
coming out of our apartment and think we forgot the gospel.

BUDDY   (*Throwing the guitar to* C.J.)   Here, kid! You can play
that gospel stuff the Sisters like. But it all sounds like blues to me.

ESSIE   At least our words is different. But we don't need no music
now—we're about to put the steaks on the stove. Anybody want
to wash up for dinner?

C.J.   (*His hand is on his stomach as if slightly nauseated*)   I do,
Miss Essie. I'm not used to drinking beer.

ESSIE   Come on, I'll show you the place.

(C.J. *and* ESSIE *exit.* BUDDY *approaches* MARIETTA)

BUDDY   And I'd like to show *you* something. I believe it's up to me
to school you.

MARIETTA   School me?

BUDDY   That's right. That gospel boy of a C.J. ain't dry behind the
ears yet. Men don't start asking a sharp little chick like you what
school you're in.

MARIETTA   Sharp?

BUDDY   Stacked, solid—neat, all-reet—boss, baby! That means—
attractive.

MARIETTA   Thank you, Mr. Buddy.

BUDDY   Don't *Mister* me. Just Buddy, that's all—Big-Eyed Buddy—
with eyes for you.

MARIETTA   Mama told me you're Miss Laura's friend.

BUDDY   Sure I'm her friend. But, Marietta, I'm gonna show you something. I'm gonna show you how fast a Harlem stud moves in.

MARIETTA   Moves in?

BUDDY   On a chick. (MARIETTA *tires to pass* BUDDY *as he approaches*)
We start like this. (*Quick as a panther,* BUDDY *grabs* MARIETTA *and
kisses her*)

MARIETTA   Oh!

(*Before she can draw back,* LAURA *appears in the doorway,
a dainty apron on. She catches them embracing, and speaks
in slow anger*)

LAURA   You said you liked your steaks rare, Buddy—with the blood
oozing out.

BUDDY   (*Releasing the* GIRL)   I do.
LAURA   And your women tender?
BUDDY   Could be.
LAURA   Huh! Miss Marietta, I reckon you ain't as innocent as you look.
MARIETTA   I tried to get past him, Aunt Laura, but he——
LAURA   Then get past, honey, *get past!* (MARIETTA *exits frightened toward the kitchen*)   As for you, Buddy Boy——
BUDDY   Aw, old chick, don't get blood in your eyes.
LAURA   Nor on my hands? (*She stares at* BUDDY *silently*)   I never knowed a man yet that didn't bleed—if cut.
ESSIE   (*Calling from the kitchen*)   Let's go, everybody—dinner's on the table!
LAURA   Come on, Buddy, get your steak.
        (LAURA *walks indignantly toward the door. Suddenly like a panther,* BUDDY *grabs her, and swings her around into his arms*)
BUDDY   Listen, Laura! You know damn well you're my woman. Can't no young girl lay a candle to you! You've got something I want, something I love. (*As he embraces her roughly* LAURA'S *struggles cease*)   I said something I want, baby! . . . Come on, give me a little sugar—right now!
LAURA   Buddy! . . . We've got to go eat.
BUDDY   Kiss now—eat later! Kiss . . . *right . . . now!*
        (*Long and passionately their lips meet*)

        BLACKOUT


MUSICAL BRIDGE:
        *The gospel music of "As I Go" rises in the darkness and carries over into the next scene.*


## SCENE SEVEN

*The glowing rostrum of Tambourine Temple in a newly converted theatre. It is a bright and joyous church. Besides an electric organ, there is a trio of piano, guitar, and drums* —BIRDIE LEE *is the drummer—with a colorfully robed* CHOIR *on tiers in the background, some* SINGERS *holding*

*tambourines.* DEACONESS HOBBS *stands before the rostrum,
an imposing woman with a big voice. On either side of her
sway two tall* DEACONS, *and also* DEACON CROW *and* BUD.
*The four men hum* " As I Go " *softly to end of refrain.
As the curtain rises, the* DEACONESS *sings.*

DEACONESS

> I cannot find my way alone.
> The sins that I bear I must atone
> And so I pray thy light be shone
> To guide me as I go through this world.

DEACONS

> As I go, as I go,
> Oh, Jesus walk by my side as I go.
> As I go, as I go,
> Be my guide as I go through this world.
> (*Refrain repeats softly under talk*)

DEACONESS  Now, dear friends, as the preliminaries of this meeting
draws to a close, we proceed to the main body of our ceremonies.
I thank God for these long tall deacons, these basses of Jehovah—
the Matthew, Mark, Luke, and John of this church—and your humble
deaconess and servant, myself, Lucy Mae Hobbs, who prays——

> As I go, as I go
> Oh, Jesus, walk by my side as I go!
> As I go, as I go,
> Be my guide as I go through this world.

BIRDIE  Sing the song, Sister, sing the song!

> (DEACONESS HOBBS' *voice soars in song as the* FOUR DEA-
> CONS *support her. On the final verse* ESSIE *enters singing*)

ESSIE

> I need some rock on which to stand,
> Some ground that is not shifting sand,
> And so I seek my Savior's hand
> To guide me as I go through this world.

BIRDIE  Keep your hand on the plow, Sister Essie. Hold your holt on
God!

> (*The refrain continues as the* DEACONESS *and the* DEACONS
> *retire to the choir stalls and* ESSIE *takes over at the rostrum*)

ESSIE  Brothers and sisters, I am humble, humble tonight, humble in
His presence. Pray for me, all of you, as I go! He has been so good
to me! I thank God for His name this evening, for Sister Laura,

for our fine Minister of Music there at the piano, for all of you congregation, for Deacon Crow, Sister Birdie Lee, young C.J., and for my daughter, Marietta, God has sent to me. Marietta, daughter, rise and state your determination.

(MARIETTA *speaks as the* CHOIR *continues to hum* " As I Go" *to end of chorus*)

MARIETTA   Dear friends, Jesus brought me out of the deep dark Southland up here to the light of New York City, up here to my mother, Essie. Jesus brought me to her, and to you, and to this church. I want to be worthy of your love, and of all my mother has done and is doing for me. And most of all, dear friends, I want to be worthy of the love of God. Friends——

I want to be a flower in God's garden,
To know each day the beauty of his love,
Take from the sun its warmth and splendor,
From gentle dews the kiss of heaven above.
I want to share each beam of holy sunshine,
Help make the world a radiant happy place,
A place of joy and love and laughter,
A howdy-do on everybody's face.
If God will give me understanding,
Lead me down the path his feet have trod,
If God will help me grow in wisdom,
Let my life be rooted in his sod.
Oh, just to be a flower in God's garden!
Oh, just to be a flower in his sight—
A tiny little flower in God's garden,
A flower in his garden of delight.

(*The song becomes a prayer as the* CHORUS *joins* MARIETTA)

Dear God, just give me understanding.
Lead me down the path your feet have trod.
Dear God, just help me grow in wisdom,
Yes, let my life be rooted in your sod.
I want to be a flower in your garden.
I want to be a flower in your sight.
A tiny little flower in God's garden,
A flower in your garden of delight.

(*The song ends softly to subdued amens. There is a roll of drums. The spotlight falls on* LAURA, *regal at one side of the stage. Tambourines shimmer as she marches toward the rostrum to the melody of* " Home to God ")

LAURA    Oh, saints of this church, blooming tonight in God's garden! My heart is full of joy! See what Tambourine Temple has done— united mother and daughter, brought this young lamb to the fold, filled Essie's heart with joy for her child! Blessed me, blessed you! What other hearts here are filled with joy tonight? Who else wants to speak for Jesus as Marietta has done? Who else?

(*A tall, scrawny old man,* CHICKEN-CROW-FOR-DAY, *emerges from the* CHOIR)

CROW    Great God, I do! I has a determination to make.

LAURA    Make it, brother, make it! Deacon Crow-For-Day! Our friend converted to Jesus! Testify, brother!

ESSIE    Testify! Testify!

(CROW-FOR-DAY *takes the center*)

CROW    Oh, I am here to tell you tonight, since I started to live right, it is my determination to keep on—on the path to glory. In my sinful days, before I found this church, I were a dyed-in-the-wool sinner, yes, dyed-in-the-wool, sniffing after women, tailing after sin, gambling on green tables. Saratoga, Trenton, New Orleans—let 'em roll! Santa Anita, Tanforan, Belmont, Miami, I never read nothing but the racing forms. In New York, the numbers columns in the *Daily News,* and crime in the comic books. Now I've seen the light! Sister Essie and Sister Laura brought me to the faith. They done snatched me off the ship of iniquity on which I rid down the river of sin through the awfullest of storms, through gales of evil, hurricanes of passion purple as devil's ink, green as gall.

BIRDIE    Green, green, green as gall!

CROW    I shot dices. Now I've stopped. I lived off women. Uh-huh! No more! I make my own living now. I carried a pistol, called it *Dog*—because when it shot, it barked just like a dog. Don't carry no pistol no more. Carried a knife. Knives got me in trouble. Don't carry a knife no more. I drank likker.

BIRDIE    Me, too! Me, too!

CROW    It made me fool-headed. Thank God, I stopped.

BIRDIE    Stopped, stopped, stopped!

CROW    I witnessed the chain gang, the jail, the bread line, the charity house—but look at me now!

BIRDIE    Look, look, look!

CROW    I lived to see the chicken crow for day, the sun of grace to rise, the rivers of life to flow, thanks be to God! Lemme tell you, I've come to the fold! I've come——

(*He sings and the whole church bears him up*)

        Back to the fold—
        How safe, how warm I feel
        Yes, back to the fold!
        His love alone is real . . .
BIRDIE  In the fold! The fold! Yes, in the fold!
CROW

        Back to the fold
        How precious are my God's ways!
BIRDIE  Where the streets are streets of gold!
CROW

        Back to the fold!
        So bright are all my days.
        (BIRDIE LEE *begins to bang her drums then leaps and dances in ecstasy as the* CHORUS *hums*)
BIRDIE  Hold your holt, Crow! Hold your holt on God! Hold your holt!
LAURA  Birdie Lee, why don't you set down?
BIRDIE  Set down? I can't set down—too happy to set down—got to stand—got to talk for Jesus—testify this evening in His name. I got to tell you where I come from—*underneath* the gutter. On the street, I heard Sister Laura preaching, Sister Essie praying, I said I got to take up the Cross and come back to the fold. Yes, they preached and prayed and sung me into the hands of God! I said goodbye to sin—and I wove my hand. (*She waves her hand*) Yes, I wove my hand to the devil—and said goodbye. That's why tonight, brothers and sisters, *I'm* gonna testify!
        (*Gradually her speaking rhythm merges into song as she returns to her drums and begins to play and sing*)
CROW  Testify, Sister, testify!
ESSIE  Tell the world about it, Miss Lee, tell the world!
BIRDIE

        I'm gonna testify!
        I'm gonna testify!
        I'm gonna testify!
        Till the day I die.
        I'm gonna tell the truth
        For the truth don't lie.
        Yes, I'm gonna testify!

        Sin has walked this world with me.
        Thank God a-mighty, from sin I'm free!

Evil laid across my way.
Thank God a-mighty, it's a brand new day!

I'm gonna testify!
I'm gonna testify!
I'm gonna testify!
Till the day I die.
I'm gonna tell the truth
For the truth don't lie.
Yes, I'm gonna testify!

I didn't know the strength I'd find
Thank God a-mighty, I'm a gospel lion.
Things I've seen I cannot keep.
Thank God a-mighty, God does not sleep!

I'm gonna testify!
I'm gonna testify!
I'm gonna testify!
Till the day I die.
I'm gonna tell the truth.
For the truth don't lie.
Yes, I'm gonna testify!

LAURA   No, the truth don't lie! How happy are the lambs of God!
Friends, I got a surprise for you, something new. I am going to
give you texts for the week—Lucky Texts—picked out with prayer
and meditation on my part from the Holy Book. And for each Lucky
Text, I want you to drop a quarter in the tambourine. Ushers out
there with your tambourines, pass among the congregation for their
free-will gifts. Now write the numbers of these Lucky Texts, and
study them during the week. That goes for you of the radio audience
too. Just call Atwater 7-4352 any time and let me know how your
blessings fall. Get your quarters and your pencils ready. Now write!
(LAURA *turns the pages of the Bible*) Psalm 9 and 20. Got that?
9 and 20. Drop a quarter in the tambourines. For each text a quarter.
Give God His and you'll get yours! Take all three numbers 9-2-0.
Twenty-five cents. You'll have no luck if you don't give God His'n.
Aw, let 'em clink! Let the holy coins clink! . . . Now ready? Next
text. What a great text—Sister Essie's favorite—Job 11:7. 7-11
or 11-7, either way. Yes, bless God, children! 1-1-7, that's right.
Job 11:7.
                (*On the rostrum a white telephone rings*)

VOICES  Thank you! Thanks, Sister Laura! Thanks! Thanks! Amen!

LAURA  Hello . . . What's that, sister? . . . You say you know you're gonna be blessed. Well, I thank you for your faith in *me*—and God . . . Now, as I sing, I invite those of you who are sinners tonight to come into this church. Who wants to touch His garment this evening?

ESSIE  Who wants the Lord to claim him for His own?
> (BOTH come forward)

LAURA  Who will come into the fold—the church that has no doors? Who wants to join Tambourine Temple?

ESSIE  And know the blessings of Christ!

LAURA  Who? Who? Who?

ESSIE  Who will come? Who?

LAURA  I know there is a lost lamb out there in this congregation somewhere.

ESSIE  Lost, lost, lost!

LAURA  Why don't you join us in this temple of the saved?

ESSIE  Yes, come into the fold.
> (*The piano begins to play very softly*)

LAURA
> There were ninety and nine that safely lay
> In the shelter of the fold,
> But one lamb was out in the hills away
> Far from the gates of gold,
> Away on the mountain wild and bare,
> Away from the tender shepherd's care.

CHORUS
> Away from the tender shepherd's care.
> (*A cry is heard in the* CONGREGATION)

BUDDY  Save me, Lord, save me! I want to be saved.

LAURA  Oh, come, brother, come!

BUDDY  Help me, Lord!
> (BUDDY *stumbles up the steps to kneel on the threshold of the rostrum as* LAURA'S *voice rises loud and strong*)

LAURA
> All through the mountains thunder-riven
> And up from the rocky steep
> There arose a glad cry to the gates of heaven!
> Rejoice! I have found my sheep!
> (*As* LAURA *reaches out her hands to* BUDDY *the* CHORUS *booms thunderously*)

CHORUS

    Rejoice! God has found his sheep!

    Rejoice! God has found his sheep!

    (ESSIE *rises, glaring at* BUDDY *doubting his conversion*)

BUDDY   I'm saved! Saved! Saved!

    (*As* "Amens" *and* "Hallelujahs" *rend the air,* ESSIE, *her head down in shame, walks off the rostrum and exits, but* LAURA *and* GLORIA *are ecstatic*)

LAURA   Converted! Converted! Brother Buddy Lomax converted!

CROW   Another sinner saved! Thank God! Thank God!

VOICES   Amen! Hallelujah! Praise God! Amen!

GLORIA   Buddy, I'm so glad you're saved. Glad you're saved.

LAURA   Stop interrupting the service!

GLORIA   Can't I say I'm glad he's saved?

LAURA   Gloria, your job is to sing. Sister Mattie, bring the church book. Let Brother Lomax sign his name.

MATTIE   (*Bringing the roster to* BUDDY *to sign*)   Now you're on God's roll.

GLORIA   So glad! . . . So glad!

    (LAURA *gives* GLORIA *a pointed look*)

BIRDIE   God's roll! God's roll! God's roll!

LAURA   Oh, yes! Oh, yes! Yes! Let Brother Buddy speak his determination. Tell 'em Buddy, tell 'em!

BIRDIE   Testify! Testify! Testify!

BUDDY   (*Rises from his knees to sing, glancing at* GLORIA *as he turns toward the congregation*)   Church, what can I say? Except that——

    The devil had a playground

    In my heart one day.

    He set up his tents of sin

    And invited me to play.

    It was so nice, so calm and cool

    That I played just like a fool.

    I almost lost my immortal soul—

    Now I've got that devil told.

CHOIR

    Devil, Devil, take yourself away!

    Yesterday I played with you

    But I ain't gonna play today.

    I've changed my playground,

    Changed my ways,

    I've changed my habits

And I've changed my days.
My feet are anchored on the gospel shore
And I ain't gonna play no more.

(GLORIA *shouts ecstatically, approaching* BUDDY *as she does,* LAURA *motions her angrily to her seat*)

BUDDY

I turn and look behind me,
This is what I see:
A world full of sinners
Just like I used to be
My heart is filled with pity, Lord,
And I feel the need to cry,
Come pitch your tents on the gospel shore
And let the world go by.

(BIRDIE, CROW-FOR-DAY, THE GLORIETTAS, *and* LAURA, *join* BUDDY *in the song while* BIRDIE *quickens the tempo on her drums and the entire* CHORUS *swings into the refrain, as all point their fingers at sin in a big finale*)

ALL

Devil, Devil, Devil,
Take yourself away!
Yesterday I played with you
But I ain't gonna play today
I've changed my playground,
I've changed my ways,
I've changed my habits
And I've changed my days—
My feet are anchored on the gospel shore
And I ain't gonna play no more!

CURTAIN

# ACT TWO

*PROLOGUE*

*Scrim of a Harlem street again.*

BUDDY *enters and jauntily takes center stage, flashing on
his index finger a diamond ring.*

BUDDY   Folks, you see this ring? Don't let it blind you. It's the Devil's
ring—I'm wearing it. God is good to the Devil sometimes. He lets
him have a few little old things like diamonds, and Cadillac cars, or
Thunderbirds. And yachts if I want them. Country houses, villas,
chateaux in France. Of course, He makes me suffer for them—by
never letting me be anything but a Devil . . . Like the comedians who
always want to play Hamlet, sometimes I would like to play God.
Or at least J.B.—but since I can't, I'll have fun anyhow—my damned
self. I play with people. Let me tell you one of my secrets. The way
to get any good man—I mean he-man—on the Devil's side is to
put your hand in his pocket with something in it—money. The
root of all evil! . . . The way to get a woman is to put your arm
around her waist with your hand *empty*—and let your sense of touch
do the rest. Don't waste money on a woman. Any woman you can
*buy* is already on the Devil's side . . . Now, let me give you folks
out there a few tips on how to be an honest-to-God devil. Just be
yourself. Don't pretend to be good. If you pretend you're good, and
put too good a pretense at it, you'll fool nobody. Then folks will
certainly think you are a devil—and not only a devil, but a hypocrite.
Your devilishness will defeat itself if you behave too well. Be a
devil right out—like me. Then folks will think you are dashing,
daring, dangerous, darling, cute—especially the women. They will
find it hard to believe you've got a tail. (It's here, but you don't see
it) . . . Another tip on being a devil, friends—don't take yourself
seriously. Smile! You can't help being a devil, so don't worry about
it. Just pick your *fleurs de mal*, and enjoy their perfume. Ha-ha!
You didn't know I read Baudelaire, did you? Beelzebub reads everybody . . . Ha-ha! M. B. Devil, that's me: Mephistopheles Beelzebub
Devil, alias Satan—nickname, Old Nick . . . I read Henry Miller,
too. And I *wrote The Carpetbaggers*. I gave Peyton those ideas for
*Peyton Place*. I rigged the radio quizzes. I'm of the intelligentsia.

Big business, too. The stock market, I fix it. Silos—I've built more out of thin air than Billie Sol Estes ever dreamed of. Pornography? I don't even own a pornograph. I *am* pornography—the gargoyle of sex—the original international playboy deluxe, and a millionaire. Money's no problem. I'm not needy—just greedy. I admit greed's a fault. Oh, well, even a devil has faults. Too bad I can't be perfect . . . But I am bad and know it. That's why I am disturbed by innocence. Innocence bugs me—especially young innocence. Just like I walked into the Garden of Eden and upset Adam and Eve in their purity, tonight I am going to—but why anticipate? Just wait a minute, you'll see—old Devil me! Ha-ha! On with the show, stage manager! (*Behind the scrim, the young voices of* MARIETTA *and* C.J. *are heard. The* DEVIL *laughs. The lights dim as he exits still laughing*) Ha! Ha! . . .

## SCENE ONE

*Living room of* LAURA *and* ESSIE'S *apartment. A summer night. The lights are dim, but the cross glows softly. Through the open windows, the moon and stars are seen. On the sofa,* C.J. *holds* MARIETTA *in his arms, just releasing her from a kiss, but not from his embrace, as she begins to sing an old Southern play-song. She pushes* C.J. *away, but he keeps edging toward her, as she rises to act out the song.*

MARIETTA   C.J., no! Be cool—as you all say in Harlem. Let's pretend we're kids again and play that little old game about being farmers.

C.J.   I know that game, but——

MARIETTA

    Little boy, little boy!

C.J.

    Yes, ma'am!

MARIETTA

    Did you do your chores?

C.J.

    Yes, ma'am!

MARIETTA

    Did you milk my cow?

C.J.
>Yes, ma'am!

MARIETTA
>Did you feed my sheep?

C.J.
>Yes, ma'am!

MARIETTA
>Did you count my lambs?

C.J.
>Yes, ma'am! Yes, ma'am! Yes, ma'am!

MARIETTA
>Um-m-hun-n-n-n! . . .
>(*As the duet continues, it is obvious* C.J. *is more interested
>in the girl than the game*)

MARIETTA *and* C.J.
>Well, little boy, little boy!
>Yes, ma'am!
>Did you feed my hens?
>Yes, ma'am!
>Did you throw them corn?
>Yes, ma'am!
>Did the hens lay eggs?
>Yes, ma'am!
>Did you count them eggs?
>Yes, ma'am!
>Yes, ma'am!
>Yes, ma'am!

>Um-hum-m-m-!
>Well, little boy, little boy!
>Yes, ma'am!
>Did you take them to the cook?
>Yes, ma'am!
>Did she bake corn bread?
>Yes, ma'am!
>Was that corn bread hot?
>Yes, ma'am!
>Was that corn bread good?
>Yes, ma'am!
>Yes, ma'am!
>Yes, ma'am!

Um-hum-m-!
Say, little boy, little boy!
Yes, ma'am!
Do you love me true?
Yes, ma'am!
Will you feed my hens?
Yes, ma'am!
Will you count my eggs?
Yes, ma'am!
Shall I make corn bread?
Oh, yes, yes!
Yes, yes, yes!
Yes, ma'am!
(*As the song ends,* C.J. *takes* MARIETTA *in his arms, and smothers her last " Um-hun-n-n!" He kisses her passionately as he pulls her toward the sofa*)

C.J.  Let me love you, Marietta, love you now! Love you like a man loves a girl!

MARIETTA  No! No, C.J., you don't mean this.

C.J.  Yes, I do!

MARIETTA  (*As* C.J. *tries to kiss her, she holds him off, speaking very gently, very softly*)  C.J., if you was to make love to me now— the way you want to, then you wouldn't want me when we got married.

C.J.  Yes, I would, Marietta. I want you now—and I'd want you any time, all the time.

MARIETTA  You would disrespect me, C.J., if I gave in to you quickly like this; I love you, C.J., but I want you to love me, too, not just— be with me.

C.J.  I got to be with you, Marietta, I got to! I got to! . . . Oh, honey! sweetheart! . . . I got to!

MARIETTA  You will, sweetest boy in the world, you will—but not tonight!

C.J.  (*Frustrated and angry, jumps up*)  Aw-wwww-ww-w! You're not all *that* pure.

MARIETTA  C.J., I'm not pretending to anything. I love you!

C.J.  I love you, too, Marietta, but I'll be damned if—pardon me, I'll be dogged if I don't want you—want you closer than you've ever been to me. If you loved me, you'd trust me. (C.J. *turns his back on her and looks out the window*)

MARIETTA    There are more ways to trust a boy than going to bed with him.

C.J.    Then you don't trust me. Look down there at the park—I'll bet it's full of kids making love. And look up there at the moon— it's happy about it. Aw, gee, Marietta, you make me feel like hell! Feel bad, like I do when I make up songs. Right now I could make up a hell of a song.

MARIETTA    (*Shrugs*) Then make up a song then.

C.J.    No! I'll sing you one I already made up. But it's not about you. And I won't be singing to you, either. I'll be singing to the moon. (*He sits in the window with his guitar and looks out as he sings*)

> Moon outside my window,
> Don't peep in on me.
> I don't want you to see
> How lonely I can be.

MARIETTA    (*Comes to stand behind him, an arm over his shoulder*) Oh, C.J., that's beautiful!

C.J.    (*Ignoring her, sings louder than ever*)

> Moon outside my window,
> Sail right on away.
> I don't want you to know
> My heart is sad today.

> Moon so round and golden,
> Moon up in the sky,
> So many lonely lovers
> Watched you fade and die.

> Right outside my window,
> Moon so bright above,
> Moon outside my window,
> Please, whisper to my love.

(*Relenting,* MARIETTA *puts both arms around* C.J. *as the song ends. He looks up—and they kiss.* C.J. *puts guitar down and takes her in his arms. At that moment* BUDDY *enters, startling them before they can release each other*)

BUDDY    Ha-ha! What's that they say? When the cat's away, the mice will play. (*As* C.J. *puts his guitar back in its case,* BUDDY *walks up to* MARIETTA *and chucks her under the chin*) How are you tonight, Miss Innocence?

MARIETTA   Please, Mr. Buddy!

C.J.   Why do you say *please* to him? Just keep your hands off of her, Brother Lomax.

BUDDY   Keep your diaper on, Junior!

C.J.   I guess it's not enough you're doing, turning the Temple into a gambling den! Chasing all the young girls in the church! And don't think I don't know you've got a bunch of runners writing numbers for you in the block. Guys like you are no good for Harlem.

BUDDY   You talk like *I'm* not Harlem.

C.J.   You are not Harlem. Harlem is a dream—the dream black folks dream way down in the deep South. And then they come here and sometimes find it's a nightmare, because men like you trick and betray them. You're related to the devil, Buddy, that's what.

BUDDY   Ha-ha! How did you guess? Smart one, heh?

C.J.   Harlem is full of good people, and people trying to be good, trying to get somewhere. Some are already there, up in the world— in the City Council, in Albany and in Washington. We've got wonderful doctors now, and lawyers and writers like Ralph Ellison, and composers like Margaret Bonds, and ministers like Rev. Dempsey, and young people—like Marietta and me, even. I'm going to amount to something, Buddy, in spite of all.

BUDDY   *All* meaning me, huh? You bore me, kid. Marietta, where's your Aunt Laura? I'm hungry.

MARIETTA   Tambourines Chorus has a TV rehearsal today.

BUDDY   Oh, no wonder I didn't see Gloria in the bar. Did you eat yet?

MARIETTA   C.J. just came to take me out to dinner.

BUDDY   Hell of a way to be eating with his tongue down your throat.

C.J.   (*Rushes toward* BUDDY)   You dirty low-down dog, you!

BUDDY   Oh, so you want to try me once? (BUDDY *picks* C.J. *up and throws him across the room*)   Now gather yourself together, Samson.
  (C.J. *slowly gets up off the floor, crouches, then rushes like a tiger at* BUDDY. *Blows are exchanged, but* BUDDY *gets the best of the youngster, shortly knocking him out cold with an uppercut to the chin*)

MARIETTA   Oh—ooo-oo-o! How could you!

BUDDY   Cut the jive, baby, let's you and me get together. Remember the first kiss you got in New York? (BUDDY *stalks* MARIETTA *as she tries to pass him*)

MARIETTA   Let me go get some cold water and throw on C.J.

BUDDY   Don't worry about C.J., he will come to. I'm the one that needs cooling off right now.

MARIETTA  Buddy! (*Frightened,* MARIETTA *darts about the living room, trying to avoid him. Finally he corners her.* MARIETTA *screams, grabs* BUDDY'S *shirt and rips it open as he holds her*) Oh—ooo-oo-o! C.J., somebody, help! Help!
> (*As she struggles against* BUDDY'S *caresses,* WOMEN'S VOICES *are heard.* LAURA *enters followed by* ESSIE, *who switches on the ceiling lights*)

LAURA  Say, what's going on here?
> (*They hear* MARIETTA'S *sobs, see the dishevelled* BUDDY, *and C.J. lying on the floor*)

ESSIE  Marietta, what's worng?

MARIETTA  Mama! Mama! Mr. Buddy, he—oh—ooo-oo-o!—I tried——
> (MARIETTA *is weeping incoherently as* ESSIE *tries to comfort her.* LAURA *picks up an overturned chair*)

LAURA  All right, Buddy, what's your story?

BUDDY  These kids tried to gang me. You got a couple of juvenile delinquents on your hands.

MARIETTA  Buddy wouldn't let me go! He—he—kissed me . . .

BUDDY  Aw, you've been kissed before.

MARIETTA  But you—but you—Oh, Mama! He ——

ESSIE  Come on, baby, we'll go in our part of the house and set down, and you tell Mama about it.
> (ESSIE *leads* MARIETTA *out. They exit.* LAURA *glares at* C.J. *as he slowly sits up, head in his hands on the floor*)

LAURA  What have you been doing, C.J., taking a nap?

BUDDY  I put him to sleep . . . Laura, pour me a drink.

LAURA  What do you think I am, a barmaid? What's been happening here?

BUDDY  When I got in, it looked to me like C.J. was trying to rape Marietta. And I always take a virgin's side.

C.J.  (*Jumping up from the floor*)  Marietta's my girl, Sister Laura, and he——

LAURA  C.J., take your guitar and get on over to the Temple to prayer meeting. Tell them I'll be along in time to wind up the services.

C.J.  God will take care of you, Buddy. If He don't *I will.*

BUDDY  That'll be the day you'll go ice skating in hell.
> (C.J. *exits as* BUDDY *laughs contemptuously*)

LAURA  Can't you leave Marietta alone, Buddy? Right here in my own house! Can't you leave Essie's daughter alone? You know, I'm gonna get sick of you one of these days—damn sick and tired of you. Gloria, Marietta, God knows who else. You're nothing but a bastard with women.

BUDDY  Yeah? How could you get along without *me*? Where would you get your ideas from? How would you keep the inspectors off of that old fire trap of a theatre you're operating in? How would you ever get on TV? Who's got recording connections like me—and Gloria—have? So stop talking jive. Come on, let's catch a little fresh air. Want a ride in my red Caddy? Want me to drop you off at prayer meeting?

LAURA  I've got a car—and I'm thinking about getting a chauffeur. I can get where I'm going.

BUDDY  All right, keep your hips on your shoulders, old chick. I've had enough yap-yapping. I'll dig you later, maybe in the wee small hours.

> (BUDDY *exits slamming the door.* LAURA *starts after him, stops, then sinks down on the sofa, in silence. After a moment, she calls*)

LAURA  Essie! Essie!

ESSIE  Yes, Laura? (ESSIE *comes to the entrance*)

LAURA  Don't you think you and me could skip going to prayer meeting tonight? They can get along for once without us at the Temple. Set down, let's talk. You always did have a calm mind. Essie, what's happening to me?

ESSIE  One thing I've decided, Laura—me and Marietta's got to move. I been thinking about buying that little house in Mount Vernon a right smart while now. Tomorrow I'm gonna make a payment on it. You was right when you said I ought to get my daughter out of here.

LAURA  I think so, Essie—since I can't get Buddy out of my life. I guess I don't want to. I love that man.

ESSIE  Marietta loves C.J., too, and he loves her. Oh, why can't Buddy let them young people alone.

LAURA  Why can't he let that Gloria alone?

ESSIE  Laura, if you don't mind my saying it, when you're trying to keep your hand on God's plow, you can't afford to let the Devil get a holt—he'll plow a crooked furrow every time and plant a bad seed.

LAURA  Looks like the more I do for him, the less he cares—and I need *somebody* to care for me.

ESSIE  Stray cats, stray dogs! You know, when I were a young woman down in Richmond, I took in a stray dog once, so frisky and friendly in the street, smart and clean-looking. After I had him two or three days around the house, I found out that dog had just about everything a hound could have. He was so frisky and leaped and jumped so much because he had fleas. He scooted and slid across the floor so funny because he had the itching piles. He sneezed so cute because he had distemper. He also had a pinch of ringworm behind his ear, which is catching to children and humans. I had to get rid of that dog I had taken into my home.

LAURA   I get your point, Essie. (LAURA *pours a big drink as they talk*)

ESSIE   Stray dogs, stray cats, stray people, you can never tell about 'em. Never tell.

LAURA   We got a church full of stray people.

ESSIE   True, but when folks is under the spell of Christ, they generally behave themselves. Yet even religion do not touch every heart in time to save it from hell. You better pray over Buddy.

LAURA   Love, loot, and likker, that's his speed. Unholy trinity! (LAURA *lifts her glass*)

ESSIE   Uh! Uh! Uh!

LAURA   But you know, Essie, Buddy's got ways of making money I never knew existed—also of making love. I wish I knew how to handle a man like Buddy. I wish I was like mama was. She wasn't soft and good like you. But mama really could handle a man, Essie, did I ever tell you about my mama?

ESSIE   Not much. But so much excitement today's tired me out. Since we ain't going to the Temple, I think I'll go to bed.

LAURA   Oh, Essie, please stick with me. Set right there and relax yourself a little if you want to. Loosen your girdle and lemme tell you about Mama.

ESSIE   (*Yawns as she stretches out on the couch*) Excuse me if I happen to sneeze.

(*By now* LAURA, *more than a little tipsy, returns often to the bottle*)

LAURA   Mama was the hell-raisingest woman in Charlotte society. She's dead now, but North Carolina ain't forgot about Mama yet. From a good family, too, but they put her out when I was born— I'm illegitimate, you know. The principal of the school was my father—married and a father twice before he fathered me. He never would graduate my mama from school after she became pregnant, which he did not consider respectable for a student to do. But do you think Mama cared? Never! She just said, "Who gives a damn?" and stayed right on there until the day she died having her thirteenth baby at the age of forty-four. Mama should have known better, but she kept on producing black, yellow, and brownskin children for thirty years. She had so many marriage licenses around the house that one overlapped the other! Every time Mama got drunk she wanted to get married. As for men, Mama could jive a man back, make him run and butt his head against the wall, lay down his month's salary at her feet, and then beg her for a nickel. But don't let a man do her wrong! Mama knew how to protect herself. Fight back like a wildcat! I *admired* my mother. I wish I had her gumption with men. If you think I got energy, you should've seen Mama. Ball all night, play all day, drink a bootlegger dry—and still looked like a glamor chick when she died. This whisky I'm downing tonight would be a soft drink to my mama. And that Big-Eyed Buddy I'm so weak about, that I'm worried as to where he's at right now—to Mamma, Buddy would be nothing but a play toy. Take a man like Buddy seriously? Not Mama! She would bust his conk wide open. They made women in them days! I take after her, too. The rest of Mama's children turned out to be nothing—wasted —all fell by the wayside except me, Sister Laura Reed. (ESSIE *is sound asleep now, so* LAURA'S *eyes turn to the past. She speaks to her mother*) I made it, Mama! Look at this place, Mama! Look at this fine silk sofa. Look at these chairs—French, Mama. Look at them drapes, the best money can buy. And what am I drinking? Ten dollar Scotch! (LAURA *fills her glass again, staggers proudly to the mirror, and lifts it to her own reflection*) Mama, you hear me, don't you? I'm gonna make a toast. A toast to your daughter, Laura. A toast—to Miss Bitch.

BLACKOUT

MUSICAL BRIDGE

*Choral singing of* "What He's Done for Me" *gradually growing in volume and intensity as the tambourines shimmer. The song continues into next scene under dialogue.*

## SCENE TWO

*Robing room under the stage of Tambourine Temple. Music and the beat of* BIRDIE LEE'S *drums drift from above.* MATTIE MORNINGSIDE, *stout mistress of the robes, sits on the lap of Laura's chauffeur,* CHARLIE WINDUS, *a tiny little man in livery, completely hidden by her enormous girth.*

MATTIE    Windus, where you left Sister Laura?

WINDUS    Setting by herself in the back seat of the car outside and she didn't look too happy—waiting to see——

MATTIE    (*Rises*)   You don't have to tell me! Buddy comes driving up nowadays in that red sports car just as brazen, with Gloria setting beside him as if she were his wife. Sister Laura's going to crack-up and all over Buddy Lomax—who everybody knows is a motherfouler.

WINDUS    " As the eagle fouleth his nest," the text goes.

MATTIE    Sister Essie's got plenty of sense, buying herself a home in the suburbs. She and her daughter seems so happy with it—a porch, a swing, a nice big yard, grass—better'n being all crowded up here in Harlem with you devilish men. The ruination of *any* young girl.

(*But* LAURA *has already appeared in the doorway. She enters*)

LAURA    You needn't hurry now, Windus. Just hold the car at the door till services are over.

WINDUS    Yes, ma'am, Miss Laura. I'll be right outside. Right there! (*The chauffeur exits*)

LAURA    Is Sister Essie here yet?

MATTIE    No. ma'am. It takes a right smart time to get down from Mount Vernon.

LAURA    Seems so. I guess everybody else has come in.

MATTIE    Two of the Gloriettas are here, but not Miss Gloria. But the chorus is all upstairs singing beautiful. Hear Sister Birdie Lee now?

BIRDIE

> What He's done for me!
> What He's done for me!
> I never shall forget
> What He's done for me!

MATTIE    That Birdie Lee! Ha-ha! Chipper as a cricket!

LAURA    I hear her attracting attention to herself. Hang my coat up carefully. On a hanger!

MATTIE    On a hanger!

LAURA    Minks don't grow on trees, Sister Mattie.

MATTIE    Sure don't, and you got a *fine* piece of skin for a lady minister.

LAURA    Prostitutes dress well, call girls and madams. I don't see why saints shouldn't.

MATTIE    No, ma'am! Saints should look the best. I'll bring your robes.

(*As* MATTIE *exits, laughter is heard from the hall.* BUDDY, *very well groomed, enters with a case of Holy Water. He is drunk*)

BUDDY   Holy Water from the River Jordan! Ha! Ha! Ha!
        (GLORIA *in dark glasses, sporty cap, and tight-fitting gown
        beneath a smart leather jacket, rushes in behind* BUDDY)
LAURA   It's about time you're getting here. Gloria, you're late. I want
        everybody on that platform—including you—when I make my
        entrance.
GLORIA  I told Buddy to hurry.
LAURA   *You* told Buddy to hurry?
BUDDY   We just stopped for a little nip.
LAURA   Well, nip yourself on up the steps with some cases of that
        Holy Water.
        (*As* LAURA *turns away,* BUDDY *pinches* GLORIA *playfully
        on the thigh. Gloria giggles and prances tipsily toward the
        robe closet*)
GLORIA  Sister Mattie, help me with my robe. It looks like I'm late.
        (GLORIA *exits*)
BUDDY   Aw, Laura, let your chauffeur lug that damn Holy Water
        around.
LAURA   He's paid to drive. This is your job.
BUDDY   Aw, well then, I might as well take off all my coats if I have
        to work. (BUDDY *tosses his camel's hair coat across the table, and
        removes his jacket as well, revealing a rich canary-yellow shirt*)
LAURA   How come Gloria can't make it here under her own steam?
BUDDY   All good-looking women like to ride on rubber—and Gloria
        *is* good looking.
        (GLORIA *returns in a Chinese sequin outfit, more like a
        night-club costume than a robe. Her cap is still on her head*)
GLORIA  I'm set to ascend the rostrum!
LAURA   About your sports cap, baby, ain't you gonna take it off?
GLORIA  Oh, that open car of Buddy's, the wind ruffles my hair!
        (GLORIA *tosses her cap to* BUDDY *and exits laughing*)
BUDDY   Cute kid!
LAURA   She can stay out of my car.
BUDDY   (*Looks at her nonchalantly*)  You're bugging me, woman!
LAURA   What?
BUDDY   (*Playfully staggering toward her*)  Do you want me to break
        one of these bottles of Holy Water over your head? Then you'd
        really be baptized.
LAURA   I'm not playing. Sometimes you try my soul, Buddy Lomax.
BUDDY   Jesus had a cross to bear, didn't He? Well, so has everyone.

Let's put up with each other's crosses. Say, if you sell ten cases of
this Holy Water tonight, we can get that color TV tomorrow.

LAURA   And who wants a color TV?

BUDDY   I do. Hey, did you see Gloria's picture in *Cue* this week?
Marty's got a thousand juke boxes lined up for her record. And
Laura, old kid, everybody in the syndicate's grinning like chesscats
the way the Harlem numbers bankers picked up business since you've
been giving out texts. What luck, huh? The third week straight
one of your numbers hit. That's got everybody talking——

LAURA   Don't try to change the subject, Buddy, sometimes I'm disgusted with you, especially when you're high.

BUDDY   Aw, cut the yak-yak, Laura. I'm gonna pack this case of
Jordan Water upstairs and listen to the rock and roll. Are you
coming?

LAURA   In due time. I've got to robe myself pretty tonight—to compete with the Gloriettas.

BUDDY   Gild your lily, baby! Drape your frame!

> (BUDDY *exits with a case of water.* MATTIE *returns with
> two robes, one green, one scarlet*)

LAURA   I'll take the red robe tonight.

> (MATTIE *helps* LAURA *dress as* ESSIE, MARIETTA, *and* C.J.
> *enter, and hang their coats on the wall. Upstairs the* CHORUS
> *is singing with a rousing beat,* " What He's Done for Me ")

ESSIE   Good evening! Music sounds great upstairs.

LAURA   Long as I don't hear Birdie croaking! I believe I'm gonna
have to get rid of that old woman.

ESSIE   Why? The way she hits them drums, the congregation loves her.

LAURA   That's just it, I want them to love *me*—and you—without
competition.

ESSIE   They do, Laura.

MARIETTA   Mama, we're going on upstairs.

LAURA   C.J. should have been up there at eight o'clock like the others.

MARIETTA   It's my fault, Aunt Laura. He came up to Mount Vernon
to spend the afternoon, and I made him a cake that was late getting
out of the oven.

C.J.   It was good though—um-mm-m!

LAURA   Cooking for him already, and you're not married yet!

MARIETTA   We will be, soon's I graduate. Come on, C.J.

> (*They exit.* MATTIE *exits also to return the green robe to
> the closet*)

ESSIE   C.J.'s a nice boy, Laura. I'm so glad for my child.

LAURA  Me, too. And I'm glad you've got Marietta in the country. Essie, powder your face a little, won't you, before you go upstairs? That spotlight on the rostrum shows up your liver spots. And tell them musicians I want plenty of drum rolls, tambourines, and hallelujahs tonight when I appear on the rostrum.

ESSIE  The spirit don't need all that theatre kind of ballyhoo, Laura.

LAURA  No. baby, but I do.

> (*Meanwhile,* LAURA *has dumped the contents of her purse on the dressing table, as if searching for something*)

ESSIE  Laura, why are you dumping everything out on the table?

LAURA  Why don't you just go on upstairs, Essie, and make your presence known? . . . Sister Mattie, come here!

> (*Puzzled,* ESSIE *exits, shaking her head.* MATTIE *bustles in*)

MATTIE  I'm coming.

LAURA  Mattie, go upstairs and tell Brother Buddy I said to come down here a minute—*now*! And suppose you sit in with the chorus and sing a little. I want to speak to him *private*.

> (MATTIE *exits singing* "What He's Done for Me." *Shortly* BUDDY *enters with mock piety*)

BUDDY  What wantest thou, Sister Laura?

LAURA  Did you take a one hundred dollar bill out of my purse?

BUDDY  Sure did.

LAURA  Ain't the cut you're getting from this church a plenty for you?

BUDDY  (*Answers impudently*)  No.

LAURA  (*Rises angrily*)  You still don't have enough of *my* money to spend on the bitch?

BUDDY  Watch your language, Sister! What bitch?

LAURA  Huh! The chick you and Marty like so much. Who's she sleeping with? Or does she rotate between you?

BUDDY  (*Moves toward* LAURA *threateningly*)  I ought to knock your teeth down your throat—and don't think I won't. Lay off Gloria!

LAURA  That slut can't even sing in tune—a cheap little rock-and roller.

BUDDY  She's no rock-and roller. She's got a contract at the Vanguard, moving on up to the Blue Angel. Next thing you know she can say goodbye to this hallelujah house and open at the Copa because Marty's underwriting her.

LAURA  If she don't stay out of my car, somebody'll be undertaking her.

BUDDY  (*Cool again, grins as he takes out a cigarette*)  Your car? (*He lights up nonchalantly*)

LAURA  Yes, I said *my* car. Who meets the notes? It's still not paid

for. My car! Bold as that slut is, it's a wonder it's not all written
up in *Jet* or some other gossip columns. Gloria Dawn—even her
name sounds phoney. A little strumpet!

BUDDY  (*Takes a deep draw on his cigarette, obviously enjoying*
LAURA'S *jealousy*)  She's young, baby. But you, pshaw, you been a
good old wagon, but you done broke down.

> (BUDDY *blows the smoke of his cigarette into her face.*
> *Hurt,* LAURA *bites her lip in silence. Suddenly tears come*
> *against her will. Upstairs the* CHORUS *is singing loudly*
> "When I Touch His Garment)

CHORUS
> When I touch His garment . . . (etc.)

LAURA  Buddy, you don't have to go out of your way to hurt me. I
just wondered who took my money, that's all.

BUDDY  You know who took it. I can have it, can't I?

LAURA  Yes, Buddy, I guess you can—anything I got. Buddy, tell me,
why is it, looks like men can't never act right? You try to treat a
man nice, and he turns around and drops the boom on you. Ain't a
woman supposed to be nothing but dirt under a man's feet?

BUDDY  That's all, in my opinion—and you feel good under *my* feet.
(BUDDY *grinds his cigarette butt beneath his foot*)

LAURA  You don't try to hide *your* way with women, do you?

BUDDY  Why try? You can't hide nothing from God, can you? Nor
the police. So why try to hide it from anybody else? The police
I can *pay* off. God you *pray* off.

LAURA  How about me?

BUDDY  (*Leaps forward savagely*)  You? I'll slap the hell out of you
if you fool with me—and make you like it. (LAURA *does not move*)
Maybe you think I won't, heh? (BUDDY *slaps her full in the face.*
*Her purse drops to the floor as she takes a step back to avoid a second*
*blow*) And I'll do it again . . . I'll slug you right into your grave.

> (BUDDY *glares at* LAURA, *then wheels to cross to a chair.*
> LAURA, *obviously frightened for her life, picks up her purse*
> *as* BUDDY *sits down. As* BUDDY *talks, she puts her purse into*
> ESSIE'S *coat pocket where her hand lingers for a moment*)

LAURA  What do you want to hit on me like this for?

BUDDY  For kicks maybe, baby—to see you cry—so I can drink your
tears.

LAURA  I'm not the type to cry, Buddy Lomax.

BUDDY  I'll make you! I guess you know, a used-up bitch like you is
supposed to put out some money to keep a man like me around.

And believe me, baby, now that you've got me, you're gonna *keep* me. I ain't gonna let you give me up. Two old saints like you and Essie might pull into the Temple wrecks out of the gutter like Crow-For-Day and Birdie Lee—but me, I bring in the young chicks. There's something about me that women go for. You admit I'm a man, don't you, kid? Heh, baby? I love you. Come here, lemme taste your lipstick.

LAURA  What?

BUDDY  Come here, I said! I want to kiss you.

LAURA  Kiss me? After the way you treat me?

BUDDY  Beat a woman till she cries, then kiss her till she laughs—is my recipe. Are you coming?

LAURA  No!

> (*As* LAURA *backs away,* BUDDY *lunges toward her like a monstrous ape*)

BUDDY  God damn you, I'll kiss you! Or kill you, one! (*His arm is raised as if to strike her. But instead, he grabs her, one hand behind her head, and forces her to lift her lips to his. With savage ferocity he moans*) You sweet rascal of God! You . . . rascal . . . of God! (*With what appears to be a passionate embrace, they kiss. But as the wide sleeves of* LAURA'S *scarlet robe sweep upward and her arms go about* BUDDY'S *shoulders, there is the gleam of a switch-blade knife in her hand, raised in fear and self-defense. At that moment* BIRDIE LEE *enters on her way to the* LADIES ROOM)

BIRDIE  Oh! Excuse me—but I got to go!

> (LAURA *jerks loose from* BUDDY. ESSIE'S *knife falls from her hand. A strange look comes over* BUDDY'S *face—as he realizes the knife was buried in his back. He cries out, puts one hand to his mouth, and finds he is belching blood*)

BUDDY  What did you—? Aw-aaa-a! I'll kill you! You dirty— Ah-aaa-aa-a! I'll—I'll—I'll kill you!

> (BIRDIE *sees* BUDDY *lunge at* LAURA *as she backs away.* BUDDY *falls to the floor flat on his face, the back of his canary yellow shirt red with blood.* LAURA *screams threateningly at the astonished* BIRDIE LEE)

BIRDIE  Oh, my God! My God! Aw-aaa-aa-a——

LAURA  (*Covers* BIRDIE'S *mouth*) Birdie Lee, don't call on God— or nobody else. Just shut up! Be speechless! If you so much as open your mouth, with my own hands I'll—(*The threatening claws of* LAURA'S *fingers sweep upwards, ready to strangle.* BIRDIE *trembles*)

Get back upstairs to your drums, Birdie Lee! And give me a great
*big* drum roll when I ascend the pulpit. You hear me! A great . . .
big . . . drum . . . roll!

> (BIRDIE *rushes off in a frightened exit.* LAURA *looks down
> for a moment at* BUDDY'S *body. Then as the drums roll
> above and the tambourines shake ecstatically, she throws one
> end of her golden stole about her throat and exits to join
> the services*)

**BLACKOUT**

MUSICAL BRIDGE:

> LAURA'S *entrance theme—shimmer of tambourines into
> mounting drum roll, crash of cymbals, then* " Home to
> God."

## SCENE THREE

*Rostrum of Tambourine Temple with full* CHORUS, *the*
GLORIETTAS, CROW-FOR-DAY, BIRDIE LEE *and* ESSIE *present.*
ESSIE, *at the center of the rostrum, sings as the* CHOIR *sup-
ports her.*

ESSIE

I'm going to lay down my soul
At the foot of the cross.
I'm going to tell my Jesus
Just what sin has cost.
I'm going to find my Savior,
Whisper in His ear,
I'm going to tell Him, Savior,
My salvation's near.

CHOIR

Oh, this world has been my dressing room,
But now at last, dear Lord, I'm going home.
Down, down in the mire
Too long my feet have trod.
Now, at last, I'm going home to God!

(*As the refrain nears its end,* LAURA *enters walking regally in rhythm from the wings, her scarlet robe swaying.* ESSIE *retires to her seat, leaving the pulpit to* LAURA. *The* CHOIR *continues to hum as she speaks*)

LAURA Move on up a little higher! Thank God! Casting off shackles, getting rid of devils, thank God! Wrestling with evil, and downing Satan! Oh, yes, this world is nothing but a dressing room where we put on our robes and prepare for Jordan, heavenly Jordan!

CHORUS Amen! Amen!

LAURA And now, directly from the Jordan River, I bring you again that precious water, that Holy Water that only Sister Laura has, imported just for you from the River of Life. Blessed water to purify your home. (ESSIE *rises with bowed head and exits as* LAURA *lifts a bottle*) While Sister Essie goes for her meditation, ushers, pass amongst the people. One dollar a bottle, children, just one dollar! Get a bottle tonight while there is yet time. Ushers, if you run out, there's more on the rostrum—just like the bottle I hold in my hand. (*A muffled scream is heard off stage. Heads turn curiously as the humming stops.* LAURA *suddenly drops the bottle with a crash, but quickly recovers her poise*) Oh, my friends, the power of this water—it almost makes me faint with glory! Buy a bottle! Buy a bottle tonight. But don't drop yours as I dropped mine. Now, whilst the ushers pass with the bottles, let's have a few testimonials. Let one and all declare his determination. (LAURA *sings*)
Who will be a witness for my Lord?
Who will be a witness for my Lord
On the day of jubilee?
(BIRDIE LEE *sings loudly*)

BIRDIE
I will be a witness for my Lord!
I will be a witness for my Lord
On the day of jubilee!
Yes, I'll stand up and be a witness!

LAURA (*Stares threateningly at* BIRDIE, *then walks over to* MARIETTA) Well, since Sister Birdie Lee seems to want to take over—Marietta, go tell your mother she can return from her meditations—and be a witness, too.
(MARIETTA *exits.* BIRDIE *projects defiance as she leaves her drums*)

BIRDIE My testimony this evening is that I want to tell you all what it means to be a witness—I mean a witness for God, and a witness for men and women, too. Lord, lemme hold my holt! I were in a trial once, a court trial—and I lied. I let an innocent man go to jail for something he didn't do—to protect my man I thought I loved. Another man served time, innocent as a lamb. Whereas the one I lied for lived to cut up, and shoot up two or three more people. In fact, that man did not appreciate what I did for him. He lived to kick my—excuse me—I meant to say—to beat and mistreat me, too. And he were so mean he wouldn't let me do a damn—excuse me—I mean not a blessed thing. I'm just excited tonight, folks. But I tries always to keep bad words out of my mouth, now that I's a Christian woman. And what I's trying to say to everybody this evening is, that when the time comes, in God's name, I know I got a determination—and my determination is——(*Her speech blends into song*)

I'm gonna testify! I'm gonna testify!
I'm gonna testify till the day I die.
I'm gonna tell the truth
For the truth don't lie.
Folks, I'm gonna testify! . . .
(LAURA *sits staring angrily into the audience*)
I'm gonna tell the truth
For the truth don't lie!
Yes, I'm gonna testify!
(As BIRDIE *finishes,* LAURA *rises defiantly*)

LAURA   Lemme tell you one thing, church, I say——
We all shall be free!
Children, we all shall be free!
Children, we all shall be free
When the Lord shall appear.
(LAURA *turns and looks at* BIRDIE *to intimidate her*)
We want no cowards in this band
That from their colors fly.
We call for valiant hearted souls
That are not afraid to die.

I mean ——
Children, we all shall be free!

CHORUS

Children, we all shall be free!
Children, we all shall be free!
When the Lord shall appear.

(MARIETTA *runs from the wings to whisper frantically to* LAURA)

MARIETTA   Sister Laura! Sister Laura! Oh, Sister Laura!

LAURA   Excuse me, saints, let me go to see what little sister Marietta wants that's so urgent. Until Sister Essie and me resume our seats on the rostrum, I'll turn the services over to our beloved deacon here, known in love to all of us as Brother Crow-For-Day. Deacon, come forward!

> (LAURA *follows* MARIETTA. *Both exit as* BIRDIE *gives a drum roll, then a contemptuous thump.* CROW *advances singing*)

CROW

> Leaning, leaning,
> Leaning on the everlasting arms!
> Leaning, leaning,
> Leaning on the everlasting arms . . .
> (*As the* CHORUS *joins in, the song rises.* Gradually lights dim to darkness, pinpointing DEACON CROW)

BLACKOUT

MUSICAL BRIDGE:

> *Choral singing continuing* "Leaning on the Everlasting Arms."

## SCENE FOUR

*Robing room. Having tried to minister to* BUDDY, ESSIE *is aghast over his body, with blood on her white robe.* SISTER MATTIE MORNINGSIDE *enters, stops at the doorway and begins to tremble at the sight.*

MATTIE   Oh-ooo-oo-o, my God! Somebody's killed Buddy! Buddy! Buddy! Police! Somebody get the police! (MATTIE *runs to the door calling the chauffeur*) Windus! Windus! Get the police quick! The police. (MATTIE *returns to stare at the body.* MARIETTA *enters*) Lord have mercy! Sister Essie's knife right there on the floor.

MARIETTA   Mama didn't do it!

ESSIE   Mattie, you know I didn't do it.

MATTIE   Sister Laura were in the pulpit—it's your knife on the floor and there's blood on your robe.

ESSIE   Buddy were dead when I first touched him, stone cold dead. I tried to see if I could help him, but he were gone.

MATTIE   You didn't try to help him when he was living, did you? Folks know you couldn't abide him. Now look! (MATTIE *shudders*)

ESSIE   Somebody took my knife out of my pocket. I left it where it always was, in my coat. (ESSIE *goes to her coat hanging on the wall. She feels in her pocket and surprised, pulls out* LAURA'S *purse*) Laura's pocketbook!

MATTIE   Sister Essie, you was the last one here.

MARIETTA   My mother couldn't do anything like that. She wouldn't! You know she wouldn't. She just couldn't! Oh, why don't Sister Laura come here?

ESSIE   (*Comforts* MARIETTA)   God will straighten things out, Marietta.
             (*The music of* "Leaning on the Everlasting Arms" *comes drifting down as* TWO POLICEMEN *hurry in followed by the* CHAUFFEUR)

MATTIE   It's her knife on the floor. See the blood on her robe! Lord, how in a minute a saint can change into a sinner! Officer, who'd of thought it of Sister Essie?

COP   Don't nobody touch the body. We'll send for the coroner. Officer, put that woman in the squad car while I go phone.
             (*The* COP *exits. As the second* OFFICER *leads* ESSIE *out,* MARIETTA *follows weeping with* ESSIE'S *coat*)

MATTIE   Poor Brother Buddy, God rest his soul!
             (MATTIE *exits.* LAURA *enters, takes off her scarlet robe, and with it covers* BUDDY'S *body. Suddenly she buries her face in her hands*)

LAURA   Oh, my God! . . . Oh, God! . . . My God!

BLACKOUT


MUSICAL BRIDGE:
             CHOIR *humming* "Bible" *with high soprano obbligato between phrases.*

## SCENE FIVE

*A jail cell. Alone in the darkness, the light gradually
reveals the anguish in* ESSIE'S *face as she sings, clasping
a Bible.*

ESSIE

Thank God, I've got the Bible in my hand . . . (etc.)
(MALE VOICES *are heard approaching*)
WARDEN   You're the first visitor she's had since your daughter came
down with her last night.
CROW   I certainly thank you, sir, for escorting me in.
(WARDEN *enters with* CROW-FOR-DAY)
WARDEN   Mrs. Johnson, your husband to see you.
ESSIE   My husband?
CROW   (*Nervously motioning her to be silent*)   Shsss-sss-ss-s!
ESSIE   Deacon Crow, I'm glad to see you.
WARDEN   I'll give you folks ten minutes together.
CROW   I thank you, sir. (*The* WARDEN *exits as* ESSIE *looks condemn-
ingly at* CROW *who begins to explain*)   Sister Essie, they said *nobody
but relatives*. I had to tell some kind of little white lie to get in here.
ESSIE   Deacon Crow, you know we ain't——
CROW   I know it. We's related only in spirit. But to tell the truth,
Sister Essie, I been kind of looking at you a right smart lately with
a manly eye. Sometimes I says to myself, "Big Mama, you look
good to me." Meaning no harm, of course.
ESSIE   Crow, this is no time for foolishness. I'm troubled in mind.
CROW   Put your mind at rest, Sister Essie. The Lord has already this
morning give us glad tidings. You gonna get out of this mess. The
church has got you and Sister Laura both the best lawyers in town.
But the big news is, Sister Laura confessed——
ESSIE   Confessed?
CROW   That she killed Buddy Lomax. She prayed all night and con-
fessed all morning—and nobody made her.
ESSIE   Poor Laura! Now she'll be behind bars.
CROW   I been behind bars fifty times. It ain't so bad.
ESSIE   This is my first time, and I sweated blood. But I guess if Jesus
could stand what was done to Him, I can stand this mite of punish-
ment visited on me. Deacon Crow, I deserve this punishment. When
I seen what was happening in our church—all that unholy water
selling, numbers and stuff—I should have riz in my wrath and

cleaned house. But no! Instead I just set and sung. That's what's been the matter with me all these years—setting, just setting—accepting what comes, receiving the Lord's blessings whilst the eagle foulest his nest—until he gets struck in the back with my own knife.

CROW   Sister Essie!

ESSIE   Lemme speak, Crow! It don't do to just set. Me, I let Buddy fill the house of God with sin, let vanities of vanities take over, let Laura parade her fur coats before them poor peoples what brought us their hard-earned money for God's work. Me, I let our church become the devil's playground. Religion's got no business being made into a gyp game. That part of God that is in anybody *is not to be played with*—and everybody has got a part of God in them. I let Laura play with God. Me, Essie Belle Johnson. Deacon Crow, if I get out of here——

CROW   You're gonna be cleared! Hallelujah!

WARDEN   Cut the noise! We keep a quiet jail.

ESSIE   Sh-sss-ss.

CROW   You're going to be cleared. You'll be out today, just as soon as your lawyer gets down here with the papers.

ESSIE   Then, Crow, lemme tell you one thing—from here on in I, Essie Belle Johnson, am gonna run my church. And I'm gonna make it what I visioned—a Rock of Goodness in the heart of Harlem. We's a wealthy church now, Crow. I'm gonna buy that old building next door for a clubhouse for our anniversaries and teas and such. Oh, joyful Rock! That empty vacant lot, we're gonna turn into a playground so our teen-agers can play basketball in summer and skate in winter.

CROW   Happy Rock!

ESSIE   And my daughter, Marietta, I'm gonna send to be a nurse—like she wants to be—so she can help me take care of the sick in our church. Whilst I pray with them, Marietta can relieve their pain. Oh, how great Tambourine Temple can be!

CROW   Amen! Amen! Amen!

WARDEN   I say, cut that noise. Your time's up anyhow.

CROW   See you at services this evening, Sister Essie.

>            (CROW *exits singing* " Leaning " *as* WARDEN *escorts* LAURA *handcuffed, dressed in black*)

ESSIE   Laura!

LAURA   I can't look at you, Essie.

ESSIE   You got to look at me, Laura.

>            (WARDEN *permits* LAURA *to pause*)

LAURA   Forgive me—after what I did to you.

ESSIE   I forgive you, Laura.

LAURA   Oh, pray for me, Essie, please. I couldn't let you go on trial for me. I told the police. I had to tell them. I confessed. Essie, I love you. Pray for me.

ESSIE   I pray for you, Laura. In my heart, I pray.

> (*The* WARDEN *leads* LAURA *away. Tears flow down* ESSIE'S *face as she clutches the bars. The light fades. Suddenly there is a great burst of music as the* CHOIR *sings* " God's Got a Way ")

BLACKOUT

MUSICAL BRIDGE:
> " God's Got a Way " *as immediately revealed in the following scene.*

## SCENE SIX

> *Tambourine Temple in a blaze of light. The* CHORUS *is newly and more beautifully robed than ever. For this gala night a trumpet, and perhaps other instruments have been added to the band. On one side of the banked platform is* C.J. *with his guitar,* MARIETTA *on the other.* BIRDIE LEE *is at the drums. Only* GLORIA *is missing as* CROW *stands singing proudly at the rostrum, backed by the* CHOIR.

CHOIR

> God's got a way!
> God's got a way!
> God's got a way!
> His wonders to perform.

CROW

> Just trust in Him,
> Just trust in Him,
> Just trust in Him,
> He'll keep you from all harm.

BIRDIE   Hold your holt, Crow! Yes! Hold your holt on God!

CHOIR

      God's love can save,
      God's love can save,
      God's love can save,
      Oh, yes, I know it can!

BIRDIE  It can! It can! It can! Yes, it can!

CHOIR

      God's got a way,
      God's got a way,
      God's got a way,
      That's unbeknownst to man.

CROW  God's way—unbeknownst to man! What I wants to say tonight is, church, let him who is *without* sin cast the first stone—if he dares! Let him who is without sin put his feet in a saint's shoes—and see if he don't tread on thorns. Thorns! See if you ain't tried by the fire. And when you have been tried, you can never be the same again. What was we all once but wrecks on the shoals of life? (CROW *mounts the drum stand*) What was we all but flotsam and jetsam in the gutters of this world? But look up here tonight on this rostrum and see if you see flotsam. See if you see jetsam. See if you see anything up here but light—light and happiness and whole-sam and health-sam. No wrecks! No flots, no jets, no rolling stones tossed on the tides of sin. Tambourine Temple has saved many a soul.

BIRDIE  It saved me! Saved me! Saved me!

VOICES  Me, too! Me, too!

CROW  And when a soul is saved in this church, it is really saved.

BIRDIE  Yes, 'tis! Yes, 'tis! 'Tis! 'Tis! *'Tis!*

CROW  And who ought to know, better than you and me, Birdie Lee, because we was down there!

BIRDIE  Down there, Crow!

CROW  Down there!

BIRDIE  Yes, we was!

CROW  Down there! Now we got to save others. Ain't that right, Birdie Lee?

BIRDIE  Right! Right! Right, I say!

CROW  Then tell 'em about it, Sister Birdie, tell 'em!

      (BIRDIE *begins to testify in song as* CROW *takes over on the drums*)

BIRDIE

      When you see some sinner leave
      Iniquity's dark den

And turn his feet toward Canaan,
Just help him to begin.
Christians, take his hand
And show him God's his friend.
Just lead him on and say amen!

(BIRDIE *descends from drum stand as* CHOIR *joins in*)

Let the church say amen!
Let the church say amen!
When a sinner comes to Jesus,
Let the church say amen!

Licker drinking brother
Drowned in alcohol,
Leave your empty glasses
And hear the Savior's call.
Christians, take his hand
And show him God's his friend
Just lead him on and say amen!

CHOIR

Let the church say amen!
Let the church say amen!
When a sinner comes to Jesus,
Let the church say amen!

BIRDIE    (*Invites* AUDIENCE *to participate*)    When I say *Amen,* let
everybody say *Amen!* Come on, sing! Sing with me!
        (*The Refrain is repeated*)

MATTIE

Listen, wayward sister,
Though you have sunk so low,
Ask—and He will wash your
Sins as white as snow.
Christians, take her hand
And show her God's her friend
Just lead her on and say amen!
        (MATTIE *shakes her tambourine*)

CHOIR

Let the church say amen!
Let the church say amen!

When a sinner comes to Jesus
Let the church say amen!
(*Chorus is repeated as* BROTHER BUD *and* MATTIE *prance across the rostrum shaking tambourines in competition with each other*)

ALL

Oh, let the church say amen!
Let the church say amen!
When a sinner comes to Jesus,
Let the church say amen!
(BIRDIE *shouts.* ESSIE *rushes in with a newspaper in her hand*)

ESSIE God works in mysterious ways His wonders to perform. Church, Sister Laura's lawyers have got the detrimentation—the charge is not murder, not manslaughter—just self-defense. So she won't go to the electric chair—just the pen. See! (ESSIE *holds up the front page of the* Daily News *with a full page photo of* LAURA. *She reads its caption*) "SEPIA SONGSTRESS OF SALVATION SHEDS HER SHACKLES. Laura Wright Reed, darling of the District Attorney's Office since her sensational expose of Harlem rackets, is free on bail." Newspapers tonight just full of how the end of Buddy Lomax unearthed a cesspool of crime in New York City and the Nation—a syndicate with pay-offs from the corner candy store that writes numbers, right on up to the cornerstone of government that protects the Martys of the underworld. Behold! Let your eyes believe what you see! Repentant—and with head bowed down—ready to serve years up the river—Sister Laura comes back to the fold.

CROW

Back to the fold . . .

BUD God's got a way! Oh, yes! He's got a way!

CROW

Back to the fold ——
God's got a way! Oh, yes!
(*As the* CHOIR *sings, with head down* LAURA *enters clad in black as she was in prison*)

CHOIR

God's got a way!
God's got a way!
God's got a way
His wonders to perform . . . hum . . .
(*The* CHOIR *continues humming as* LAURA *kneels*)

LAURA  Church, I know my punishment is coming, got to come.
I know it will. But help me to bear up, children, help me to bear
up. Tonight I'm out on bail, that's all. I still got to face the jury,
stand trial, and take my punishment. But thank God, for a little
while, I'm free, and back again with you, my friends, with you. And
I have come to confess to God, before this church and before the
world tonight, that I have sinned, I have sinned, sinned, sinned . . .
(*Her anguish turns into song*)
>I have sinned,
>Now I bow my head in shame,
>Not for what sin did to me—
>But to my Savior's name.
>I have sinned,
>Now I must atone
>For others I have led astray,
>Not for myself alone.
>I could bear my agony
>If all the hurt were mine,
>But I have used the dust of sin
>Others' eyes to blind.
>I confess—confessing
>That all the time I knew
>When I was sinning, God,
>I was sinning against you—
>Against the one who loved me most—
>Lord, God, against you.
>(*She speaks against the music*)
>Mine was a sumptuous kind of sin
>Wrapped in diamonds and fur,
>Scattering money to the wind
>Like frankincense and myrrh.
>Mine was a giddy kind of sin,
>Laughing without care
>While others in this world I knew
>Found no happiness anywhere.
>Mine was a lustful kind of sin
>Close, close in lustful arms.
>Mine was a hungry kind of sin,
>Hungry for a body's charms—
>Not stopping, no, not thinking
>Of another's harms—

The harms I brought to one who prayed
That I might know God's way.
The very ones who trusted me
Oh, God, I did betray. Ooooo-ooo-oo-o!

(*Sings*)

I have sinned, sinned, sinned,
Now I bow my head in shame,
Confessing that I know I've sinned
Against my Savior's name,
Confessing all the time, I knew
That I was sinning against you—
Against the one who loves me most,
Lord, God, against you.

Oh, pray for me, Church! Sister Essie, all of you, I beg sincerely, pray.

CROWD    We'll pray! Got to pray! Must pray! Amen!

LAURA    Church, can I pray with you?

CROWD    Pray with us! Pray! Sister Laura, pray!

LAURA    Can I sing, too, with you?

CROWD    Sing with us! Sing! Sister Laura, sing!

LAURA    Can I try to find my way back to salvation with you?

ESSIE    Laura, you can. Church, in the name of His charity and His forgiveness, I request Sister Mattie now to place upon this come-home-again-lamb, her robe. Help her, Sisters, that she might be robed in the love of this Church.

(SISTERS *of the church surround* LAURA *as she is robed*)

CHOIR

God's love can save,
God's love can save,
God's love can save,
Oh, yes, I know it can.

CROWD    So glad! Amen! So glad about God! Glad! . . . Glad! . . . Glad!

ESSIE    My heart is so full tonight—and for more reasons than one. Sister Laura back with us, and all you out there to witness her confession.

CROW    With that confession she'll be out in a year.

ESSIE    Now, another thing, you all don't know it, but you gonna have a matrimony here tonight. A surprise! Deacon Crow-For-Day come forward. (*A whisper of excited talk runs through the* CHOIR *at the expected marriage of* CROW *and* ESSIE) Deacon Crow, are you prepared for your function?

CROW  I is . . . And you, Essie Belle Johnson?

ESSIE  I am.

CROW  Then may I escort into your presence and the presence of Tambourine Temple our Rose of Sharon——

> (MARIETTA *rises and casts off her robe to reveal a wedding gown of white as a* CHOIR MEMBER *places on her head a veil of orange blossoms to the surprise of the church*)

And the Little David of our Church——

> (C.J. *doffs his robe to come forward in a summer tux with boutonniere.* DEACON CROW *takes his arm, while* ESSIE *leads her daughter by the hand to the altar*)

—that they might be united by the sweet honey of love.

CROWD  Thank God! Amen! Hallelujah!

LAURA  The marrying mother, Reverend Essie Bell Johnson! I am so glad I am here to witness this occasion.

CROW  Sister Essie, before you unite these children in holy wedlock, have you got a word to speak?

ESSIE  Deacon Crow, Sister Laura, church, everybody—my heart is too full to speak. Just gimme my tambourine. Let the music say it for me. Children, gather around and——

ALL (*Sing*)

> If you've got a tambourine
> Shake it to the glory of God!
> Glory! Glory! Glory!
> Shake it to the glory of God!
> Tambourines!
> Tambourines! Tambourines!
> Tambourines to Glory!

WOMEN

> If you've got a piano
> Play it to the glory of God!
> Glory! Glory! Glory!
> Play it to the glory of God!
> Piano
> Tambourines
> Tambourines! Tambourines!
> Tambourines to Glory!

LAURA

If you've got a song to sing
Sing it to the glory of God!
Glory! Glory! Glory!
Sing it to the glory of God!
    Song to sing
        Hallelujah!
        Hallelujah!
    Piano
    Tambourines
Tambourines! Tambourines!
Tambourines to Glory!

MEN

If you've got a drum to beat,
Beat it to the glory of God!
Glory! Glory! Glory!
Beat it to the glory of God!
    Drum to beat
    Song to sing
        Hallelujah!
        Hallelujah!
    Piano
    Tambourines
Tambourines! Tambourines!
Tambourines to Glory!
(*There is a joyous singing, beating of drums, blowing of trumpets, and great shaking of tambourines as the curtain falls*)